He Got Hungry and Forgot His Manners

He Got Hungry and

A Fable

Forgot His Manners

Jimmy Breslin

Ticknor & Fields / New York / 1988

Copyright © 1988 by Rodene Enterprises, Inc.

ALL RIGHTS RESERVED.

For information about permission to reproduce
selections from this book, write to
Permissions, Ticknor & Fields,
52 Vanderbilt Avenue, New York, New York 10017.

Library of Congress Cataloging-in-Publication Data

Breslin, Jimmy.
He got hungry and forgot his manners: a fable /
Jimmy Breslin. p. cm.
ISBN 0-89919-311-0
I. Title.
PS3552.R39H4   1988   87-27989
813'.54 — dc19   CIP

Printed in the United States of America

S 10 9 8 7 6 5 4 3 2 1

For Frances Curtin Breslin,
who spent so many years
gasping for breath in these places.

He Got Hungry and
Forgot His Manners

1

OWARD BEACH is a white finger sticking into Jamaica Bay alongside Kennedy Airport, which is the reason Howard Beach first became famous, and everybody now wishes that nobody had ever heard of the place at all, but it certainly is too late for that. "Howard Beach don't speak up until something happens," Angie Cirillo, twenty-four, said one day. "Then, when they do speak up, they say the wrong thing. I don't want no mention of Howard Beach anymore. Why do you have to talk about a place that's safe for a girl living by herself? That's more than a neighborhood where the coloreds live could say."

One reason why Howard Beach might be safe for Angie is the presence of her uncle, Anthony ("the Slap Giver") Cirillo, who lives upstairs in the same house. Protection, however, too often safeguards us from all parts of life except desolation. On many evenings, Uncle Anthony the Slap Giver can be found sitting on the front stoop, thus causing those with an inclination to visit Angie to remain on the far end of the street. It also might be stated that Howard Beach may be so safe for other single girls because, although many hard-working people live there, Howard Beach also has a severe overcrowding of gangsters. One feature of their presence is that the best medieval customs are kept flourishing, one of these being death before dishonor.

But to be factual about Howard Beach's fame, I must begin with the fact that Howard Beach originally became known for the planes that fly in the sky right over its roofs. When most Howard Beach residents bought their homes, there were only propeller planes, whose sounds were bearable. Residents were proud of the planes and always urged visitors to look up into the sky to see the beautiful planes. When jets replaced the propeller planes, the flight path onto the main runways brought jets only a couple of hundred feet over Cross Bay Boulevard, the main street running through Howard Beach.

The jets went right over the New Park Pizza stand on the corner of Cross Bay Boulevard and 156th Avenue and smack over the roof of the all-electric house owned by Ralph Turchio. Ralph's roof is only seven blocks from the start of the Kennedy runway. "When the plane goes over my house, I can see the people in the window."

Suddenly noise directed even the smallest of tasks. When speaking on the phone, people developed what became known as the Howard Beach wait. Every twenty seconds the one on the phone had to say "Wait a minute" and let the plane go over the house. After a couple of years, legitimate young men in Howard Beach were having difficulties with the Fire Department physicals, for it was being reported out that some Howard Beach applicants were unfit by reason of not being able to hear a fire alarm go off.

In 1976, when the French and British introduced the Concorde plane, which makes more noise than a direct hit, Ralph Turchio and others in Howard Beach tried to fight it. "I'm a human being," Ralph Turchio said.

One day in Paris, Valéry Giscard d'Estaing, the President, said on television, "Howard Beach, that is where the fishes are."

At his home, Ralph Turchio jumped up. "What is he, tough?"

All of which first made Howard Beach famous and might explain how people in Howard Beach act, although nobody is buying that this year. Particularly after what happened on the night of December 19, going into December 20, of 1986.

First, Alitalia flight 610, coming from Rome, originally due in by midafternoon, arrived hours late. In the rear of the plane was a little priest with a long nose and uncombed black hair. With him was an ebony apparition, a man so huge that Rome airport police boarded him early, so as not to frighten the other passengers, and hid him in the rear, where the apparition sat on the floor, his legs being much too long for a regular seat. As the huge man was terrified of the plane, the priest threw a blanket over his head and the man fell asleep. When the plane landed, the black man pulled the blanket off his head and stood up, and immediately there was panic in the aisle and people clawed at each other to get off the plane.

About which we will tell you all, and how this determines the course of the priest's life, but for now here he leads his friend off the plane and to the line to the first booth, the one where you show passports if you are a foreigner. D'Arcy Cosgrove, the priest, wore a black raincoat, as did the man with him, whom he called Great Big, although the raincoat on Great Big was so small that the man could not think of buttoning the front. Cosgrove presented both passports, and the clerk, head down, glanced at Great Big's African book and seemed to think that was fine and he stamped it. But when his eyes fell on Cosgrove's, on the harp engraved on the cover of all passports by the Republic of Ireland, the clerk in his booth made a motion.

Immediately, Cosgrove and his friend Great Big were surrounded by a number of uniformed customs and immigration service officers who led the two into a large bare room that was crowded with young people who were unmistakably Irish. So many thousands of them enter America illegally, flooding into the country in the greatest numbers since the century began, that to immigration people the Irish are simply Mexicans who swagger.

When Cosgrove and Great Big entered the room, all the young Irish flattened themselves against the far wall. Immigration agents pushed through the room, severely questioning the young, and when they got to Cosgrove they were highly suspicious and demanded proof that he was a priest, and when he was able to show that, and do so grandly, with papers from the Vatican that looked so impressive that the immigration man nearly genuflected, the agent concentrated on Great Big.

"Who is this man?" the immigration agent asked. He spoke in a normal tone and his face was placid, but Great Big immediately growled. He knew the man hated him. Cosgrove spoke to Great Big in French, which is the usual way the two communicated. Great Big knew French from missionaries, and Yoruba by birth, but he was used to the loneliness of the bush country and was taciturn in any language. Yet he had marvelous instincts about the human face and sound during conversation and someone could speak in normal tones and with a placid face, just as this immigration clerk was doing, and still say something bad about Great Big and there was some instinct, some fear that caused Great Big to resent the moment, sometimes bitterly.

It was quite a while before Cosgrove and Great Big cleared the waiting room in which the Irish were detained and went on to the baggage area, where on line in front of them was a stumpy man from the Rome Alitalia flight. He had two huge brown suitcases, which he attempted to carry past the baggage inspector, who nearly tackled him. The small man, surprised that he was being stopped, having been previously assured that no such thing could happen to him, put the bags down on the counter and simply walked away. "Hey," the inspector called. The man shook his head and held out his hands. "Not mine." The baggage inspector inserted two fingers into his mouth and blew. Agents fell out of the walls and onto the small man. The baggage inspector went through the suitcases and found package after package of white powder.

"I suppose you're going to tell me this is your headache medicine," the baggage inspector said.

The little man clapped both hands to his temples and began rubbing. He was soon gone in a swirl of agents.

Cosgrove put his black bag on the counter and the inspector dug inside and suddenly held a trophy aloft, a large box of Tums, a box containing forty-eight rolls.

"What drug is this?"

"Tums," Cosgrove said.

"You are certain of this?"

"Absolutely."

"Why do you have so many of them?" the customs man said.

"Because he gets indigestion sometimes," Cosgrove said, pointing to Great Big. Great Big was anxious about his Tums and he reached out and tore a roll of Tums out of the customs man's hands and upon sensing the customs man's combination of fear and officiousness, Great Big opened the pack and handed the customs man a couple of them. The customs man sniffed them. Great Big threw a couple into his mouth. The customs man shook his head. "You've got too many of them for me. These got to be tested."

"Why don't we just leave them here?" Cosgrove said.

"You got to stay, too. Because if these are heroin tablets then you got to go to jail for twenty years."

Cosgrove and Great Big were put in a room where they fell asleep on the floor. Hours later, a customs and immigration man stuck his head in. "You're right. Tums for the tummy." Cosgrove nodded. "Where are they?" The agent threw up his hands. "We needed them for the test." He said they were free to go. When Cosgrove and Great Big walked out to the night-empty airport terminal, Cosgrove went to the newsstand and bought a dozen rolls of Tums.

They then walked out into the American daylight and Cosgrove stopped and took a huge breath, as any good fighter does before the thing begins.

The priest, D'Arcy Cosgrove, was a soldier of his church, a man bristling with celibacy, who was picked personally by the Pope out of all the priests of the world for his background and belief that sex was the greatest threat to America, and therefore the rest of the civilized world. The Pope has made virtually an equal number of speeches about masturbation and multiple nuclear warheads. As America was the world leader, and also the nation most publicly tormented by sex, the Pope viewed the country as the great battleground for world survival. The Pope was putting together in his mind a plan to flood America with priests who had the proper view of sex — that it was absolutely intolerable — and he was sending as the lead man of this invasion D'Arcy Cosgrove, who, in the memory of the Pope and most others, was by himself in this matter.

Cosgrove was pure Irish, as we will tell you later, and he had been raised on the teaching of Saint Thomas Aquinas, whose view of the worth of women still rules the church even though Aquinas issued it centuries ago. Aquinas stated that Catholics must always be ruled only by men, because to begin with, the fetus of a female received her soul from God several weeks after the male soul, and that the female soul never has had the "eminence of degree" — which sounds fancy but really means "dirty whore bitch" — necessary for the Sacrament of Holy Orders, which is how men become priests.

Even if a woman were included in the ceremony of receiving the Sacrament of Holy Orders, Aquinas wrote, the Sacrament would not take on her soul and she would never be a priest. This was a natural part of the Catholic view that all life resides only in the male sperm and that nothing can ever be done to interfere with the male sperm making its way to its natural terminal inside a woman. Contraception is not used to prevent the woman from getting pregnant, according to Rome. Rather, it is one more plot against the highest order on earth, the male sperm. With this as his only philosophy, Cosgrove might have been the finest sex fighter the church ever produced.

When the Pope was in Africa, he was amazed and supremely delighted to see the little priest who rushed about the ranks of bare-breasted black women, the usual number of whom hadn't had a decent meal in a year, throwing white cloths over their dirty naked breasts. All through his journey, every time the Pope looked up, there was the priest, throwing a white cloth over a bare chest. This, the Pope thought, is a man who sees his faith in its clearest light: the poor we shall always have with us; therefore, look past their temporary affliction, their bones sticking out and their dry tongues, and attack the true sin, sex.

This helped give the Pope the fire to stand in front of a great crowd of shoeless, 150,000 at least, with women as far as he could see with breasts covered, many with white cloth, and his eye was attracted to these clouds of dust in the ranks of people and, sure enough, here was the little priest, pounding along the ground, slapping cloth onto nipples. And so the Pope took the Devil on under the sun. He told the crowd of 150,000 to practice celibacy on the African continent. They must never use birth control.

"Deny yourself of sexual pleasure," he told shoeless Africans who lived in huts in the sun. Everybody in the crowd listened respectfully. Then the Pope blessed a hippopotamus and the crowd cheered. They thought the hippopotamus was going to stop having sex in the river. Then everybody went home to their huts to have sex. The Pope, sensing this, was disappointed.

Next he went to South America, and on the way home he

stopped at the island of St. Lucia in the Caribbean. The island had 140,000 people, half at average age twenty-five, the other half at age four, and Prime Minister John Compton had been instructing his people that birth control was a civic duty every bit as much as fire prevention in order to prevent people of the island from having the baby next door for lunch.

Arriving at St. Lucia, the Pope, his eyes afire, was expected to make a powerful call for celibacy by the sea, and for no birth control for those allowed to have sex, for nothing ever to interfere with the male sperm, but only a week before this, the Prime Minister of St. Lucia had delivered a strong address to the island legislature about the urgency for population reduction by birth control. Therefore, the Prime Minister would be unable to stand mute if the Pope were to deliver a statement unalterably opposed to that of the island's civil authorities. Which put the Pope in shock only momentarily, for he was an establishment politician — in his own Poland he had sold out Walesa the labor leader as if it was a good thing to do.

Now on the island of St. Lucia, he wavered, stammered, and finally told a crowd of five thousand that "our faith invites us to promote the dignity of the Christian family in accordance with God's unchanging plan. The future of the nation belongs to them. To prepare for the future, it is right that you should aspire to greatness." As this meant exactly nothing, it pleased everybody, and the Prime Minister was especially thankful.

On the way back to Rome, however, the Pope was furious that he had not hammered the sin out of the crowd, and he thought about that little priest covering all those black breasts in Africa. Perhaps the priest could work St. Lucia, the Pope thought. No, America was still the place that needed an attack on sex the most. He thought of dispatching men to fight in America long after any one Papal visit. There were some decent celibates trying to run his church in America, the cardinals of New York and Boston foremost, men who understood that sex was the first sin and probably the only sin and that those who failed the church were the ones who took their eyes off the main event, sex, and let them wander over such irrelevancies as race and hunger.

Race was silly for American Catholics to worry about because few blacks were Catholic. Nor was hunger something to fret over, for it was only a cause of temporal death, which all must experience, but sex causes eternal damnation. So the Pope sat in Rome and thought sourly of America and of ways to help bring this fresh, hectic, brazen country into line with the sound, eternal thinking of old Europe, particularly Eastern Europe.

And then, from nowhere, on a dark night, with his first soldier, D'Arcy Cosgrove, standing in Kennedy Airport, Howard Beach exploded and gave the Pope an international reason to get his hands on American morals.

If you will remember when I started telling you this, I told you that Howard Beach is a white finger of land that sticks into Jamaica Bay by Kennedy Airport. Which is a precise description. On one side of the finger is the airport and surrounding the airport are neighborhoods called South Ozone Park and Jamaica, quite black. And on the other side of the white finger, but very close, the bay water runs into marshes with seven-foot-high mouse gray bullrushes.

These tall weeds are constantly watched, or sure should be, for any motion, because beyond the bullrushes there is a parkway and on the other side of the parkway is the start of the Borough of Brooklyn, with a neighborhood called East New York, which starts the longest stretch of non-white poor in the United States. As we will see later on, any waving of weeds, any thrashing sound, always should be regarded as threatening. When blacks appeared in Howard Beach in cars and shopped in the daytime at Waldbaum's, nobody cared as long as they were gone by the time the lights came on. As vespers are not conducted in Howard Beach, the people see no reason for black strangers after dusk.

And now the thing that happened on this night, as Cosgrove and Great Big were landing at the nearby airport, all began with an eighteenth-birthday party in the basement of a house in Howard Beach. There were at the party boys and girls, most of them Italian Catholic. The birthday boy was Jewish. So were his parents, who were present. Lewd Jews. For as a birthday treat for his son, the father had contracted for the services of a woman known as Cindy the Cop, who was an entertainer for social functions. For a fee of $115, Cindy the Cop drove in from Long Island and arrived in Howard Beach wearing a policewoman's uniform, police hat, tunic with gold buttons, badge, and on her smacking good hips a big fake gun. She stood on the basement steps and announced, "You're all under arrest. Put up your hands." Then she wiggled and said, "Let me see if I can make something besides your hands stick up."

The young people at the party were drinking Southern Comfort and Budweiser beer chasers. Cindy the Cop, with the family beaming and the kids going berserk, peeled off her badge and gun and everything to the skin, head to toe, and one of the young boys waved a twenty-dollar bill and screamed, "What would you do for this?" and the rest of them went into — and now I will quote directly from a subsequent intelligence report to the Vatican — "a frenzy of overexcitement caused by the rush of temptation through their young and therefore vulnerable bodies."

The young people did sit in the basement and go crazy getting hard-ons, no question about that.

And then, as the Vatican report noted, sex destroyed life. When Cindy the Cop finished her act and flounced up the stairs, the young people, half drunk, sex berserk, went out into their cars and a couple of them got onto Cross Bay Boulevard where three blacks, whose car had broken down, walked in the night. One of the cars full of whites nearly ran over the blacks, who said fuck you to the car, and the white young men in it said, "We'll be back, niggers," and the blacks waved in disdain and walked on to the New Park Pizza stand, which is a low hut with a glass front and a cement floor and wooden picnic tables.

The whites did return. In force, drunk with whiskey, crazy from Cindy the Cop. When the blacks came out, the gang of whites chased them with baseball bats and a tree limb or so and the blacks ran. Whites chased blacks through Howard Beach. One black ducked through a hole in the chain link fence running along the parkway. The whites chased after him and in blind fear he ran onto the parkway and was hit by another white guy who was driving home from Brooklyn. The white kept going. He explained later that he thought he had hit a dog. On the streets, the other white kids kept chasing and beating the other blacks.

All over Howard Beach on this night there were Christ-
mas decorations on the lawns and the brick ranch houses
were festooned with lights. Brilliant spotlights showed
Santa Claus and the reindeer flying over roofs.

And out on the parkway, police flashlights played on the
dead body — a black killed at Christmastime in Howard
Beach.

2

WHEN THE BUS CAME to the curb, the woman, a mean-looking woman, with a scarf the color of stale mustard pulled tight around her pinched face, pushed in front of Bushwick Taylor. In her hand she had a dollar bill, which was useless and she knew it. Fare must be dropped into the box in change or a token to discourage holdups; drivers have a sign pasted right on the fare box stating that they carry no money to make change. Of course the woman knew all this, but she pushed on anyway with the dollar held out to the driver, who wouldn't even look at her. Immediately, she turned and thrust the bill at Bushwick.

"Mister, you got any change?"

Bushwick had four quarters in his hand and, as he was so used to giving away things — he does that for a living — he unconsciously held out his hand and the woman snatched the change, handed him the dollar, and went off for a seat. Bushwick stepped onto the bus with the dollar. He went through his pocket for change, but he had none. The driver told him to get off the bus.

This was how the morning started for Bushwick Taylor, whose real name was Fred, but nobody ever called him that. He was originally from Bushwick Avenue, and as he took the nickname of Bushwick early in his life, he retained it when he moved to another neighborhood in Queens. This morning he was at his usual bus stop, the B55 bus stop, at Sixty-eighth Street and Myrtle Avenue.

He went across the street to a delicatessen and asked for change, caught the next bus, dropped his quarters into the box, and asked the driver for a transfer. He rode this first bus, the B55 bus, for fifteen minutes, with his face against the window and his mind full of yesterday's ache. Late in the afternoon, he had taken a call at his desk from a woman who said that she had four children on the street with her and no food for the last two days. Bushwick said to her, "Prove it to me." When the woman asked how, Bushwick said, "Put your kids on the phone and let me hear them cry." He always started out with the proper smart remark, but then at the odd moment, such as this, he became dazed. He had to get over this weakness, for if he was to succeed in the city's chief industry, the Poor, he had to ignore their pain of the moment and understand that most of these people forget immediately, which is why their suffering usually is overrated.

On this morning, it took Bushwick an hour and a half to get to his job at the New Opportunity Hot Line, a place where the poor call for food when they have no other out. Offices are on the fifth floor of an old creaking building on Church Street in downtown Manhattan. Leaving the subway in Manhattan, he saw nobody waiting at the change booth, and he seized this moment to buy a pack of tokens, ten for ten dollars, so he would have no more trouble with fare boxes. This left him with seven dollars until payday; he became apprehensive when he realized what he'd done. He believed strongly that working with the hungry could turn him into a client. "You could catch hunger quicker than a cold," he told himself.

Bushwick Taylor, age thirty-five, had long black Irish hair that framed a tough face that always seemed to be looking for humor. Bushwick closed his eyes when he laughed. He was a rock composer and singer and his best work ("Why Make Me Different?") was done with his rock group called the Fourteenth Street Line. The best date the rock group could get, however, was at the Dry Harbor Recreation, an old bowling alley used as a club on weekends. So Bushwick started working part time answering phones and doing other such jobs at the New Opportunity Hot Line. The callers are mostly women with children who learn about it from other hungry out on the streets, and there are so many tens of thousands of them in this city, women with children and without as much as a piece of bread. No food is kept in the offices, but the workers, such as Bushwick and two women, interview the hungry over the phone and direct them to a food pantry, usually in the basement of a religious institution, where there are limited stocks of canned vegetables, some canned meats and Spam and beef stew, and sacks of rice.

———~~~———

There were three ways to work in the Poor business. One was to take a grubby government job and live a frozen life at a fixed salary; there were in New York City some five hundred thousand city, state, and federal employees, most of whom worked directly on the Poor. Then there was the more leisurely way, a position at one of the dozens of foundations that each year gave away as little as possible, as low as five percent of a total trust fund that earned close to ten percent a year. The five percent in grants kept the foundations free of taxes and the ten percent in earnings ensured that the size of the staffs and their salaries expanded, and the length of service they could expect was at least long.

The last and most preferable way to work at the Poor was to be anywhere on the staff of a most prestigious and amazingly powerful organization, the New Opportunity Partnership. When New Opportunity was first formed, Sam Daniels of the *New York Times* wrote,

> The formation of a private non-profit corporation, the New York Opportunity Partnership Corp., which is a private civic group whose membership includes the city's leading business executives, was greeted yesterday with praise for its "awesome" undertaking by political leaders. The new organization, to be known as New Opportunity Partnership, is seen as a cooperative venture using federal government and state and city money for private developers to build affordable housing on a cost-plus basis, cost plus profit. New Opportunity is pledged to oversee the city's insoluble problems. One answer to the questions may be that the city itself owns large parcels of land and could make them available for development by New Opportunity at nominal fees.

This was a private group of the rich, led by David Rockefeller, using all the federal housing funds in a city of the Poor. New Opportunity went along with a calmness befitting its moral superiority, while at the same time using exciting language, particularly the federal Urban Development Action Grants, carrying the bang-up initials UDAG. These grants were supposedly for immediate rebuilding of devastated city neighborhoods — action grants, government making a frontal attack.

Big bang! The thing worked magnificently. The first action grant was supposedly to fix up an RKO movie house at 181st Street in the Bronx, but when the movie manager, Francis X. Walsh, said, "There will be niggers in the balcony no matter how you fix it up," the action money stayed on the bench. Later, the best UDAG quick-action money, tens of millions, right from the taxpayers, was put into play building a new hotel for a nice rich company in Times Square. Not a whimper from the taxpayers, either, which is how it should always be done. The total control and ability to suppress nearly all public complaints made New Opportunity Partnership a magnificent success. It surpassed anything ever seen in the city and there was such perfect control that the governor sent his wife to serve tea at a function in order to get the promise of a tiny amount of funds that he then in turn could boast of as the start of a great program to help the public. Meanwhile, the federal housing money was in action right where it belonged, smack on the thigh of a good fellow rich man.

Everything was fine until the 1980s, when the distance and difference between rich and poor in New York became so vast that it threatened the rich with being seen as barbarians. Many — such as Bushwick Taylor — started working full time, conducting studies on the "plight of the Poor."

Bushwick even wound up doing actual work as a result of a fire in the Flatbush Arms Hotel, a welfare hotel in the most miserable section of East New York. The fire started on the eleventh floor, where three children in an end room, none of whom were in school because they were ashamed to give their hotel address in front of other children, spent the day collecting the small empty vials dropped by crack users in the hotel hallways. At the end of the day, the children, ages eleven, nine, and seven, had three plastic garbage bags filled with the vials, which they sold to a crack pusher. They asked for a nickel apiece. The crack pusher, a private security guard hired to keep order in the hotel, paid them with a ten-dollar vial of crack.

The three kids went into a room and started smoking the crack in a glass pipe. They had to use many matches to keep the crack smoking, and one of the matches, still lit, fell on a mattress. The flames from the mattress made no noise until they touched an old paper shade, and the three children turned around and tried to get out, but only the oldest made it; the other two were trapped in the room and the fire spread over the entire floor.

When firemen arrived, the sidewalks were crowded with tenants who had fled the place. In one crowd in front of the hotel, a woman screamed that her children were missing. The owner of the hotel shook his head and said to the firemen, "Don't worry about the kids. They are all gone. Dead! We tried to look. Believe me. Forget the kids."

It took long minutes, maybe twenty, before the flames seemed under control. The building was sealed and the firemen who had been fighting the fire from the top of a hundred-foot extension ladder came down and caught their breath. The remainder of the fight would be made from inside the building. The ladder was one story short — ten feet — for the eleventh floor. One of the firemen who came off the ladder, Georgie Larson, walked over to the wrench on a hydrant and he was starting to shut off the water when, right away, a man on the sidewalk, just a guy watching a fire, said to him, "Kid in the window." Larson looked up and there in the top floor, the eleventh, a kid was standing on a window ledge. Suddenly the room behind him danced with flames.

"Kid in the window," Larson screamed as he ran. He ran up to his truck, Ladder 265, and hit the ladder and started going up.

"Kid in the window!" A lieutenant named Albanese was behind him, screaming and running.

Georgie Larson went up the ladder. Up, up, up, his head down, his legs pumping, cursing and spitting and screaming to God that somebody had let this kid go back up to the eleventh floor and the motherfreaking fire started up again. Larson looked up and saw the kid standing there, a black kid — what could he be, twelve, maybe? — in some kind of a jacket, and Georgie Larson hoped it was a good one, a jacket that you could hold on to. The kid also was holding a box of some kind in his hands, and Georgie Larson didn't care about that, he was only thinking about being able to grab on to that jacket and hold it, and Georgie put his head down and pumped harder, and now he got higher and he saw that the flames from the room were all over the windowsill, and they were licking at the kid and the kid was flinching and he screamed and looked right down at the sidewalk, this kid did, and he was going to jump to get away from the fire.

Georgie Larson screamed up at the kid, "Don't jump. I'll get you. Don't worry. I'll get you."

Now it was personal for Georgie Larson. He had spoken to the kid. And what Georgie Larson was going to do, he was going to go up these few more steps, right to the top of the ladder, then reach and somehow, by jump or snatch or rope or miracle — who cares? — get this kid from the ten or twelve feet above the end of the ladder. I'll get him, Georgie told himself. He's mine, mine, mine, mine, mine.

He was almost at the top and he saw the kid's face, saw that he was holding this thing in his hands, and then there was a sudden rush of wind and the flames inhaled, sucking back inside the eleventh-floor room and the kid was on the windowsill with fire dancing on his back. There was a liquid sound and a fiery tongue came out of the window and into the sky, and the kid on the windowsill stood in the middle of the flames. Every part of the kid was afire, flames crackling on his jacket shoulders, hair blazing like a pile of leaves, and the kid jumped with the box or whatever it was in his hands. He went out into the night air covered with flames. Georgie Larson took his shot. He held the ladder with one hand and swung most of his body right off the ladder, a leg hanging in the sky, and he grabbed for the fireball. He caught the kid by the shoulder. The jacket shredded and the kid, a fiery pinwheel, fell eleven stories.

When Georgie Larson came down the ladder, he went out to the curb and sat down in the dark. A few minutes later, Jack Russell, an old guy from Engine 52 in Brownsville, walked over and said, "You know what the kid snuck back to get?"

Georgie Larson looked up.

"A cat," Russell said.

"Cat," Georgie said.

"That's what he had in the box. He had a cat in a box. I guess that was all he had in the world."

The story of the kid with the cat in the box, and the fact he was the fourth dead kid of the night in a welfare hotel fire, was regarded as a threat by those at the very top of the New Opportunity Partnership. The Poor are the most important people in New York, for their social welfare billions blow through the air for all the well-off to grab; where are the rich supposed to get their money from, the rich? In order to tell each other and outsiders that they were trying to prevent so many of these particularly alarming things from happening, and interfere with the orderly flow of poor money into rich bank accounts, in order to keep suffering, tempers, and crime down to an acceptable level, or at least find a way to deflect the effect of publicity and allow the rich to function, New Opportunity Partnership attempted to put a better veneer over the Poor and began trying to assist millions to go through the act of dying each day without noticing it so much. Of course they were not going to change anything. Nobody ever did a thing like that. But they were going to appear to try, so that those of station and grace could continue to live in order in a city covered with a roof of gold. It is not the streets of New York that are paved with gold; let the imbeciles trudge the streets for a lifetime and they will get nothing. The gold in New York is in the sky, and when people of substance desire something, they reach out and snap off a piece of the sky.

———

When Bushwick got to his desk, an old gunmetal gray desk in a small crowded room that had no lobby, the elevator doors opening smack onto the first desk, the woman next to him, Jane, who was a radical gone gray, brought out a flask of rum and offered it to Bushwick. "Christmas drink?" He refused, for he knew that even a little drink at this hour would put him in bed by noon.

He nodded to the girl he liked, Sarah Carter, who was at a desk in the corner, talking angrily on the phone. Bushwick knew that she was from either Vermont or Ohio. Lanky, and perhaps an inch taller than Bushwick, she was wearing an Ohio Wesleyan sweatshirt, which is where she received high honors in her undergraduate studies in preparation for the Methodist ministry, which she intended to pursue to ordination, and while at it, to write new hymns for the Methodists and any Protestant church that needed them, thus keeping the level of music at a consistent high. She found out later, however, that the Methodists would not ordain her as a minister because her midwestern board refused to classify her work as religious. Feeding the hungry in New York has become a business, the Methodists said, and as proof showed that the city in 1986 had the first professional soup kitchen workers in memory.

Sarah Carter suspected that the Methodist board had some notion that she might be a lesbian, which couldn't have been further from the truth. She liked men all right, as long as they didn't get in the way. Even so, Bushwick had taken Sarah out for a beer and they talked about music and had a very good time and, after a few more beers, Sarah allowed as how she could fall in love with him, maybe.

Now, in the office, Sarah hung up and rubbed her face with her long hands. "Every time Bethany calls!"

"For what now?" Bushwick said.

"Sanitary napkins."

"Come on."

"You come on."

Bethany was a Catholic hostel in Brooklyn for homeless mothers.

"She asked me for fifty boxes. I said to her, 'Sister, I'll call around for you, but do you really need all that many? You only have ten girls, a box should take you through a month.' Know what she said to me? She said, 'I want them here as a sign of hope. Wouldn't it be marvelous if they ever used them all up?'"

"A miracle," Bushwick said.

"And her girls get pregnant over there every half hour," Sarah said.

The one next to Bushwick, Jane, with the flask of rum, had a caller with three daughters in the Bronx and no food. He said he was going to kill himself. Jane told the man to forget about killing himself, that he'd best worry about feeding the kids. "Now just get a pen and take down where you have to go," she said. When she finished, she went to the rum flask. "The official New Opportunity manual says you can't drink in the office." She took a slug of rum and held out the flask; Bushwick again refused. The phone on his desk rang and he began his day.

The call that stuck this time came in the middle of the afternoon, from a woman who said, "You the ones got food?"

"If you have a legitimate emergency," Bushwick said.

"How do I prove that to you over the phone?"

"Put the phone against your stomach and let me hear the growl," Bushwick said.

She didn't understand this and merely continued her story. "I had welfare until two weeks ago."

"Then what?"

"Failed my face-to-face."

The face-to-face is the most important test many adults in the city must take. Every couple of months a recipient must appear at the offices of the local income maintenance center and bring all records, including birth certificate, to prove that in the last six months an uncle in Aiken, South Carolina, didn't keel over and leave her the odd $500,000. After which she must pass a short written test failed by many because they don't know how to study and have totally ignored the pamphlet "Read to Eat." Others never even show up, for while welfare women know the day their check comes and wait in the street in front of their buildings for the mailman, the face-to-face notices always arrive unexpectedly and of course the buildings have no mailboxes since long ago kids pried the whole metal rack off the lobby wall. Therefore, the woman never knows about the face-to-face notice. Under the rules, she has fourteen days to appear for the face-to-face or her name automatically comes off the welfare computer, and then nobody can do anything about that.

The New York social services computer center is located on two floors of a building running an entire block, from Eighth to Ninth avenues, on Manhattan's West Side, where, at 4:00 P.M. each day, each welfare computer terminal, hospital Medicaid terminal, food stamp center, child services office, day-care center, every social services computer terminal in the city, thousands of terminals, transmit to the main control center, the lights on all the panels in all the rooms on both floors of the control center blinking in the torrent of names and addresses and statuses coming in from the offices that serve millions of people.

At one big Univac mainframe, down near the Ninth Avenue end of the building, while a fat female technician sits with a Walkman on and listens to Minister Louis Farrakhan's rap record against the Jews, the Univac mainframe in the cool hum in front of the fat technician erases names of face-to-face failures. Off the printout, off the terminals, off the mailing addresses, off the list at the local income maintenance center, off the notices list, and finally, their names race into this one room. At one Univac mainframe, here are all these smaller machines, cabinets with light blue sides and white tops, handling Job 3433, Task Term 00966, ZRZC 94 CMDOZOP25, which cause 250,000 checks a minute to spit out. Suddenly, at the next mainframe there is a speedy ripple of red lights and at that instant, with another clerk sitting and dreaming, the face-to-face losers drop off the computer that writes the checks. They now must turn to the safety men, the New Opportunity Hot Line workers.

Once, on a New Opportunity junior management training tour of the computer center, Bushwick blundered into a room lined with instruments and long racks holding hundreds of tape drums, and the fat technician ripped off her Walkman and pointed to Bushwick's coat, a brown down jacket with frayed cuffs. "Read that sign!" On the wall was a huge notice that read, NO BULKY COATS ALLOWED! Bushwick unzipped the down jacket. She shook her head. "They be walkin' out of here with one of these drums under their coats."

"It looks like a film library," Bushwick said.

"Film all right. The whole world be on them tapes. Be walkin' out with even one drum, the city be stopped dead."

She looked around in agitation. "How come you got in here anyway? Guard supposed to stop you."

"I used that door," Bushwick said, pointing to the one he had used.

"You be comin' in the back way. You here already?"

"I'm on the junior management tour."

"Well, you be in a *sensitive* room."

Bushwick, holding the jacket out so she could see he had no tape drum under his armpit, left the room.

And now Bushwick was sitting in the fifth-floor office of the New Opportunity Hot Line, and the woman caller said to him, "I made my face-to-face, but the computer says I wasn't there. The caseworker says she knows I made my face-to-face because she was the one giving me a face, but the computer says I didn't. Don't make no matter what I says or the caseworker says, if the computer say I wrong, then I don't get my check."

As the woman was calling from the Bronx, Bushwick told her to go to the Saint Nicholas of Tolentine Center on University Avenue, which kept Spam and canned vegetables. Good they did, too, for there were so many hungry in the rich city that many pantries ran out of food before noon. As most callers have no carfare and have to walk, Bushwick jealously guarded his secret pantries, such as the Tolentine center.

The woman thanked him. Then paused. Bushwick flinched, for he knew what was next. "I don't want to be getting ahead of myself, but I was wondering about Christmas food."

"You mean Santa Claus?" Bushwick said.

"He be my man."

"Santa Claus committed suicide," Bushwick said and hung up.

At 3:00 P.M., Jane again held out the flask. "Christmas drink?" Bushwick shook his head. "I still can't do it on an empty stomach."

He went down to the Greek lunch counter where he bought a ham and cheese sandwich, which cost him $2.50. This left him with four dollars and change until payday. "You are now running a bit tight," Bushwick told himself. He congratulated himself on having bought the tokens earlier. He brought the sandwich up to the office. "Some call it lunch. To me, this is early dinner," he said to himself.

At which point the elevator doors opened and looking straight at Bushwick were a woman in a raincoat that sure wasn't good enough for the cold outside and two little girls with wool caps pulled down and the lower half of their faces covered with mufflers. Only the eyes appeared. The eyes were locked on Bushwick's sandwich. Immediately, Bushwick slid the sandwich across the desk, intending to duck it. He saw the two pairs of eyes follow the moving sandwich. The group moved out of the elevator and advanced on Bushwick's desk. Right away, the woman started explaining how she had been knocked off the computer and didn't have a quarter and still had all these people to feed. Bushwick tried to listen and at the same time protect his sandwich.

"It taste good?" one little girl said. She held on to the desk with one hand and swayed back and forth. "We be hungry."

Her sister stood behind her and nodded.

He tried to outlast them, but the two little girls stood there until they stared him out of the sandwich. He ripped it in half and handed them the halves.

"Where do you live?" he asked the woman.

"Brooklyn."

"How did you get here?"

"The cop let us on the subway."

"I have a pantry on Sixth Avenue and Thirteenth Street in Brooklyn. Do you know where that is?"

The woman shook her head. "Be far from us."

Bushwick looked at the clock. "I have a pantry here in Manhattan. Saint Francis Xavier on West Sixteenth Street. It's open until four o'clock."

"The cop let us on the subway?"

"I don't know."

"I be tired. Kids be tired."

Bushwick sighed. Slowly, painfully, his hand came out with the pack of subway tokens. He wrote down the address of the food pantry on a slip of paper. He handed tokens and paper to the woman.

"I won't say Merry Christmas to you because I have more brains than that," Bushwick said.

The woman thanked him and walked out. Bushwick swung around, his old chair creaking, and his hand went out for the rum flask from Jane. Bushwick took a great swallow. The rum burned down his throat and into his empty stomach. He knew the second swallow would go down easier. It sure did. The third went even better than that. The only slug that gave him trouble was the last, when he raised the flask and found it was empty.

"Sarah."

"Yeah."

"You take me out, Sarah?"

She nodded and put on her down jacket and they went into a Blarney Stone on Church Street, which was packed with postal workers and Wall Street messengers and they drank with their coats on and in the smoke and heat and soon Bushwick began to rub up against Sarah. "Nobody in your house?" he said to her.

"My mother."

"So come out to my house in Queens," Bushwick said.

"Don't push me, Bushwick," Sarah said.

"You told me you might want to. I'm ready."

"I only told you I was thinking about it. Please don't push me."

They each had another couple of big beers and Bushwick took Sarah's hand and she said, "I'll come to Queens with you. But I don't know what it's going to be like. I told you, I was only thinking. Don't blame me if it isn't good."

"Don't worry," Bushwick said. "It's new for me, too. I never was with a minister before."

They had a couple more drinks on empty stomachs, then left. Later, at the end of the ride home, Bushwick suddenly awoke in the Q11 bus and found he was in the middle of Howard Beach. "I thought you knew where we were; I never was here before," Sarah said.

They got out in front of the big Tilerama store on Cross Bay Boulevard. The bus stop for the ride back up to Myrtle Avenue was across the street, in front of the New Park Pizza stand. There was no bus in sight and Sarah said she was hungry in the winter night. Bushwick took her into the pizza stand and the counterman, who had sparse gray hair and a sour face, looked down at his hands and waited to hear the order.

Bushwick opened his mouth to speak. But at this moment a plane came in so low that the plane's landing floodlights bathed the room in blinding white light. The counterman put his head under the ledge. Pizza tins rattled uncontrollably. The pizza baker in the back dropped to the floor. Bushwick looked outside, where a man in a blue zipper jacket and a New York Jets cap looked excitedly into the sky and a woman in a red coat wrote determinedly on a clipboard. Both wore earmuffs. When the most shattering of the noise was gone, the man and woman rushed into the pizza stand. They went behind the counter to the pay phone alongside the oven. The man dialed a number and said, "Spring Rock Civic Association here. We want to complain right now —"

"Alitalia 747," the woman said.

"Alitalia 747. Coming onto your runway right now. Right over my roof in Howard Beach and onto your runway. What? I can't hear you. I got a earache. The lawyer'll complain personal at the FAA office tomorrow morning."

He hung up. "Rome," he said.

The woman nodded. "Rome plane. Every night. They want us to die."

"So the lawyer goes in tomorrow, that's all," the man said.

It is funny how complaints can coincide with each other so smoothly and obviously that even if it is supposed to be a coincidence anybody with sense knows that there is no way for it to be such. For on this very day, as the New Park Pizza counterman and baker, Bushwick and Sarah the Minister, the two watchers from the Spring Rock Civic Association, and the airport FAA noise control man who took the call know so well, they were present at only part of what actually occurred. For over in Manhattan at this moment on this night, in the computer center, on terminal and printout machine, terminal and printout after terminal and printout in all the cool rooms and floors, there was a rush of blinking lights and the paper in the printing machines squealed and on each printout was the phrase, and you can check all the printouts from that time on December 20, 1986, check them all out and see that they are on file, each computer said, "Unexpected Footprint."

Now right here you should know that such expressions are part of the terminology of computers and yet for these words to appear suddenly at this precise hour can be explained by no technician, but instead only by those with the wisdom to believe in the power of mystery, and to understand that the phrase "mysterious warning" should never be taken for granted, for it is as real as the center of the sky from which it comes.

3

T HE MONSIGNOR in the Vatican who had plucked
Cosgrove out of Africa was an ambitious man who
had performed the initial part of his task with
speed in order to impress superiors. He had things
moving in weeks when usually they took months. When
Cosgrove indicated that he had to think about placing a lay
person, some large African who had assisted him, the mon-
signor wrote that Cosgrove simply should bring the African
along. Anything but delay.

When Cosgrove got to Rome, the monsignor in the Vati-
can immediately had him attend orientation courses at the
Vatican Secretary of State's office. There, a lecturer stated
that Rome was going to put its hand directly into the reli-
gious and political life of all American Catholics and, even-
tually, into the secular life as well.

The new American technology, which was being dis-
played as a way to think past what the arrogant Americans
described as nature's mistakes, actually was only another
way of thwarting God's will. "If these people are left alone,

someday a woman can enter a booth, the same sort of booth we use for passport photos, and she can press one button that will make her pregnant, another button to find out if the baby is perfect, and if it is not absolutely perfect then of course there would be another button to push and a ray would come out of the machine and destroy the fetus in the womb. And most certainly if the woman wanted a boy and the machine told her it was a girl, why, press the button, and the girl is gone. Tomorrow we will try a boy."

Cosgrove, who had studied the latest decrees, said to the lecturer that he had one observation. "If for some reason, blocked Fallopian tubes being the most common, I suppose, a woman who desperately wants a child, as does her husband, and cannot have one, then because of the compelling force of this love, I'm trying to understand why it is so morally corrupt to remove the egg from the woman, fertilize it with her husband's sperm, and then replace it in the uterus. For this is love with which we are dealing, not human selfishness or disorder. It would seem to me that there are mitigating circumstances."

The lecturer, a squat man, exploded. "To give sperm, the husband must masturbate!"

"Oh," Cosgrove said. It was his last defiance of his church.

On his last day in Rome, Cosgrove asked the monsignor about conditions in America besides the fantastic immorality of sexual technology. The monsignor was suddenly impatient. "What exactly would you like to know?"

"Perhaps it is because of my recent past, but I am thinking of hunger."

"In America! Why, many priests who come to this very office where we are sitting after having been in America tell me that they were forced to overeat in that country in order to prevent food from spoiling. Even with that country's great technology, and you certainly have heard of it this week, they still do not have enough refrigeration to keep all the food they raise. Why, of course you know that the Papal ban on eating meat on Friday really ended after people from America beseeched His Holiness to allow them to eat such meat, not out of selfishness but out of concern for the ranchers who had so many cattle on their hands that there was no room for grazing grass to grow. The Pontiff was afraid of food riots in reverse. Can you imagine people fighting because there is not enough being eaten? That is America."

"Then I'm thrilled to the bones to go there," Cosgrove said. "The wonderful man I'll be going with has simply starved for too many years in Africa. The man went with virtually nothing to chew. He now has a nervous system unable to handle the slightest feeling of being hungry."

"The man suffered quite a bit in Africa?" the monsignor said.

"Oh, dear Lord, yes. Shocking," Cosgrove said.

"He must then beware of people forcing him to overeat in America," the monsignor said.

Once the monsignor had set up Cosgrove's urgent trip so speedily that he was certain the Pope would hear of it, he was through, for he had never been west of Rome and had no idea of what was happening in America or what this Irish priest was actually going to do there. "It is the idea that counts," the monsignor assured himself. "A man representing the Pope's determination can have an effect just by sitting there." The monsignor wrote to a very close friend from seminary days who was stationed at the Papal delegate's office in Washington. The letter was long and admitted confusion and begged for help. The letter also contained a grievous omission: the monsignor in Rome neglected to insert a check.

He got what he paid for. Not only did the Papal delegate have difficulty understanding the complicated letter, and of course I must reiterate here that he was wounded by its absence of respect, a check, but the delegate also was deeply suspicious of motive. If this supposed friend, the monsignor, was sending a man over here on such a mission, then it was plain to the Papal delegate that the priest would roam the land and extort money from other priests at will. For what other reason was he coming except to collect money for the monsignor by using the very name and seal of the Vatican as a weapon?

The idea of this offended the Papal delegate who, because he was affiliated directly with the Vatican, received gifts from the very same priests this other man, this horrible little Irishman, was going to extort. And he was to be in Howard Beach! Of course, that would be only as a start. The Papal delegate thought of collections at a big, spanking white, cash-money parish such as Howard Beach parish. A special messenger from the Vatican, indeed! If any treasuries were to be raided, the Papal delegate had one question: Where's mine? So the Papal delegate made arrangements to house Cosgrove at Saint Lucy's on Cozine Street in the East New York neighborhood of Brooklyn, which in actual measurement is only yards from Howard Beach and illustrates again that a miss truly is as good as a mile.

The Papal delegate then said that he was going to Seattle for some time, because the cardinal there had performed as all hated Americans do in Rome's eye and had of course been disciplined. In the meantime, this Cosgrove was to receive neither money nor special consideration. "He is a tired man who is accompanied by a friend. They should enjoy the rest."

~~~~~~~

So they had come to America. Cosgrove and the huge black, Great Big, were driven along desolate streets at the end of an El line in East New York. Cosgrove was astonished. There were old abandoned two-story brick houses and homemade wood houses often flanked by empty lots that were covered with auto tires, old couches, bottles, garbage cans, and scrawny but mean dogs yanking at garbage. Many abandoned buildings had doors and windows covered with cinder blocks to keep them from being used and set afire by crack smokers.

The cabdriver asked a cop in one patrol car for directions and drove for a couple of blocks, each block getting worse and the cabdriver more nervous, until he turned onto a street that seemed to be a country lane. The street dipped into a black gully and the driver backed up and drove out of the area and onto a more populated but particularly horrible street, Dumont Avenue, where there was a row of dingy stores, fronts covered with iron grates. The corner store was burned and abandoned. Inside, in the rubble, a boy stood with his hands over a fire that was coming out of a steel drum. The boy had on a white baseball cap worn backwards and a black jacket and pants. Cosgrove had the cabdriver stop. Cosgrove shook off the depression at finding himself not in a city of gold but in one of misery and he said, happily, "Bright lad in his clubhouse. He'll know."

The cabdriver refused to wait and demanded money. Cosgrove paid him $12.50 and had Great Big stay with the suitcase on the sidewalk while he stepped into the burned-out store to see the boy. Cosgrove's foot caused piles of broken glass to chime. The boy, wiry and silent, watched Cosgrove approach.

"Good lad. What's your name?"

"I be Baby Rock and I be bad."

"Suppose you tell me exactly how to get to Saint Lucy's."

"Don't know."

"It's somewhere right near here, I'm told," Cosgrove said.

The boy began to whistle and beat the palms of his hands on his pants legs as if playing the drums. He looked out the open storefront. "Somethin' real bad be comin'. I don't look for trouble. I just stay here till trouble find me."

"Well, you certainly have a fine clubhouse for yourself," Cosgrove said.

"No club here. This be my house," the kid said. He went over to a couch with the insides coming out of several holes and suddenly jumped into the air and landed on the couch. He pulled a torn khaki blanket over him. "Good night!" He closed his eyes. Then he bounced up. He wore white sneakers with the laces open. "Only thing I can't do here is eat. I'm waitin' for the brothers bring me somethin'. They eatin' at the federal program. I can't go there and eat. I be too old."

"People are never too old to eat," Cosgrove said, smiling. .

Baby Rock shook his head. "You got to be under fourteen to go in the federal lunchroom. You be over fourteen, they don't let you in. They say your mother get food stamps for you."

"Then just go home to your mother."

"She be havin' no room."

"I can't believe that."

"Be believin' one thing," Baby Rock said. "You stay here, little old man, they vic you."

"Vic?"

"They be makin' you a victim."

The boy began beating his hands so rapidly that the slapping sound echoed on the vacant street, causing small dogs with nervous eyes, who had been rooting in the garbage, to jump at the curb. Watching the street in its silence, Cosgrove felt sure that the place was an error, an aberration in one corner of New York, one so insignificant that it was overlooked in the rush of life in a place that had to be so rich and busy.

"My friend Calvin be here, he vic you for sure," Baby Rock said. "Calvin passed away, Calvin don't care about nobody. He be robbin' and stealin'. That's why he passed away. Calvin tries to vic a cop right in the schoolyard. If my other friend come around here — he be Manslaughter — he vic you for sure. What your name, little old man?"

Cosgrove introduced himself. Instead of listening, Baby Rock clutched his stomach. "Growlin' like a bear. Know what I had to eat all day? Had nothin'."

Cosgrove felt certain that the boy was using his youth well, for of course America was not Africa and nobody was hungry, nor was it the O'Connell Street bridge in Dublin, where the tinkers show you babies and claim they are starving. But, fair game, Cosgrove thought. Smiling, he pulled a couple of singles out of his watch pocket. "Good lad."

"My man!"

Baby Rock took the money and ran through the glass piles and stopped dead when he saw Great Big outside. "What team you play for?" When Great Big didn't answer, Baby Rock shook his head. "You way bigger than Jabbar." Baby Rock ran for the corner and was gone. Cosgrove and Great Big were left on an empty sidewalk and had no idea of which direction to walk when a car with lettering on the front door saying AL DI LA CAR SERVICE stopped. The driver called, "What do you want, get beamed up?"

Cosgrove didn't answer.

"You want crack? You don't get no crack here. I'll take you get some."

"I'm looking for Saint Lucy's Church."

The driver, noticing the collar, decreed that he had merely been fooling about the crack and told Cosgrove to get in. But when Great Big followed, the driver jumped out onto the street. "He's a savage," the cabdriver said.

Said it with a tone and face that prompted Great Big to growl. Not a low growl, either, but one so advanced that it had already reached Great Big's throat. Cosgrove, in sheer fright, shouted at the driver. "This is my charge! You are to drive him with me! Do you understand!"

The cabdriver, surprised by this intensity, chortled. "You act like it's a matter of life and death."

Cosgrove said, "It certainly is!"

The cabdriver shrugged and got into the cab. The cabdriver wore a blue windbreaker with a New York Mets insignia and the name "Buster" printed on the front. "I'm just like Keith Hernandez. I never got convicted for drugs. That's my name, too. Buster. You know why they call me Buster? Because I bust people in the mouth."

Baby Rock came racing back around the corner with a can of grape soda in one hand and a bag of potato chips in the other. "You goin' for a ride?" When Cosgrove said yes, Baby Rock said, "I be ridin' too."

He tumbled into the back seat and offered the bag of bright orange potato chips. Great Big got two fingers into the bag and removed half the chips.

Baby Rock hid the bag behind him, then slapped his thigh. "Manslaughter's tool. Manslaughter axed me to hold on to his tool. Manslaughter told me hold it till he be around lookin' for his tool. He just have to wait for me. Say, my man." He looked up at Great Big. "When you play on the team, they go get you a whole lot of fine white females?"

At this, the cab turned a corner and was at the Chief from Howard Beach's restaurant. "I got to see a man," Buster announced. "You know who I'm going to see? Look at you, you don't even know where you are. You think I'm just a driver? Huh. I'm connected." He studied Cosgrove. "You don't know what I'm talking about, do you? I'm in the big outfit."

"Is that your cab company?" Cosgrove said.

"No, great big outfit. You think we just got cabs? You think Big Paulie got such a big outfit in Staten Island? Forget about it. We're the big outfit. Big Paulie don't like it, he could go screw. I say what I want about Big Paulie, if I make Big Paulie mad, even better. I'm with the Chief. The Chief got class."

The cabdriver swaggered into the restaurant and, through the window, Cosgrove saw him stand frozen, listening to orders, then bolt for the door. "You got to get out right away unless you want to wind up in the city," Buster yelled as he ran to the cab. "I go straight to the city for the Chief. I can't go a block out of my way, even for a priest."

"I be stayin'," Baby Rock said. "I never saw the city in my whole life." To Brooklyn, the city is Manhattan.

"Why, that is a grand idea," Cosgrove said. "We'll ride to the city with you and then you can get us home."

Buster the Cabdriver had the car moving when he said, "It'll still cost you. The Chief don't lose a dollar. They seen from inside that I had people in the back. They make a fortune using these cabs with no customers in them. The Chief is a multimillionaire, he still wants twenty dollars.

"Even with all that's coming in right here in this cab, and I'm not talkin' about you, I mean real business, he got twenty of these cabs, you think he cares, he still wants everything down to loose change. Don't ever go into a candy store with the Chief. He embarrasses you till you die. The Chief steals butterscotch rolls! How do you like that? How do you like him? How do you like the Chief? I tell you what else he does, he gets in a candy store. Then he takes the fuckin' newspaper. Excuse me, but that's what he does. He takes newspapers he don't even want to read. Just as long as he can rob them. I shouldn't even tell you because I took an oath not to say anything."

Buster drove to a parkway and onto a boulevard and soon they were on a bridge coming into midtown Manhattan in the full of evening. Lighted glass towers pierced the night blue sky. At the summits, the white light of the glass towers was so intense that it flooded the sky, turning it in places into gold. Or this is what it looked like from a distance, and it was a most important perspective, for the sky is the most important property in New York in the 1980s. Great Big hung his head out the window like a huge dog and pretty soon his hand came out waving at the sight. Cars in the next line either swerved away or slowed down so they would not have to ride near this apparition.

Baby Rock was on his feet and leaning out the same window. In the excitement, he dropped his potato chips on the floor. As he bent over, he again patted his thigh. "Manslaughter come to find his tool, find me be gone. He be so riled, he get another tool and shoot me."

"Over a tool?"

"This be a tool." Baby Rock pulled out an ugly black pistol and held it up.

Buster the Cabdriver saw this in the mirror. "The little nigger heists me." He stopped the cab so suddenly that Baby Rock was thrown to the floor.

Cosgrove snatched the gun. Buster jumped out and dodged through the bridge traffic. Cosgrove followed him out of the cab, waving his arms. "It's all right. Please come back!" In one of Cosgrove's waving hands was the ugly black gun. Buster sprinted for the other side of the bridge.

Cosgrove noticed the gun in his hand. In headlights and horns, he stepped to the bridge rail and looked at black water that was far down. The edges of the river were ablaze with light, but in the middle the water was black and soundless, yet even through the night air, Cosgrove could see that the black water was running smoothly.

Baby Rock came alongside him, reaching for the gun. "Be Manslaughter's."

"We can do without this," Cosgrove said. He was ecstatic that he could make such an understatement at a moment of high fear. He was terrified to touch the gun and he held it far away from him. "Yes, we can do without this." He flipped the gun out into the air.

Baby Rock wailed. "Manslaughter's tool."

Cosgrove followed the gun through the night air; he saw nothing but thought he heard a splash. He threw his arm around Baby Rock. "Isn't that a beautiful sight? A gun going to its death. You must always remember that it is the only thing to be put to death. You must respect life. You must never use birth control."

Baby Rock looked at him. "You don't have a gun?"

"Wouldn't touch one except to do this."

The boy looked at Great Big. "You ain't dressed, either?"

Great Big didn't understand the question. As he did not answer, Baby Rock took it for a negative.

"Don't care how big a man is, he ain't big unless he be dressed. Got himself a tool. Manslaughter, he smaller than me and he blew away a man big as a door."

Baby Rock jumped into the front seat of the cab and said he was going to drive to the city. Great Big got in, and Cosgrove was half in and pausing to say he thought this was a bad idea when Baby Rock got a foot on a pedal and that was it. He made the cab leap forward and Cosgrove pitched onto his stomach on the back floor. Baby Rock sent the cab whistling down the bridge and onto streets ablaze with light.

Baby Rock went through red lights and green lights with equal speed, and then he decided to stop the cab while running at top speed. The cab screeched and Baby Rock screamed with glee as it spun completely around and stopped with an explosion against an island in the middle of the street. The street was a ground fire of light and had flower beds in the middle. A street sign said, PARK AVENUE. Baby Rock left the motor running. "Gotta get me another soda from the store. Drivin' make me thirsty." He rattled the few chips left in the bag. Good lad. I'll buy him another bag at the next store, Cosgrove thought. The three walked the avenue and Great Big stepped into one of the plots and threw himself on the grass and gazed up at the glass buildings, each of which reflected another's light, and the series of reflections met in a sky that to his eyes was a fiery gold. When there was no candy store in sight, the three walked back toward the cab and saw two patrol cars parked at it.

"I be bookin'," Baby Rock said, walking away quickly, jamming the potato chip bag into his pocket, getting ready to race. Cosgrove, feeling it prudent to claim his suitcase at another time, nudged Great Big and they left with Baby Rock. They walked onto a street where restaurants sat blazing in yellow light for as far as the eye could see. At the first, Baby Rock and Great Big pressed their faces against the window. At a table alongside the door, a man in a blue striped shirt was talking to a young woman, who listened intently. The man waved his hands grandly. Baby Rock opened the glass door and reached between the man's gestures and snatched a piece of roast beef from his plate. Baby Rock walked on and took a large bite of the meat, which was quite strange to him.

"What you call this?" he said, looking at the meat.

"My dinner!" the man said, suddenly appearing in the cold without an overcoat. Baby Rock started running with the roast beef sticking out of his mouth and his hands pumping. Great Big grabbed for the meat and missed. Baby Rock's legs were of such thinness that he could swing them across each other like scissor arms and whisk around groups of people. Baby Rock left Cosgrove and Great Big behind as he ran on his young legs to the corner, where a patrol car rocked to a stop and a cop jumped out with his arms spread. The arms closed like gates on Baby Rock, whose squall was unintelligible because of the roast beef in his mouth. The second cop, the driver, seeing Great Big, pulled out his gun. When Cosgrove ran up, the cop holding Baby Rock said, "Did he rob you, Father?" Cosgrove, thinking quickly, told the policeman, "Oh, no! He's my altar boy. His idea of a practical joke."

The policeman was just about to let go of Baby Rock when there was a noise and here came Buster flying up the sidewalk, flying up so excited — "You stole the Chief's cab! I could go to Leavenworth what I got in my cab!" — that he failed to notice the police. Buster did not touch Great Big. Buster did throw a tremendous punch into Cosgrove's face. Buster certainly could punch. Cosgrove went down on the back of his head. One of the cops reached and hit Buster over the head with a nightstick. The nightstick also could hit. Buster went onto his knees like a penitent.

Great Big, his huge hands only inches away from Buster's throat, stopped and bent down to assist Cosgrove. One of the cops spoke into his hand radio and soon the street corner was alive with cars and more and more police and one of them, a sergeant, looked at the group and pronounced everyone under arrest. Baby Rock started to run and the sergeant grabbed him by the collar. Several police, looking up at Great Big, pulled out their guns.

A police van arrived and they were all pushed into the rear. When the doors were slammed, Great Big kicked so hard that they parted slightly, even against such thick locks. Baby Rock sat and shook his potato chip bag, trying to get more out of it. Great Big reached for the chips and Baby Rock slid into a corner. The van lurched for many minutes and gave one great lurch and stopped. The doors flew open and Cosgrove saw that they were in a garage with police cars and vans. A fat cop with a clipboard looked at Cosgrove's collar and said, "What are you, a fake priest or a fag priest?"

Inside, in a large room with pale yellow tiles, a desk lieutenant with gray hair and a long, bored face that needed a shave inspected Cosgrove's identification and did not look up.

"What is this about?" Cosgrove said.

The lieutenant, reading, said, "Order me around in church. This is my place and you do what I want. Right now I want you to shut up."

The lieutenant read aloud from a sheet. "You have violated penal code 120.05, assault on a police officer; 205.30, resisting arrest; 147.50, theft; 125.27, attempted murder of a police officer."

Buster suddenly cried out, "Are you people crazy? If I touch a cop, I'm a dead man. You know what I mean? I come from a law-and-order outfit. I'm good people. You know what I mean? But this black nigger savage" — Buster swung around and pointed directly at Great Big — "he tried to kill the cop!"

Great Big was extremely furious at Buster. Over at the fingerprint table, a young man with light hair and a thin mustache and a young woman in a leather jacket were pushed aside for Cosgrove's group. Buster inked his fingers and rolled them expertly on the fingerprint card. Buster's rolling motion pleased the cops greatly, as it is poor form to press the fingers straight down. When Great Big put his thumb on the fingerprint card it went right out of the space. The cop taking the prints said, "This destroys the print, don't it?" Another cop said, "Send it up anyway, I guess."

They were taken through a doorway and inside was a row

of six cells. Cosgrove, in the first cell, could hear the others locked in. A cop with a huge belly, whistling, keys jingling, walked past. Cosgrove asked him what would happen now. The cop said the fingerprints had to be transmitted to the state capital at Albany, where they were checked to see if anybody had any prior criminal record. "It takes a little while," the cop said. He walked out.

Buster called out, "The Chief blows up when he finds what happens to me. Serves me right, even havin' a nigger in the car."

Great Big sensed what Buster was saying and called out to Cosgrove in Yoruba that he hated Buster and wanted to kill him. Buster, hearing the strange language, said, "What did that animal say about me?"

"He wanted the time of day," Cosgrove said.

"Eleven-thirty at night already," Buster said.

Cosgrove sat down on the hard bench. He rolled his raincoat into a pillow and put his head back. He stared at a yellow tile wall that was covered with scrawling he could not read and with drawings of huge penises. He took off his glasses, rubbed his eyes, and, saying his evening prayers, fell asleep.

He was awakened by the cell door opening and the light-haired prisoner walking in. The prisoner held out a hand to keep Cosgrove where he was. "We could be here for days," he said. "They're all backed up."

"And how did you have the misfortune to land here?" Cosgrove asked.

The light-haired guy made a gun out of his hand.

"I'm sorry you had to do such a thing," Cosgrove said.

"The trouble is, somebody got hurt," the guy said.

"Oh, dear God, what a shame. Hurt bad is he?"

"A she. She worked in the cashier's office. Food March supermarket. Dizzy bitch tried to slam the door in my face. I don't know what happened. She gets shot. I shouldn't even be talking to you. I shouldn't even be talking to myself, but I have to trust you, you're a priest, right?"

"Oh, of course I'm a priest and I say nothing. But, dear God, this unfortunate woman you shot, is she all right?"

"They told me she only got hit in the arm. She's all right."

"Thank God. I'll pray for you, lad. And the young woman you were with outside?"

"That's my girlfriend."

"She was a participant? Oh, the poor misgui — "

"No, she had nothin' to do with it. They're lousy bastards for arresting her, excuse me but they are. I was asleep with her in her apartment and bing-bang-boom, they come in through the door, off the fire escapes. All over."

Cosgrove's eyes widened. "Are you telling me that you were sleeping with a woman to whom you were not legally married?"

"My girlfriend."

Cosgrove shook a finger. "You should be ashamed of yourself!"

He rolled over so he would not have to look at the light-haired prisoner again.

In the morning there was a shout, and a Hispanic cop opened the cell doors and told them to come with him. "Your prints were no good," he muttered. When the cop looked at Great Big, his arrogant lips became more pronounced. Great Big, in turn, had an anger rising out of an empty stomach.

"Do we get food?" Cosgrove asked.

"You get something at dinnertime," the Hispanic cop said. He supervised their fingerprinting and brought them back to the cells. No food materialized.

Later, another cop looked in. "Do you have our food?" Cosgrove said.

The cop laughed. "What are you, freeloaders? You got your sandwiches."

"No we didn't."

"Oh. Then they'll get you something soon."

The next time the door opened, midafternoon light spilled in and several new cops walked in and handcuffed everybody to a long chain. When no cuffs would fit over Great Big they put leg shackles on his wrists and attached him to the chain. Great Big was next to Buster on the chain. He bared his teeth and growled. Now a cop holding a small Puerto Rican by the shoulder walked up. The Puerto Rican wore a rainhat pulled over his eyes. He had a pencil mustache. "Come on, you fuckin' spic bastard," the cop said. The Puerto Rican, seeing Great Big, resisted. "Man, don't put me near no black nigger bastard."

Cosgrove asked about the fingerprints. One cop said, "We used to get the prints back right away when the central office was in police headquarters. In Albany they got only civilians. They go to lunch and dinner while you guys sit here. Sometimes the farmers up there take days."

They were taken down the staircase to the garage and into another van and this time for a long ride and finally, after much lurching, the van doors were opened and they were in another garage, one much older, and this time they were taken down a flight of stairs and into a grimy dungeon with a bare light in a ceiling painted sickly green. They were pulled off the chain and shoved into small filthy cells by a black cop with a bald head.

"I be hungry," Baby Rock said.

"Don't play with me," the black cop said. "I'm a cop, not a brother."

"I be hungry, not be playin'."

"You'll be fed."

The door slammed and Cosgrove began to pray in the dim light. And for the first time, the dull hunger in his belly kept him awake.

Now there was a kicking and rattling of the cell door by Great Big. He kicked and rattled for the next eight hours, for by now he had Africa in his belly. Cosgrove, knowing this, prayed for help.

Sometime in the middle of the next morning, a cop looked in and shouted, "We're moving you all out."

Cosgrove, expecting to embrace freedom, got up and was met with the sound of more chains rattling. The police brought in chains of the size used on trucks during snowstorms. As they were led out of the cell block, Cosgrove said that they were truly hungry, but nobody listened to him. They were again in a van and this time found they had been taken back to the original police station. Great Big said in Yoruba that he was starving. This disturbed Cosgrove. Buster, whose eyes were glazed, stumbled into Great Big, and when Great Big elbowed him away, Buster, with a fury that caused him to lose all caution, kicked Great Big. A furious whine came out of Great Big and Cosgrove had to place his head on Great Big's chest to calm him.

The four suddenly were nearly dragged off their feet by a squad of cops yanking the chain as if mooring a ship and taken through a door and into another dark cell block. Cosgrove was put in with Baby Rock. He heard Great Big and Buster the Cabdriver being put into the same cell.

"What of food?" Cosgrove said.

"We'll get you sandwiches in a few minutes," the cop said.

Cosgrove, for the first time since the African dust, had hunger cramps, severe ones, and as he doubled over in the cell he suddenly thought of Great Big. Alarm raced through his mind. Some hours later, a young cop with large brown eyes and black curly hair looked in.

"Our sandwiches," Cosgrove said.

"You got them already," the young cop said.

"We did not. The last lad who was in here promised us sandwiches."

The young cop ran his hand over his head. "He told you?"

"Yes."

"He went home. You got a new tour now."

The young cop slammed the door and Cosgrove sat through the hours, trying to pray, with Baby Rock now squalling and, in the last cell, Great Big starting a tremendous attack on the barred door. He got something loose, for the door began to make even more of a racket. Finally Great Big stopped and Cosgrove went into a coma. He partially heard a snarl and an inhuman scream, but as he only heard it partially, he passed it off as more normal suffering.

"All right, let's go."

The cell door was open. The cop took Cosgrove and Baby Rock out to the deck, where a fat red-haired cop sat in his lieutenant's white shirt. He held up white slips of paper.

"You know what these are? These are desk appearance tickets. You got to appear in court on March twenty-third."

"What do we do until then?"

"You go home."

"But we have been held all this time?"

The red-haired cop looked at papers. "Well, you know there was all that trouble getting fingerprints. Then the charges had to be changed. They were excited the first night. We had to rewrite them to menacing and harassment. That's only a misdemeanor. So you got lost in the system a little. Sorry."

"What about the other man with me?" Cosgrove said, turning to the open cell block door.

"Oh yeah, him, too," the red-haired cop said. He nodded and the other cop stepped into the cell block and, without bothering to look inside, opened the door and Great Big stepped out. The cop slammed the cell door and locked it without deigning to look inside. "We got to hold the last guy. This Buster. He got a long sheet and the district attorney wants to see him," the red-haired cop said. "Now go over there to the desk and the property clerk will give you back your belongings. By the way, it's a little late, but I'll wish you a Merry Christmas."

Cosgrove signed and was given his wallet and passports and the three — he, Baby Rock, and Great Big — stepped out of the station house into a cold evening. Cosgrove, on a whim, went back into the station house and yelled at the desk officer, "I'll have you know that we had not a morsel of food during our captivity!"

The desk officer failed to pick up his head. Cosgrove, Baby Rock, and Great Big began walking until they came to a coffee shop and they went in and sat at the counter and

Cosgrove ordered huge stacks of pancakes. Baby Rock ate until he got sick. Cosgrove wolfed them down. After about twenty minutes he happened to notice that Great Big was toying with the food and eating none of it.

Great Big began to push the pancakes around the plate in disgust. He opened his mouth and gave a loud burp. Cosgrove switched his fork to his left hand without missing a chew, dug into his jacket pocket, brought out a pack of Tums, and rolled it across the counter to Great Big, who dropped all of them into his mouth.

After Cosgrove paid the check, Baby Rock said that once they found a subway he could get them back to East New York. He asked two white men, who were unsure. A black delivery boy knew the line they wanted immediately and Baby Rock led them along Fifty-seventh Street and across a splendid avenue where a gold tower rose so high into the sky that Cosgrove grew dizzy looking up at the top.

A couple of blocks later, they saw a man standing in an alcove alongside the entranceway to a building still under construction. He had tangled hair hanging into a face covered with dust. Blank gray eyes were sunk into his gaunt face. He was wrapped in a greasy, once-pink blanket, which he clutched in front. In back, the blanket hung only to his waistline and underneath that the baggy pants were ripped and his bare bottom, stung red by the cold, was out for all to see. Including a woman who stepped out of a Bentley that was almost too rich for the eyes. Cosgrove's blood quickened. He ran up and yanked the blanket down, causing it to drop from his front and the man to bawl, "You want me to freeze to death?"

Cosgrove turned from the gray-faced man in disgust. He

addressed the elegant woman alighting from the car. "How can they permit such nudity in a civilized country?"

The woman, Octavia Ripley Havermeyer, was taken aback by the sight of the huge man with this rumpled priest, and also the young black boy. This was obviously a homeless mugging team; she walked on rapidly. Stepping into the sweeping lobby, however, she did have the vision of a night in summer with all these homeless people walking completely naked about the streets. They could depreciate real estate values simply by displaying their private parts. This certainly was something to think about.

All Bushwick knew was that the building was next to the Russian Tea Room on West Fifty-seventh Street. He wore a jacket he had borrowed from Roberts, who worked in accounting, and a tie purchased from a street peddler. Earlier, called by the New Opportunity office and asked to appear at the fund-raising party, he had suggested that they take Roberts, who at least could wear his own jacket, but the New Opportunity P.R. woman said they needed exactly what Bushwick could bring them, somebody a little seedy from working with the Poor, thus authenticating the reason for the party, which was to raise blocks of money for the soup kitchens.

The party was being held after the opera in the penthouse apartment of an unfinished building whose address was given to Bushwick as "next to the Rush" and when Bushwick didn't know what that meant, the P.R. woman had laughed and told him, why, of course, the Russian Tea Room. The building was a shaft of smoked glass set on the ground so that it appeared to be marching to the left obliquely.

As there was not enough room to plant the entire front of a building on Fifty-seventh Street, the builder one day stood at the drawing board, tilted the blueprint, and told everybody to start putting the place up. He immediately applied for tax relief from the city, which he got, and on top of the tax break he asked for permission to make the building four stories higher than the permit specified, and four stories higher at the same tax rate, or absence thereof, and of course he got exactly what he wanted because New York taxes and land were being given away in the 1980s with more speed and efficiency than any bowl of soup. When Bushwick got to the building, scaffolding hid the entrance, where two smiling young women sat at a desk and checked his name on a list and handed him a hard hat.

"I don't work here," Bushwick said.

"Oh, you must wear one," one of the young women said.

When she looked at the hard hat, she saw an oh-so-gay costume for the evening, a dress-up in the uniform of a workingman. When Bushwick looked at the hard hat, he saw the bus to work at six in the morning.

The elevator operator was a young man in a tuxedo and white hard hat. "Here's another workingman," he said.

"Only I work," Bushwick said.

The elevator opened to the penthouse, where people sat at tables with a triangular setting of candles four feet high that allowed them to have the simultaneous thrills of seeing diamonds flashing in and out of near darkness and then, whenever they felt like it, they could tilt their white hard hats for all to see that they were working-class jaunty.

Bushwick stood in the foyer uncertainly, until a smiling young woman with a clipboard walked up to him and he asked for the managing directress of New Opportunity, Octavia Ripley Havermeyer, and the young woman said, "Why, of course, she is right inside," directing him to the master bedroom, where Octavia, about sixty-three, with short gray hair and head held high in order to draw her neck as long and tight as a goose's, stood and admired the place and then stepped into the bathroom, which was a tile arena.

"Oh, I'm so glad you could come," she said to Bushwick.

"Thanks for having me," he said.

"Not at all. When we have these fund-raisers, we need field workers so people can see exactly what we do. This one was so poorly planned. We have all the givers but promotion completely forgot about getting you people." She shook her head and sat down on a French Provincial chair, which was placed in a seating area outside the shower. "My feet hurt. I went to the podiatrist today and he made me these little pads that I put under my toes. That eased the pain somewhat. But I'm afraid I'm going to be wearing these horrible old ladies' shoes. Custom-made, luxurious boats." She sighed.

"I just wanted to ask you one question," Bushwick said.

"Of course."

"Is this a real bathroom?"

Hearing this, Octavia gave a tight little smile. What else could the room be but a bathroom? A long room with a high ceiling that had spotlights in it. The walls and floor were marble and there were two gleaming sinks, floor-length mirrors, two separate compartments for toilets, a large area for a shower, and another for a sunken tub. She looked at Bushwick and thought, Of course he doesn't understand all this. How could he? He has never seen anything, much less been trained in how to regard it.

She thought of the time, at dusk of a spring night, when she had sat on the great lawn at Pocantico Hills and Nelson Rockefeller squeezed her arm and said, "Now, fella, it's the old story. For every action, there is a reaction. And on balance, you have to go with the people who have ownership. Perhaps when they react, they overstep, but you always have a next time with them. Maybe you can bring them back in line a little. But once the ones who own nothing overstep, what is there to bring them back? They're right inside someplace they never were in before, and they sure don't want to leave. It's that simple. Right there goes your whole game. On balance, fella, stay with ownership."

As she certainly owned enough herself, Octavia Ripley Havermeyer decided that her mission here in later life was to work for the Poor as long as they stayed in the alley. That wasn't a bad deal for anybody, she felt. Her name was familiar in both social and financial circles and at the same time she threatened nobody and had much time — she was a widow of twenty-one years — so those important in the city were content to allow her to assemble the huge organization, agency by agency, and pose as directress. This allowed her an office and the services of a staff and the only time she had to drop pretenses and understand her true position came when David Rockefeller arrived at the New Opportunity offices. Rockefeller security people had the hallways cleared, and any secretary out walking papers to another office was shoved into an alcove, for Rockefeller preferred serenity and silence as he walked to his private suite of offices. Octavia Ripley Havermeyer was alert enough on those days to remain in her office and thus spare herself the humiliation of being asked to clear the hall for David Rockefeller.

Now, on a French Provincial chair in the shower area, regarding her aching feet, she said to Bushwick, "Why don't you just go out and . . . mingle?"

"Because to tell you the truth, ma'am, I'm a little leery. I don't know one person. What's here, a lot of politicians and things like that?"

"No politicians. These are all new builders and they don't know quite so much about anything. They run themselves and that's it."

"What am I supposed to talk to them about?"

"Nothing. Let them talk. The only thing anybody really cares about is the rents. Only the rents. That's all that is really sacred. Otherwise things run for the usual motive. Sheer jealousy."

She said this firmly, as one who understood the alliance that ran her city. She had seen it for herself on the afternoon in the walking ring at Belmont Park racetrack before the Belmont Stakes, the walking ring for this race a gathering of only the rich and known. A group of builders and the governor, his face red as a lobster from luncheon wine, laughed uproariously at one another's jokes. It was clear to Octavia that each was insanely jealous of the other. Who is this scruffy little wino to be so important, the builders obviously thought, at the same time feeling terribly uncomfortable in the presence of a true star of what the builders regarded as the real world: politics. That day Octavia had seen that the governor was uneasy in the presence of those who could make so much money in a world politicians find most mysterious: private business. It was by using this jealousy and fear that people such as she, at the top of New Opportunity, could work with much success over long days and weeks.

Now, in the penthouse apartment, she took Bushwick by the arm and led him into the dining room and introduced him to people and Bushwick kept saying "Pleasure," and he didn't remember one face or one word, and as he was terrified of taking a seat at one of these round tables with all these lacquered people, he made his way to a huge picture window and here, thirty-five stories down, was a streak of fire running straight up the island of Manhattan, the great avenue at night, the firelight rising so high that it turned the air to gold. They have so much money they end the night, Bushwick thought. Below he saw a brilliant white circle, the ice rink in the middle of the soft darkness of Central Park. Perhaps two hundred tiny forms skated in a slow circle.

A man was standing alongside Bushwick, a man curried and combed, wearing a rich double-breasted blue pinstripe. "The one thing disappointing to me about this building is that they close the rink and shut off the lights at night. You can't look at the people skating," he said.

"That is a shame," Bushwick said.

"I wonder if there is somebody we could call to keep the rink open at least until one A.M. or so when I go to bed. Keep it crowded with skaters, give me my view."

"You live here?" Bushwick asked him.

"I'll be moving in as soon as the decorator finishes," he said.

"Maybe we'll force people to skate all night," Bushwick said.

"Well, I don't see how you can make them."

"Use convicts," Bushwick said.

"Do you really think you could do that?" the man said.

"Better than sitting in a cell all night."

"I suppose it is. But wouldn't the security be too costly?"

"Not if you locked the skates on their feet. Then they couldn't go anyplace," Bushwick said.

"Wouldn't that be amazing?" the man said. His mind was at midposition between ludicrousness and actuality and for the moment he had no idea which was correct.

"Is your apartment like this one?" Bushwick asked the man.

"Pretty much so."

"How much does one like this cost?" Bushwick said.

"Five million."

"For that you should get ice skaters all night."

"I've got till next year, anyway," he said. The man's hand waved at the elegant room. "It'll take them till spring to finish the building and my apartment. In the meantime, I'm trying to survive in hotel living."

"Which one?" Bushwick asked.

"The Carlyle."

"You can survive there," Bushwick said.

"If you call four rooms surviving."

"Dear Fred Taylor, what are you doing there?" Octavia Ripley Havermeyer, hands on her hips, scowled at Bushwick like a schoolteacher.

"Talking."

"But there is a whole table full of people who want to talk to you. Come now."

She led Bushwick to one of the large round tables and sat him down.

The man next to Bushwick nodded. "How do you do? My name is Sidney Golden. I own 246 Park Avenue. That's a nice office building, fifty-four stories. I own 813 Park Avenue. That's a residence. Twenty-one stories. That's who I am. Tell me who you are."

"I'm Fred Taylor. I own some things, too."

"Where?"

"In Queens."

Octavia Ripley Havermeyer, unsure whether Bushwick was being serious or outrageous, but taking no chances, leaned forward and broke in.

"Does anybody know a good foot doctor?"

"I can find out from my wife," Golden said.

"Fred Taylor, did you try the salad?" Octavia said.

Satisfied that Bushwick's mouth was full and that Golden would talk about foot doctors for five minutes or so, Octavia relaxed. Oh, she could have talked buildings with the man all night, but for what? Her family had owned the land under Golden's buildings since the 1800s, and Golden's ninety-nine-year lease would expire in the year 2036, at which time the land and all that was on it, the big beautiful buildings worth hundreds of millions, would revert to the Havermeyer family. "This family came here from Rotterdam to rule," her grandfather had always insisted. The only way to rule was to retain control of the land. Octavia Ripley Havermeyer's antecedents were among the thirteen original members of the Dutch West India Company and thus belonged to the handful of adventurers who founded New York. They were the first to push into the desolate lands of upper Manhattan, where Octavia owned parcels of most priceless land, from the core of the earth to the top of the sky, and thus was worth a fortune that would be handed down to her family for entire centuries to come.

Next to her, Golden, living for the moment, was lustrous. At fifty-four, he had dark wavy hair with curls on each side. He and his barber allowed some gray, so he would look distinguished, but not so much that his twenty-five-year-old wife, who professed such desperate love for him, would decide he was too old and take the complaint to her lawyer. The twenty-five-year-old, in a Bill Blass black that was a size too small for her, sat a table away.

Golden spoke in low tones to the man next to him, Robert Whalen, another major builder.

"I have the feeling that they simply have more teeth."

"How could one set of teeth be different from another?" Whalen said.

Octavia said, "You must forgive me for interrupting, but I do so want to pick up the thread of your conversation."

"We're talking about dogs," Golden said.

"Oh, how cheerful. Are you showing at Westminster?"

"Not quite," Golden said. "I have been having trouble with teeth. I can hardly believe it, but the dogs I like best, good young Dobermans, have plaque, just like humans do. The plaque pushes the gums back and loosens the teeth. Just as if it's your grandfather. My God, if there's one thing I can't stand, it's a Doberman with loose teeth."

"Dobermans are so sleek," Octavia said.

"The sleekness doesn't attract me. The original reason I went to Dobermans was that I fell in love with their teeth. I thought they had more teeth than other dogs. They remind me of sharks. Teeth growing all the way down the throat. Break off one set of teeth and you have another just waiting to catch onto you. So I wind up with dogs that have plaque. You know what? To scrape away plaque, you have to put the dogs to sleep. You can't tell one of them to open his mouth. Have to knock him out."

"If Dobermans get plaque, then get another breed," Whalen said.

"The Dobermans are the only breed on earth."

Octavia Ripley Havermeyer looked with some alarm as Bushwick picked his head up from the salad and said, "How many of them do you have in your kennel?"

"Kennel? I got twelve of them out on the street around my buildings."

"Oh, to keep people away."

"Of course."

"The drug addicts and criminals?" Octavia said hurriedly, particularly when she saw Bushwick's scowl.

"No, the homeless," Golden said.

"Whatever it is that they pretend to be," Whalen said. "Who knows what they are? Why don't they sleep in subway stations where they belong? I guess they're all on drugs. But there is no way to have decent real estate with them hanging around every nook and cranny of a building. You ask them to leave and they just sit and stare. But when you have a man patrol your building with a dog, they go away and they don't come back."

"The dog sniffs out their drugs," Octavia Ripley Havermeyer said, her voice at least strained.

Golden smiled slowly. "My dogs don't sniff. My dogs bite."

Octavia Ripley Havermeyer understood the subject, protection of property, but here she had the sudden burden of

Bushwick sitting at the same table. Why did they have to send this young man from the office to this party? They usually had people silent and unconcerned and so happy to get a meal in splendor that they suffered through anything. But this young man clearly was agitated and about to do something bold.

"They can't very well with sore gums," Octavia said, her voice a little tense as she tried to think.

"That's why this plaque has me crazy," Golden said.

"I still think you should try German shepherds," Whalen said. "They are a bigger dog. They might even have bigger teeth."

Golden shook his head. "You take a German shepherd. As good as they are, there is still a quality about a German shepherd that you want to reach out and pet him. You don't do that with a Doberman. You look at them and what do you think of? Mafia. That's what they are. Mafia dogs. And with those yellow teeth sticking out of that black mouth. That's for me. A couple of my good alert guards swagger around with the dogs and these other people simply leave."

"If the dog bites the guard, he got a lawsuit against you," Whalen said.

Golden shook his head. "Not my guards. You ought to see them. I have twenty-five former Rangers who guard the buildings."

"Who pays them?" Whalen asked.

"I take it out of the tax fund. I was supposed to pay thirty million in taxes for the first three years. The city cut it to nineteen million for me. It gives me something to play with. You should see them. They wear berets and fatigues and polished boots, just like in Vietnam. They have some kind of pride. They were fighting in Vietnam. Now they're keeping people away from a building. But those boots are polished."

Octavia, voice more strained, said, "This is all well and good for dinner conversation, but tell me, Mr. Golden, what happens if the dogs actually do bite a person?"

"That's exactly what I pay for," Golden said.

"They have actually bitten people?"

Golden said nothing.

"Can't these people sue you for a fortune?" she asked.

"Not these people."

Her lips immediately trembled with indignation, but Octavia also had her usual difficulty in understanding that what she was hearing was real. For the world that she had small glimpses of, the one out in the streets, and this one here, with which she was most familiar, were in such contrast that the differences frequently stunned her, and at times such as this, when some man next to her said the most atrocious things, she was capable of having proper emotions but at the same time found her insides inert, as if they had just fallen from a horse.

Octavia arose and put a hand on Bushwick. "Dear me, I forgot that you had to get something signed. If you gentlemen will forgive us." Bushwick, who had an idea the party was over, picked up a piece of chicken with his bare hand and ate it as he walked out of the room with Octavia.

"Oh, I don't know what I can possibly say to you except that these men contribute money that does reach the poor dears with whom you deal."

"I guess so," Bushwick said dully.

"I am so mortified!" Octavia said.

"I don't know what to tell you," Bushwick said.

"It's part of what we have to bear," Octavia said.

"Not to insult you, but I don't know how anybody can sit here and listen to these people," Bushwick said.

"For now, please try to understand how ragged my heart is about tonight."

"You don't mind if I go?" Bushwick said.

"Oh, of course not."

"Because I would've had to go anyway, I guess."

She smiled and touched his arm and he walked out of the apartment and she went back to the table, feeling quite relieved. She also immediately changed the conversation from dogs to show horses.

4

B ABY ROCK headed straight for the lights of a sub-
way kiosk: when sick, go to a doctor; when black,
head for the subway. Baby Rock went up to the
change booth and asked the man which side the
Brooklyn train came in on. "This is the side."

Baby Rock slapped the change tray. The clerk was about
to push out a token when he saw that Baby Rock had left
nothing. He loped up to the turnstile and put the fingers of
his right hand on the turnstile and, just using the fingertips,
nothing else, went up into the air, spun spectacularly, and
went over the bar backwards, laughing at the change booth
man. Great Big walked up to it and merely stepped over.
The two were gone down another flight of stairs to the train
platform. Cosgrove ran to the turnstile, thought the jump
was too high, and thought just for a moment before drop-
ping to his knees and crawling under, and that was all the
change clerk needed to summon a cop.

A metal door alongside the toll booth opened and a young

cop in a leather jacket, with a radio in one hand and a summons pad in another, appeared. Cosgrove smiled benignly and said that he appeared to have lost his money. The cop smirked. "I'm not the police upstairs. I'm transit police. We don't care if the Pope shows up here. He got money or he can't get in."

Cosgrove was amazed that the subway police would not honor a priest. Then, looking at the cop and seeing unmistakable Italian features, he understood that the situation would not change. "Priest hater," he muttered.

Suddenly, there was noise from the staircase and a crowd of people came down, many of them white, apparently coming from a theater, for they held programs, and the young cop began to watch over them, particularly when a few blacks also appeared. Still, he never really took his eye off Cosgrove.

Baby Rock came back up the stairs, saw the problem, took out a matchbook, folded it, and stuffed it into the coin slot. Then he stood there. An old woman, carrying purse and theater program, came up, dropped her token, and tried to go through the gate. It didn't move. She looked at the coin slot and shrugged and pushed the turnstile again. When nothing moved, she walked purposefully back to the change booth to complain. Baby Rock bent over the change slot, put his mouth on it, and sucked the token out of the slot. He put his hand to his mouth, dropped the token into his hand, and handed it to Cosgrove. "My man, let's make the train."

When they got off at the last stop, in East New York, a subway worker told them how to get to Cozine Street. Following directions, they found themselves passing Baby

Rock's store. He jumped inside and threw the blanket over himself. His white sneakers showed from under the end of the blanket and he passed out.

Cosgrove and Great Big walked through the last of the night and again came to the part of Cozine Street where the street dipped, but this time, following directions, they walked in the darkness and came up the hill on the other side and a block down they came to an old church, dull red brick, with a similarly old rectory attached to it. Alongside the church litter was spread across a lot that ran into a stretch of vacant land that led far out to the bay, and beyond the bay, as the sky indicated, there was more water, endless water, the ocean. Cosgrove rang the bell; it was some time before an old pastor peered around a curtain, saw Cosgrove, and with much unsnapping of locks opened the door.

"You were due last week."

"We got lost."

"Well, I'm in bed. Who is this with you?"

"My friend."

"Well, you and your friend come in. I'm sleeping."

Cosgrove looked at the sky and the empty land running out to the water. "I want to stand here for a minute," he said.

"Have it your way. I'll be in bed. Lock the door after you. You never know who comes in here, day or night."

Great Big followed the pastor into the house, folded himself up on the floor, and was asleep.

~~~~~~

Cosgrove stood on the stoop and looked at the sky and thought for a moment that he was back where he was born, in Dunboy in Ireland, in the western part of county Cork, in a hut atop a cliff that was a hundred feet over a cold and angry Atlantic. The ocean waves slapped high on the side of the cliff and threw white salt water far up, all the way up to the tough grass in front of the hut. The cliff where the hut sat formed one side of Dunboy Bay, which is so deep and almost so endless that it should be considered an elbow on the ocean rather than a separate body of water.

On the rectory stoop in East New York, Cosgrove remembered a spring day when he had stood in the saltwater spray at the cliff as gray clouds spread high in the sky, and through them came a single shaft of light that poured across the ground around him as if it were the hand of God. Looking down the bay, he saw a section of clouds darker than night, thunder sounding in them, thunder loud enough to startle people many miles away, as deep orange lightning exploded in the black clouds, the bolts turning yellow-white as they darted to the land. Farther down, at the shoulder of the storm, bright sunlight covered several miles and washed the air blue and caused the land to appear fresh green and the white huts to glare like mirrors. The sunlight ended suddenly at a dull gray sky that covered the town of Dunboy, whose narrow streets and low stone buildings sat in a wonderful drizzle. Usually, in less than an hour, these different forms of weather changed places, with the sun momentarily on the town and the lightning out at the mouth of the bay, where it flashed down and struck the cliffs. As a child, he had often hidden inside his mother's coat when a hailstorm trapped the two on the road while they walked home from the store. The hailstorm came at the end of a bright spell. Life inside the hut was lived in the relentless whistle of wind that was exciting and even comforting for a short while, but then became torture that left an imprint on the bones.

This weather controls the Irish brain; the fact that from youth to graveyard a person does not have the freedom to step out from under his own roof without drowning so restricts the people that madness sprouts like mushrooms. As the reason for madness is so obvious — look up at the clouds — it is deliberately omitted from most of the academic and medical research on Irish genius and instability. Mix weather with the still-lingering effects of Jansenism and sometimes there can be trouble of great magnitude.

Jansenism is a religious teaching that says love is really felonious assault on God. When the British outlawed religious training in the seventeenth century, young men were smuggled to Louvain University in France, where Cornelis Otto Jansen, a religious fanatic, taught his theories and sent priests sneaking back to Ireland, where they dressed like civilians and told the Irish that even holding hands was sinful. Jansen was condemned by the church as a heretic, but his doctrine lasted in Ireland and then was transported to America, particularly to all the eastern states where, hundreds of years later, a state the size of New York, with a population of fourteen million, could not get full sex education into all of its public grammar schools because of the grip held on the government by Catholics.

Any religious mania is assisted by the rain that has doused the race for so long that finally in a lifetime a person shakes a wet head to throw off the excess water and finds that this time the inside of his head does not stop swiveling. Frequently, religion and weather combine to destroy people before they can reason.

D'Arcy Cosgrove was eleven years old when he first thought of becoming a priest. One day a recruiter for the Redemptorist order came in and made such a stirring presentation about the glories of serving God and self-denial that when D'Arcy went home for lunch, he was utterly convinced. His mother was at the stove with steam rising all around her. "Mum, I'm going to be a priest," D'Arcy said.

"No you're not," his mother said, stirring pots in the steam.

Then one day, when D'Arcy Cosgrove was twelve, his mother suddenly began to weep during a rainstorm on a February afternoon, and when the tears did not stop for several days, his father took her on the five-hour bus ride to Cork City, where in the long red-brick mental hospital on the Lee Road the female attendants interested her in making moccasins.

At first it was difficult for her to move her hands. After several weeks, however, she stitched with a country girl's deftness while women attendants reveled in her progress and lectured to her that upon her return to the hut on the cliff, she must continue making moccasins, selling them anywhere, just keep working, and then one day male attendants came in while she made her moccasins and said this was her scheduled day for shock treatment. The female attendants tried to protest, but a male attendant leafed through his documents and said no, this was the day on which she must have her treatment.

As the Irish are a third-paragraph race — the first two devoted to the weather and then in the third the news that your mother has just died and you had best hurry home for the funeral — the idea of talking out a mental illness with a psychiatrist was completely alien at that time. For any disorder of the head stronger than a common headache, the subject was strapped to a pallet, as D'Arcy Cosgrove's mother was, and hit with enough electricity to light a street. The insides of her head were shaken like dice in a box, with the predictable result that the same dice came out, but with different numbers on the top. She returned from shock treatment unable to make moccasins but now quite adept at shrieking in the night.

"To make a long story short, the Devil sits on her mind," a male attendant told the husband. They sent the mother home with him.

In July the sun broke through the clouds and remained for several days of a fantastic heat wave, climbing to 74°. D'Arcy Cosgrove found his mother on the floor with blood running out of her ear. She was taken to Dunboy Hospital, where she died of her hemorrhage. The local newspaper, the *West County Telegraph,* ran a headline saying, WOMAN IS VICTIM OF MASSIVE HEAT WAVE.

Rain returned for the funeral, streaming off the casket as it was carried down the church steps. Helping carry the casket, D'Arcy Cosgrove resembled the land on which he was raised. His flesh barely made it across his rib cage, just as the earth at Dunboy was spread so thinly over hills that when rain lifted and light fell on the hills, the sheer rock glinted through the thin covering of soil.

Later, D'Arcy's father, left with four children, sat with Bill O'Connell, proprietor, the Landmark Inn, and had a gloomy drink. "The boy mentioned to me that he wants to be a priest," D'Arcy's father said.

"To tell you the truth, I'd sooner be cut in pieces," Bill O'Connell said.

"What am I going to do with him home?" D'Arcy's father said. "He's best taken care of in a seminary." And so D'Arcy Cosgrove went off to become a priest.

The priest in Ireland, as he stood at the altar with Christ, God the Father, and the Holy Ghost inches away in the tabernacle, was considered by all as superior in station, knowledge, and celibacy. He was a great soldier who made a chapel of his body, which he mortified by forfeiting the pleasurable side of his organs as the first offering each morning.

When he left Dunboy for a religious boarding school in Toome, in the center of nowhere, D'Arcy wanted to be a missionary priest — not uncommon, for travel is exciting, and the Irish love to save distant blacks. Blacks in person are something else.

This does not diminish the national desire to save blacks who are far away; in the West country, in towns such as Dunboy, there were signs for the "Black Babies Fund." Meanwhile, in the fields outside the same towns, the Irish homeless, the tinkers, sit on the ground with children coughing and mothers ancient and dying at forty and fretfully watching the road where, so often, townspeople who have donated to the Black Babies Fund come rushing angrily with torches to set the tinkers' wagons afire.

D'Arcy had seen only one black in his life, at a circus that came to Limerick. The circus black was a man whose ebony skin fascinated D'Arcy as much as what he did, which was to eat fire. The man came out in tights, bare from the waist up, and held a flaming torch to his lips. D'Arcy watched to see if the flames reflected on the man's skin, which they did not. The black man eased the torch into his mouth and snapped his mouth shut. The crowd wailed and screamed, the noises turning into delighted laughter as the man opened his mouth and brought out a dead torch. "Your man here just ate your fire!" the barker screamed. D'Arcy ran forward and reached out and placed his hand on the ribs of the black man. He then retreated to the edge of the crowd and examined the hand carefully, to see if there was any evidence of contact with the black.

At the school in Toome, boys were housed and taught in one building and girls in another, and as both supposedly were on their way to religious orders, both sexes were required to walk with eyes downcast so as to prevent accidents and then late one afternoon, for no reason at all, a whim in the rain, D'Arcy, walking alone, heard footsteps and he found himself facing a girl with a full mouth that spread even fuller into a smile that caused him to move toward her. Such a step spread a deliciousness through his body and he intended to experience it fully, and obviously so did the girl, for they met mouth-first and a nun came out the door to grab the girl and a priest yelled out the window.

D'Arcy never saw the girl again. That night all the school priests sat in a large room by candlelight and considered whether D'Arcy should be banished or beaten. When it was over, the prefect of discipline took D'Arcy to a room in the basement, a cold room with a puddle on the floor, and beat him with a hazel rod.

Even when he went on to a seminary in Tipperary, he still was required to ask each day for a special penance for his sex-crime sin.

In the seminary, he also found that the students had to address one another as "Mister" in order to keep cold formality in daily relations and diminish the Devil's ultimate threat, homosexuality. Whenever any student placed a foot in another's room at night, particularly in February, the most dangerous month for sin, Monsignor Fagan, pacing the hall, would roar, "Sodomites!"

Time and time again the seminarians were forced to read Rodríguez's description of punishment for sexual transgression by a priest: suffering that would be magnified a thousand times because the priest had betrayed the personal trust of God. Along with this suffering would come an added torture, a sexual desire that would never be satiated through all the millions of years and the millions of years that followed them.

This terrified him forever. Home for a month, he picked up a copy of the American *National Geographic* magazine in order to read about his future parish, Africa. The magazine's covers were usually ripped off by the town librarian. On this hot day, Cosgrove found a copy that the librarian had neglected to rip off, a cover of a proud African woman, her bare breasts beckoning to all to buy the magazine in the name of natural history. Cosgrove ran out of the library with the magazine and on the way home, looking at it intently, he found himself hard between the thighs and he swerved off the road at the secret house that he and the other kids had played in, a crumbling stone building that sits in tangled brush. He sat on the dirt floor and he knew he was supposed to be reading about lions or pottery in the Congo, but instead he was fixated by the two roaring big brown tits on the cover of the *National Geographic*.

He had been in such a hurry to get off by himself that he neglected the significance of where he was. It had been a British granary in the 1840s, when the wheat crop owned by the British was excellent, although the potato crop used to feed the Irish was blighted. The potato had been brought to Ireland by the British from Peru in the sixteenth century. There were many varieties of potato in Peru, but the British brought only one, known as the clone, which was susceptible to fungus. When the fungus struck the clone, the Irish, with no second variety of potato, merely planted any potato eyes that seemed to be uninfected and prayed that the next crop would be clean, which it wasn't and over a million died in the West of Ireland and two million others fled, most to New York and Boston.

And in the West of Ireland, through the many years, the tale of the famine was passed along by a town storyteller, but always a renegade storyteller, not one welcomed by the general populace, for the stories he told on this one particular subject, handed down through all the years, were invariably horrifying. The renegade storyteller would stand in an alley or at the edge of a field, away from the decent people, and tell of cannibalism on the west coast, around the very town itself, yes, perhaps in the very town itself, the storyteller intimated. People dying of starvation, their mouths stained green from eating grass, became crazed and took man's unthinkable step and ate a friend. Each time a storyteller whispered the word *cannibalism,* somebody would flee from the audience in horror and report the storyteller to police and church. Over the decades, many of the town's storytellers were either chased out of town or thrown into jail.

Of course the official records of the famine, as opposed to oral storytelling, showed that at the very height of the famine, the British continued to fill sacks with grain and ship them to Southampton. Soon there weren't enough Irish in the town with the strength to work the wheat fields. So, with ceremony, the British donated the granary to the Irish people for use as a Children's Home. This was in the British tradition of covering horror with reasonable language; it had a proper name, Children's Home, but its function was to serve the entire area as a morgue for children who died of starvation.

The official records for the entire famine in town were kept in one of the damp stone buildings used by British government workers during the years the Irish lived in subjugation and starvation. The British stored the records in the cold wet attic of the three-story government building in the town square, only feet from the waterfront. When the British left the town in 1916, the garrison commander sneered at the people and said they were rabble and that the only history of the town's ever having been on the face of the earth would come from the civilized manner in which the British kept records. "We put the history of these years on proper paper, thickest parchment, and it will outlast every one of you buggers and the bloody children you produce."

With that the British departed, and their records sat in a building which went unused for over a quarter century. During winter months, the stone walls of the attic where the records were kept became so damp that the stones turned green with mold and water streamed down the walls. Whenever anybody talked about the building, the subject was demolition, not rehabilitation.

The records were forgotten, and so was the ruin of the old Children's Home, where at this very moment, D'Arcy Cosgrove was flat on his stomach and somewhere in the earth under him were the bones of hundreds of children who had starved to death, and as he looked at the *National Geographic* cover, he wiggled around, face down, and unbearable tension filled him and then he was relieved and he had no idea of what had happened except that his underwear was stuck wet to him. He felt great depression. He ran from the building, for one of the truly greatest of sins, masturbation, had been committed in it. He rode his bike to the Well, which consisted of a circle of mean rocks at the foot of a section of cliff that was only ten feet above the water.

At low tide the rocks were high out of the water. On a flood tide the water covered the rocks and the water inside the rocks was five feet deep. An incoming wave caused the water in the Well to rise to nine feet. A leap from the cliff, timed with the incoming wave, but still made with the marvelous fear that the wave would recede and leave the rocks high, ended with a plunge into nine feet of freezing water. But it took a leap of perfect aim, and great timing, and therefore it was not a suicide, punishable by interment forever in Hell, but a sporting chance at life or death and some tried and lived and now, staring at the water, Cosgrove remembered a day in the heart of a fall rainstorm when Paul Daley, forty-seven, who lived with his mother, was found draped on the rocks.

Cosgrove knew that never could he confess to this monstrous sin, and under the rules of the seminary, he could confess only to one of the priests in charge, thus eliminating the hope of finding some ancient country priest in a haze. Cosgrove thought of his sin and stared at the water, assured himself that it wasn't suicide, and jumped. Immediately he screamed Christ's name, for he knew that he indeed had meant it as suicide, but he did not want to die and he hit water and went into such dark sea green that when his eyes were open nothing could be seen, not even the rocks that brushed his shoulders as he rose. After this, confession at the seminary was painful but bearable. And always he carried in his mind the vision of the granary as the center of sin.

The next morning a young boy banged hard on Cosgrove's door and told him that the pastor needed him immediately. When Cosgrove got to town, he found the pastor and the mayor and an old man, the owner of the town's one great estate, which ran for a quarter mile along the waterfront. They wore concerned looks and talked quickly.

"How is it that I didn't know?" the mayor asked the old man.

"Because I was told nothing. The woman's barrister got on to me over the phone and told me how they had arrived at my name, through my own barrister in London, of course, and I became properly concerned when I was told that she was just around the bend out there, spending the night with Lady Glassniven."

"And good Lord, here she is," the pastor said.

All looked at the old government building, where at the open green wood front doors stood an old woman, a wisp of a woman, obviously a regal woman, in a tweed suit and with chin properly raised, but also a woman of great industry, for while she had on a tweed suit, she also was wearing dirty work gloves. She walked with a high ladder against her shoulder and it was a struggle for her, but she refused to allow any signs of effort to cross her face. She carried the ladder through the two large green wood doors and into the old empty building.

"She must be stopped," the pastor said.

"If she isn't, we'll all die in shame as we stand here in this very spot."

The pastor spoke to Cosgrove. "Here, lad, you're young

and vigorous and able to know what you read. Come off with me and we'll talk."

He took Cosgrove for a walk and instructed him carefully, after which Cosgrove went into the old building, climbed the stone staircase, and found the old woman on the ladder, her gloved hands testing the old wood trapdoor in the ceiling that opened to the attic.

"Here, let me," Cosgrove said.

Nimbly, he went up the ladder and when he could not budge the old trapdoor with his hands, he gathered himself and used his head as a hammer and the door burst open. He crawled in and assisted the old woman. They stood in the dampness and pale light and looked at rows of wood filing cabinets lining the walls. The woman walked over to a cabinet and pulled it open. She took off her work gloves and put on glasses and her long fingers went into the file and brought out a packet of papers bound with white cord. On the cover sheet, printed in large letters, were the words PO-TATO FAMINE, JAN., FEB., 1847. The woman went into her purse and brought out a small pair of scissors and snipped the cord. Then she sat on the cement floor with the papers in her lap.

"You're sitting on a wet spot," Cosgrove said to her.

"I shall gladly hazard pneumonia for just a glimpse of this," she said.

She began to leaf through the pages. Suddenly she jumped up and went to another file cabinet. She pulled out packets, inspected them and gasped, and went almost frantically to the next cabinet, after which she slumped to the wet floor, closed her eyes, and sat motionless. Many moments of silence later, she said, "My God!" Then she said to Cosgrove, "Do you have any realization of what we have just found? I suppose you don't. Do you know my name or what I am doing? I guess you don't know that, either. Don't know why you should. Fine young man sent to help me and help you did. If you only knew how much. What is your name?"

"D'Arcy Cosgrove."

"Well, D'Arcy, I am a writer. I have been working on a book on the British military and the reasons for so many stunning and bloody failures on the part of leadership which is supposedly the world's brightest. In my research I found that the leadership is far from the brightest because traditionally British officers paid for their jobs. The reason for the Charge of the Light Brigade, for example, was stupidity on the part of an insufferably stupid man named Lord Cardigan who had the money to buy himself a field command, which he used with such ineptness that many fine young men were killed. Dastardly! 'Theirs not to reason why.' Rubbish! In researching my work in London, I was told that Lord Cardigan had been a landlord here in the West of Ireland and I wondered just what sort of a landlord he was. Probably one of those who drove everyone from the land.

"I decided to come here for a fortnight and see if there was the slightest trace of the man remaining in the towns about. I had heard there were records kept here and I received permission in Dublin and here I come today, seeking the records of a landlord, and what do I find? My God!" Her voice dropped. "Young man, we have here in this room, apparently, a daily record of the greatest famine the world has known." She leafed through the packet of papers on her lap. "Will you examine this! My English are much like the Germans, you know. They both keep the most damning records about themselves. See the paper. It has withstood moisture for over a century. Look, look!"

She rubbed her fingers over the paper that was still thick and white. The writing on the paper was impossibly neat. "And look at this, just at a glance mind you, but here is the name of ship, master, owner, cargo, wheat grain, and the date of departure from this bay. And here is the list of those who died of starvation at the very same time. What dreadful animals these government administrators were. Oh, my dear young man, we've only been here, what is it now, a half hour? I am totally exhausted. I must go. I am staying here at Lady Glassniven's home. I must pull myself together for tomorrow. It seems to me that I have months to spend here. My book on the military pales next to this work. Such a trove!"

Cosgrove helped her down the ladder and saw her out of the building. He went over to the Landmark Inn and borrowed a hurricane lamp from the proprietor and then went to work.

On the third night in the wet attic — he came back when the old lady was gone — Cosgrove found the first of the entries he had been told to find. The light from the hurricane lamp danced across pages 111 and 112 of the month of November 1845. There, in neat yeoman's writing, probably done with quill pen, was this recording:

Maj. Anthony Guest of the Queen's Own was dispatched to the beachfront to find a tribe of people engaged in battle with each other. Many of the natives were armed with strange-looking clubs, which they wielded with insane anger. Maj. Guest cautioned his troops to beware of the crowd, lest one of the natives, whose mouths seemed to be foaming with possible communicable disease, would bite them. He also instructed his troops to be on the ready for these strange clubs, of a boomerang sort, he thought. Maj. Guest then pretended to charge the crowd, with much huzzahs and sabre waving. Sensing they were unable to defend themselves against His Majesty's forces, the natives fled. Whereupon Maj. Guest was able to find one club that had been dropped. Reporting back to barracks, the club was given to Capt. Harrison, brigade surgeon, who upon examination reported that it was not a boomerang at all, but identified it as the elbow bone of a human being. Capt. Harrison left barracks with a special investigative party. In the course of his patrol he was rendered unconscious and suffered a severe head injury in that a native emerged from behind a boulder and dealt him a heavy blow to the forehead with another club. Warrant Officer Pegsworth described it as a human bone, another elbow bone. Back at barracks, Capt. Harrison, upon regaining consciousness, was astonished to see that he had been hit with not an elbow bone, but with a thigh bone and knee joint attached. Capt. Harrison marvelled at how shiny the bone was. It had been picked clean before being used as a weapon. He particularly noticed that there was not even gristle left in the joints and crevices. Capt. Harrison is of the opinion that people with extraordinary small teeth ate the meat on the bones. He wonders if teeth shrink during starvation.

At night's end Cosgrove brought the paper across to the pastor, who dropped it into the turf fire without reading it. It was on the fourth night of finding such small reports that Cosgrove found a lengthy report, written the following year, by another medical officer, Colonel Devers, who noted,

Apparently, those who are destined to live through this are those who partake of human flesh. Where and how the natives obtain this flesh is unknown to us, but we have witnessed few funerals. The cooking of such flesh, it can be reported, is done on a spit over a fire and that the natives, upon chewing the grilled flesh, do so without breathing through the nose, thus eliminating any sense of taste as they swallow. Upon eating, they take huge gulps of water and walk about for some time, breathing only through their mouths. We report herewith that the Irish are so ravenous that they overeat during these meals. I watched a man eat a huge liver the other night and attempted to tell him that one can only digest so much and that this portion, an entire liver, was entirely too much for him but he simply chomped away (these people are quite thick-headed), and afterwards he was distinctly uncomfortable from having overeaten.

When Cosgrove mentioned this to the pastor, the old cleric watched the fire until every last bit of white paper was in flames. He trusted no one with a document such as this. Back at the attic, the writer mentioned one day to Cosgrove that she continually arrived at places where there were distinct gaps and she had difficulty in understanding why, for the British had kept such meticulous records. Still, she would of course continue with her work on the famine, and she read on. Cosgrove, after several weeks of clandestine research, came to the last packet and reported back to the pastor that his work was done. He was congratulated and told that he would have letters of commendation from every important figure in the religious and secular community sent to his seminary.

In the final days before Ordination there was one meeting after another with church people describing religious opportunities in Ireland, with the last, apparently regarded as the most important — for all the prefects from the seminary also attended — being given by a Redemptorist who had spent his life, and a long life it was, too, as a missionary in Africa. The priest was gaunt and had a slack jaw and spoke in a monotone, which indicated that he had his speech quite well memorized. He spoke of the sheer thrill of having so many souls to save and of the indescribable beauty in which such opportunity was presented. The ancient priest finished and acknowledged applause, particularly from the prefects, and was about to leave the room and head for sherry when Cosgrove stood and asked, "How can a new missionary expect to be received by the people in today's Africa?"

"That is an excellent question and I will be glad to answer it for you," the missionary said, the first life in his voice. "I first went to African mission duty while there were still members of the last Yellow Fever Commission, which had expired in the year 1915, I believe, living in Ghana," he said. "The African peoples were thoroughly delightful and thankful for the presence of all of us. There was in my time on the continent only one recorded case of cannibalism, and this involved a Presbyterian missionary from Belfast. The cannibals were particularly cruel to him, I believe. They had of course long since made their peace with the established Catholic mission people, but these Protestants, particularly of the northern strain, the Presbyterians most prominent, never did seem to catch on with the locals. Therefore, it could be said that, at the time, a Protestant missionary did risk life and limb, as a matter of actual fact.

"The cannibals had unimaginable savagery in that they removed the Presbyterian's leg and immediately packed the wound with mud in order to keep the Presbyterian alive — oh, barely alive, to be sure — but the heart was still beating and this kept the Presbyterian from spoiling. The cannibals

had their leg of Presbyterian and the next day another clus-
ter of savages came around and sawed off the Presbyterian's
other leg and packed this wound with mud, too, and then
the following day here they are, right back for your man's
arm. I understand that the witch doctors in charge were dis-
appointed because the Belfast Presbyterians all tend to be
quite gaunt and there was very little meat, particularly on
the arms."

"How long did the minister live?"

"Oh, for a day or two, I should imagine, and then when
his heart gave out they of course had to devour whatever
there was of him immediately. I've been told that there was
considerable rancor over the face, for the Presbyterian had
this typical Ulster nose, long and made completely of bone
and cartilage and with virtually no real flesh to eat. The na-
tives did make a business of going around and chewing on
the nose, as a dog worries a bone, but the nourishment from
the nose was so minimal that many people maintain that it
was the absolute end of cannibalism, and we can thank the
Presbyterian and his thin frame for the cessation of this
practice. Nevertheless, you do raise a good point. I don't
believe it is very helpful for a fat Catholic to roam around
the jungles, even today."

"Can we be sure that there are no more cannibals?" Cos-
grove asked. "I don't wish to offend by suggesting that I am
not willing to lay down my life for my God, as I certainly
have more faith in me than that, but I just like to know the
things for which I should prepare myself. Or are the rewards
greater if I simply carry my faith into the unknown?"

"Knowledge is always better," the old missionary said,
"but in this case I do think it is irrelevant to worry about
cannibalism because from all the reports we get, it seems

to be completely gone from the entire continent. I would stress, however, that you do not waddle off the boat fat and sassy in the face of millions of people who don't have quite enough to eat. Oh, the inner peace of having served."

The missionary, now truly thirsty, left for his sherry.

Cosgrove, on his way back to his room, told himself that he must think at length and thus thoroughly about the possibilities of serving in Africa. And when he did arrive at this conclusion that he would serve on that dark continent, he began to practice saying Perfect Acts of Contrition at most incredible speed, just in case the savages swung the ax and packed his wound with mud and sat around a fire devouring the first leg for dinner.

Cosgrove gave his senior sermon to eight hundred in the dining hall. It was a test that often caused many seminarians to faint, but during dinner Cosgrove walked brazenly to the lectern and started a prepared speech on Barabbas: "It was morning in Jerusalem."

A bishop shouted, "And moonlight in Mayo!"

The bishop stuck a potato in his mouth and his jaw worked happily as the hall rocked with laughter. Cosgrove shrugged and went on and did so successfully.

In pageantry that only the Roman Catholic Church is able to produce, with chalices and vestments, with bowing and prostrating in candlelight, and with music, ancient music, Gregorian chant, Cosgrove's hands were anointed with oil and as the Sacrament of Holy Orders entered his soul he could turn wine into the blood of Christ and a wafer of bread into His body.

He had a month at home before leaving for Africa. He

heard his first confession a week after he arrived in town; the confessor was a man who told him, "Father, I have committed adultery."

D'Arcy made a strangling sound. "How many times?"

"Oh, only once in my whole life, Father."

"With whom did you commit such a sin?"

"With a woman in the town."

"Do you know this woman long?"

"Oh yes. She lives next door."

"For how long?"

"Twenty-seven years."

Cosgrove couldn't wait to get away from his own, a race of amateur and professional liars, and get to Africa.

5

WHEN THE DOOR flew open, the counterman at the Cross Bay Pizza stand looked up and the Chief, the boss of Howard Beach and other communities, walked in. This pizza stand was two long blocks from the New Park Pizza stand, but the only difference to the eye was that one sign read NEW PARK and the other CROSS BAY. The New Park managed to become famous on this night, but at the moment, nobody knew that or certainly cared, for the Chief needed nobody to create excitement for him.

The Chief stood directly under the fluorescent light so everybody could see his head of gray hair, close-cropped but still standing high, brushed, curried, and combed so much that the top of his head gleamed like a sword blade. He had heavy eyebrows on a gaunt face dominated by a prominent nose that stood for all the centuries of Rome. He wore a dark blue suit and a white shirt. His neck still was young and thick. The eyes were colored brown venom.

"Hello, buddy," the counterman said.

"Buddy, my balls," the Chief said.

Dominic the Counterman began to quiver.

"Where's what you owe me?" the Chief said.

"I got nothin' right now," Dominic said.

"You got two hundred twenty dollars for me?" the Chief said.

"I ain't."

"You either got two hundred and twenty dollars for me or I take your fucking ear home with me."

Dominic began to stammer.

"Don't fucking talk to me," the Chief said.

Two days before, the Chief and Dominic had made a bet on the Knicks-Chicago game and the Chief made Dominic take the Knicks and five points and, for the privilege, lay eleven to ten. Dominic was not such a complete moron that he would bet the Knicks on his own. But the Chief walked in and said, "I want you to bet the Knicks against me. I want the Chicagos." Dominic winced, but agreed. The Knicks lost by their usual twenty or thirty points, and now the Chief was here to take Dominic's money home. There is no money too small for the Chief.

The Chief felt good. He had just been to a big cocktail party thrown by Network Records at the Waldorf-Astoria hotel in Manhattan. All the little bald record people had flocked around him at the cocktail party and some of them even touched his arm, in order to feel the biceps of a real gangster. Of course they introduced the Chief as their distribution consultant, but everybody understood that just beneath the title and the smiles it caused was the knowledge that his idea of distributing was to rip from the nose. Yet the record executives couldn't stay away from him at the party and indeed had invited him to the party for just such a thrill. They stood around him in a semicircle, and this caused the Chief to expound. "I have to have a big bet going for me every day. If you don't bet, you could be walking around lucky all day and not even know it."

They all laughed at that one. Isn't it marvelous, they said to each other, the way such a primitive can simply hurl these phrases out? Of course, because the Chief was there the record people suddenly began to talk about violence, steering away from the Mafia but going to street crime, muggings, and quickly Bernhard Goetz was the central topic. "Kill the black bastards come up to you on the subway!" one man said. Another said, hesitantly, that it was perhaps dangerous to do that because even if you thought the four kids were going to kill you, you still might wind up in the can.

The Chief smirked. "I'd rather be tried by twelve than carried by six."

It was an old line, maybe the oldest of the street expressions that the Chief ever heard, but the record people laughed and slapped one another's backs and looked with wild admiration at him. Of course, if they hesitated to pay him big money he would take them into the men's room and cut off their heads.

And now, stopping off in the Cross Bay Pizza stand before going to his home in Howard Beach, the Chief grunted as he watched Dominic try to imagine an excuse, which was impossible because the whole world knows how Dominic handles himself when he is in tight. Hanging in the Chief's Mafia clubhouse over in East New York, alongside a picture of Frank Sinatra, is the page from Dominic's cross-examination when he took the witness stand as a defense witness for himself. Dominic had a night job with the Automatic

Detection Burglar Alarm Company and during the hours Dominic worked, many fur coats were stolen from warehouses whose burglar alarms were shut down for testing at the moment the robbery occurred. One day the cops crashed into Dominic's house and found a sable coat in the closet. A rat kid district attorney questioned Dominic on the witness stand in Part 4, Queens Supreme Court:

Q. I show you this coat, Mr. Cafiero, a sable coat. Can you identify it?

A. It is a coat that got fur.

Q. Is it your coat?

A. That kind of coat is for women and some guy wants to be a woman.

Q. What was it doing in your closet?

A. I never look in the closet. I got bad asthma and my closet has too much dust in there. I never open it.

Q. You are telling me that you never knew this sable coat was in the closet. A twenty-thousand-dollar coat.

A. Never. I'm not kidding.

Q. Do you know the coat was stolen from the Continental Fur Storage in Forest Hills?

A. I never put no coat in my closet.

Q. Did you help take it out of the fur vault?

A. How could I do that when I was the only one working on my job that night? I had to be at work all night.

Q. And what was your assigned task in the office?

A. I told you, I was the only one.

Q. The only one to do what?

A. The only one to turn off the alarm system and check that it works. Nobody else.

Q. And do you have any idea why the alarm system for

the Continental Fur Storage was turned off at the ex-
act time a burglary occurred and that a fur coat from
that burglary turns up in your closet?

A. I couldn't steal. I had to stay in the office for the
switches that make the alarms go on and off.

Q. Thank you, Mr. Cafiero.

A. For what?

Q. For the conviction.

And now, standing behind the counter at the Cross Bay
Pizza stand, Dominic looked up at the Chief and, shaking
his head, Dominic went into the cash register and counted
out two hundred twenty dollars. Dominic sighed as he
looked into the register and saw how little was left. "Boss
break my head when he sees this."

"Tell him," the Chief said.

"Tell him what?"

"Tell him some big nigger come in here and held you up.
Go ahead. Now give me two pies to go home."

Dominic put two pies into boxes and as he handed them
to the Chief, he said, "When you get in the car remember
not to put one box on top of the other. Keep them apart so
the weight don't make one box squash down. I don't want
you getting home and calling me up and saying, 'Hey, why
is all the cheese all stuck together?'"

"Good man," the Chief said. He slapped the counter in
lieu of payment, picked up the boxes, and left.

The Chief was elated that he had taken the two hundred
twenty dollars from the counterman. Earlier he had col-
lected ten thousand from Network Records and another
thirty-seven thousand from a guy who had borrowed money
in order to get in a drug deal. The thirty-seven thousand had

to go into the all-city Mafia pot, but all the rest of the money was the Chief's personal score. Each sum he collected that day was worth killing for. If Dominic hadn't had the two twenty for him, the Chief was going to have somebody come in the back door later that night and cut Dominic's head off. When he was out of the place, Sarah asked, "Who is that delightful man?"

"Saint John the Baptist."

"He's crude."

"I'll say he's cruel."

Once outside, the Chief got into his Lincoln town car, the official Mafia boss's car, and drove home. He lives on the last street in Howard Beach, in a house that sits right against the bullrushes and swampland, beyond which is East New York. At night, when the wind blows in hard from the bay, the bullrushes wave and shake with so much noise that you think somebody is coming through them.

———

Bushwick and Sarah went home to Bushwick's house, and Sarah had an exciting time. In the morning they talked on the way to work and Bushwick told her that he loved her and immediately Sarah began to cry. "Oh, I don't know what to do," she said. When Bushwick asked her what was the matter, she said, "Maybe what happened to my father frightens me. My mother always reached out in her sleep to touch my father. Then one night he wasn't there. He died of a heart attack on the way home. After that, my mother made me sleep with her. If I got up and wandered around while she was still asleep, she'd wake up right away and get hysterical. Maybe that's what's bothering me. I'm afraid that if I stay with you, I'll put my hand out one night and you won't be there."

Bushwick said, "Look at me. Thirty-five years old. Don't I look like I'm going to die any second?"

———————

One day at work Sarah said, "I still don't know. I think I better go back with my mother for the time being." And Bushwick said to her, "Do you know what I was thinking about when we weren't talking on the subway? I was thinking about that it was time to get moved up to a better department. I might as well surrender and think about working all my life like everybody else. Go into the housing action grants. Start working so I can support you and the children."

Sarah was both thrilled and frightened by this and was glad when she was removed from the vortex of this controversy by the day's first phone call, which was from a woman in the Flatbush Arms Hotel who said she didn't have a can of corn left in her room.

In the late afternoon of this day, D'Arcy Cosgrove awoke in his bare room in the rectory, looked down, and shook Great Big, who was asleep on the floor, for the beds simply were too small for him, and the two arose and had tea and, as it was late afternoon, cold chicken and salad served by a grumpy old woman. D'Arcy said Mass for himself, after which the two went out for a walk with the old pastor. Cosgrove was concerned that he had received no word from the Papal delegate. As they left the rectory, which had a broken gate and was joined at the hip to the old church building, late afternoon had begun to slip into the first darkness. One light showed on the street, in the ground floor of a building directly across from the church. The old pastor called and the window opened and an old woman pressed her forehead against bars that were an attempt at Spanish grillwork but were closer to state penitentiary. "I'm about to go marketing," the woman said.

"It's nighttime already," the pastor said.

"Oh, I thought it was time to go marketing. I get so mixed up by the clocks. If it's nighttime, then I'll say good night." The woman shut the window.

A couple of blocks down, on what once had been an avenue, Cosgrove noticed that their footsteps were the only sound on a street of burned-out five-story apartment buildings whose front doors were sealed with cement. The apartment buildings stared with tin eyes at the emptiness and garbage.

The old pastor said that once this had been the center of the parish, but many people from North Carolina moved up and the parishioners had fled. "Now we have only a few left, and if one dies we don't even get the funeral. The relatives come here from Long Island and whisk the bodies away. I don't think our church has long to go."

As they walked along the deserted streets, they came up to a man in his early thirties who stood guard over three Lincoln town cars parked at the curb. A leather jacket was open to reveal a neck as thick as a boar's and ablaze with gold chains. He chewed gum as if being paid for the labor. The place he stood in front of was a small restaurant, with Christmas tree lights strung across the top of the small bar. There was no name on the window. The pastor murmured that the place was no good, but in the chill, Cosgrove had to use the men's room.

Instantly, the gum chewer blocked the way until he saw Cosgrove's collar. His fierce look became a little softer. "I help you, Father?" Cosgrove gave his destination and the guy nodded. "Tell them I said it was all right." Looking up at Great Big, he said, "He ain't coming, is he?" When Cosgrove said no, the gold chains relaxed. The pastor and Great Big waited outside.

When Cosgrove stepped inside, he found a long, narrow room with a few tables and the walls covered with horse-racing pictures, one large one of Frank Sinatra, and next to it a sheet with questions and answers on it. The place was empty except for three men seated at a round table in the rear. One of them, the Chief, looked up as he saw the priest walk in.

"Help you, Father?"

"I was told it was all right to use the men's room," Cosgrove said.

The Chief nodded his approval; then he looked at the waiter, who stood at attention in front of him.

"Garlic toast," the Chief said.

"We don't have garlic toast tonight," the waiter said.

"Make it. Then you'll have it."

The waiter nodded and went into the kitchen.

At the table with the Chief was a young man of about thirty whose eyes were not quite alert. When he opened his mouth to talk, the man sitting next to him, wearing an expensive and understated banker's suit, put a hand on his son's hand to stop his words. Clearly, he wanted nothing said that would arouse the Chief.

"The boy here is out of college and he and a couple of chums start this little business and, by golly, don't they have union trouble right off."

The Chief nodded solemnly.

Cosgrove walked past them and into the men's room, whose walls were so thin that he could monitor the conversation.

The banker said, "Now we're all for unions, but these are just college kids starting out and I said, 'Oh, you can't bother that man. He does too many favors for people as it is.' Except he gets a phone call and he was told that some people were concerned."

The son said, "Dad, they said they were going to strangle me until my eyes popped out."

The father said, "Whatever. So I said to myself, 'Well, I think I better now just go down and see my old friend the Chief in person.'"

The Chief said, "What was the name of the guy called you up?"

"Anthony Capanegro. Local 1731."

"Now you're in the Son business, right?" the Chief told the young guy.

"No, the bank messenger service."

"But you got the service because your father's got the bank. That puts you in the Son business. It's the biggest business in the city. Someday, the city'll be so old that you guys'll be in the Grandson business. I tried to get my own kid in the Son business. I go up to the school where he was going, they had this parents' night, and I give the geometry teacher five hundred and I tell him, 'I don't know what my kid is doing taking geometry, a subject like this, but he wants to be a lawyer. I know you need a father a lawyer, and this kid got no father a lawyer, so I'm buying him into the Son business. Here, you pass him so he can go to law school.'

"I push the five hundred on him and I go out. I tell you, I had to give a guy a good fucking beating that night. You know what happens? The next day the kid comes home with the five hundred from the teacher. Now what do you think the rat-bastard teacher does? My kid comes home with an *F* in fucking geometry. Fail. Fuck you! How do you like that rat-bastard teacher? I says, 'All right. They don't want my kid in another line of work. They want him to be my son and stay in my business.' His mother screamed. So I told him, look for something. He went to Fort Pierce in Florida a couple of years ago and opened a newspaper store and sold guns in the back room. Then they made his place legal. He's a legitimate businessman. He sells guns."

Cosgrove finished using the bathroom and washed his hands. The Chief and the banker and son concluded their business. "Now I got four whole percent of a messenger business," the Chief announced.

"Of course," the banker said.

The Chief laughed. "I tell you what you do. When the guy calls up again, you tell him that you give the money over to me. He'll understand. You won't hear from him no more."

Father and son were walking out of the place as Cosgrove emerged from the men's room. The Chief never noticed Cosgrove. His eyes were fixed with a murderous stare on a man being shoved into the restaurant. The man was over-weight and had thick eyeglasses.

"Here comes Rudolph Valentino," the Chief said.

The fat guy stood nervously.

"Did you take Rocky's niece out to the back of the garage and make her do something with you?"

"No."

With a great noise, the Chief shoved the table and stood up. "You're going to get the beating of your life. If you lie, you die!"

"I'm telling the truth. I never made her do nothing. She couldn't wait to do me," the fat guy said.

"She wanted to? She's twelve fucking years old!"

"Yeah, but she's nice," the fat guy said.

The Chief threw a punch that made a sound that filled the room and Cosgrove, leaving hastily, thought that the Chief was a great man. Why, if killing were not such a final sin, the fat guy should be killed. Whoever this big shot was, he certainly had some proper morals, Cosgrove thought.

<hr />

The next morning Cosgrove left the rectory again and he recognized the streets ahead as Baby Rock's landscape. Great Big was with him and they walked to the burned-out store, where Cosgrove saw a high bundle under the khaki blanket on the old couch. The bundle began to thrash quite a bit. There was youth panting. Cosgrove immediately thought of the Curragh racecourse phrase "sound of wind and limb." Great Big, however, smacked his hands together in glee. Great Big thinks he sees Africa, Cosgrove thought, and of course he is wrong, for even here in this desolation, no matter how rare a scene in a nation smothered with wealth, a flying blanket cannot be what it seems.

The whole couch took a mad jump and the high, happy voice of a very young girl said, "Make me feel good all over."

The bundle under the blanket broke into two and Cosgrove saw Baby Rock with his baseball cap on; also peering from under the blanket were two luminous dark eyes in the deep tan face of a small girl. Baby Rock and the girl stared at the fire licking out of the oil barrel a few feet away. Cosgrove saw that the girl, whose hair was pulled into a long braid, was wearing a pink snow jacket, and this comforted Cosgrove. But the girl, seeing Cosgrove, closed her eyes in embarrassment and pulled the blanket over her face. Certainly, Cosgrove thought, he was absolutely right at this moment to recall the memory of his bed in Ireland, with all four children snuggled against the cold, watching the turf fire, and squalling the moment anybody disturbed the blanket and allowed cold air to pierce the warmth.

"And who do we have here?" Cosgrove said heartily.

The little face, with large dark brown eyes and a nose with just enough nostril width to pay respect to the centuries, came out from under the blanket. "Go 'way from me."

Baby Rock twisted the white baseball cap from backwards to frontwards and pulled the bill down so that it covered all but his mouth, which formed a smirk. "My lady," Baby Rock said.

Again the girl hid her face under the blanket. Cosgrove laughed at Baby Rock's incongruous remark, for she was only a child. Cosgrove asked her age.

"I be eleven," the little girl said from under the blanket.

"And what is your name?"

"Seneca."

"And why are you not in school?"

"Baby Rock be lettin' me oversleep."

Cosgrove shook a finger at Baby Rock. "Your lady was relying on you to ring her doorbell and you forgot."

Now Seneca sat up. "No doorbell here."

"Then he should have knocked on the door."

"What door?"

"The door to your house."

"Wasn't at a house last night."

"Where were you?"

"I be here with Baby Rock."

"You were here all night?"

"Sure was."

Cosgrove smiled tolerantly. Little girl trying to shock him; of course the child knew not of what she spoke. But when she and Baby Rock looked at Great Big and the three began to snicker, Cosgrove had a momentary vision that, through shock, the little girl was trying to lead him, an old man in her eyes, into reality. No, dismiss this thought. This is the pure work of the Devil. "Dear little girl, you shouldn't use those expressions because you sound stupid. You are too young to know anything of these things."

"Fuck all around," Seneca said.

Baby Rock picked up his head and said, "Soft and warm."

He and Seneca giggled, which told Great Big all he had to know and Great Big jumped up and down.

Cosgrove had no idea of what he was thinking until he heard himself say it. "Why, as a matter of actual fact, today is a great blessing. You two must be married immediately."

"What for?" Baby Rock said.

"To consecrate all your further acts."

"If I get married, do I get welfare?" Seneca said.

"Oh, I'm not sure of these details. What's important is that, dear God in Heaven, you two wonderful children get married."

"When you married, they give you a place to go for dinner?" Baby Rock said.

"God will provide," Cosgrove said.

"What street is the man on?" Baby Rock asked.

"Oh, we'll find all that. We must get you married first. Think of what would happen if you had a child out of this."

"We only be doin' it a few times last night," Seneca said. "You got to do it a whole lot of days before you get a baby."

"Who told you such a thing?" Cosgrove said.

"Girl on my block. She know."

"Well, she's wrong. And you should get married immediately. I'll come home with you and talk to your parents."

Seneca frowned. There was wriggling under the blanket as she obviously pulled on clothes. "I'm not marryin' Baby Rock. He isn't my boyfriend. My boyfriend be Manslaughter. I be tellin' him."

Seneca threw off the cover. She was dressed for a grammar school hallway, in snow jacket, corduroy pants, and white snowboots, and she swung off the couch where she had spent the night with a boy who wasn't her boyfriend and she walked out to the street.

Baby Rock jumped up. "You got me in bad trouble. She tell Manslaughter I'm here and he be comin' around lookin' for his gun that you threw away. Manslaughter only wants to be strapped with that gun. He be bringin' his second gun. Shoot me twice. First for losin' his gun, second time for messin' with his lady. I got no gun to shoot him back."

Baby Rock caught up to Seneca on the sidewalk and when she said that she wouldn't tell Manslaughter if Baby Rock would buy her a cherry Danish and a grape slurpy, Baby Rock asked Cosgrove for a dollar fifty. Cosgrove, with six dollars on him, said of course he could have the money and Baby Rock and Seneca led him around the corner onto a desolate street where it seemed nobody lived.

There were houses with bricked-up doors and windows and others with tin nailed over the openings. It was a street without even a stray dog on it. Standing alone was a narrow grocery store with a yellow tin sign proclaiming, BODEGA. Inside, there was barely room for people to get past each other. There were rubber gloves atop the bread, a basket of sweet potatoes on the floor, a stack of cans of roach killer, a shelf of canned peas, a gum machine, cases of warm beer, a cooler filled with beer, soda, and margarine.

The Puerto Rican behind the counter had a mustache and wore a black leather jacket that he seemed to like very much. He glanced down at it, then looked in suspicion as Baby Rock fingered the packaged cake shelf, and then glanced down at the jacket once more. The jacket made the Puerto Rican's shoulders seem square and powerful, although he had a small face and neck. He watched as Seneca reached into the cooler for a slurpy and Baby Rock picked up a cherry Danish for Seneca, and for himself, his best meal, Cheez Doodles. The Puerto Rican relaxed when Cosgrove put money on the counter.

Cosgrove saw the Puerto Rican's eyes widen. Cosgrove saw Great Big bend over and open a large bag of potato chips. Great Big held them up and poured them into his mouth. Great Big bellowed. He liked the potato chips. His arms spread almost from one end of the store to the other. Great Big gathered everything within reach, which was quite a bit. Great Big, roaring in delight, clutched a mountain of canned peas, roach spray, potato chips, bottles of warm beer, and giant plastic bottles of Pepsi-Cola. He

headed for the door. The Puerto Rican shouted. Cosgrove
tried to block the way, but Great Big simply kept walking
and carried Cosgrove out onto the sidewalk. The Puerto Ri-
can tore off his black jacket and, sure enough, he didn't
have those wide shoulders that he did with the jacket on.
Still, he was courageous. He jumped Great Big from behind
and rode Great Big's back all the way to the curb. Where,
in frustration, he sunk his teeth into Great Big's back. Great
Big dropped his treasure, reached behind him and grabbed
the Puerto Rican, and scaled him like a stone into the mid-
dle of the street. Which is exactly how the Puerto Rican
went, too. Once he skipped on the top of his head. Then he
bounced on his forehead and that took care of that. The
Puerto Rican was part of the asphalt.

A woman in a white beret and a maroon down coat with
the top button missing darted off the stoop of an empty
house and into the bodega. She came out with three huge
boxes of Pampers. A chubby woman with light hair tore
along the sidewalk and into the bodega. She was coming out
with Pampers piled high when the first two kids ran past her,
one on either side, and she tripped and fell with her Pam-
pers and suddenly there was a stream of kids, four and six
years old, kids appearing from everywhere, running, run-
ning, running, into the bodega and coming out with potato
chips and soda and rubber gloves and bread and cans of
lima beans. Cosgrove went to help the Puerto Rican, who
got to his feet and walked like a blind man away from the
store.

Cosgrove then ran into the store to prevent more damage
and he was in the doorway when he was knocked down on
his face and kids in sneakers ran across his back. He got on
his hands and knees in roaring noise. The floor was packed

with scuffling feet. Children moved along the walls without any visible support, like crabs, cleaning the top shelves of canned corn and toilet paper, another shelf of Chef Boyardee and bags of rice. There had to be fifty of them inside the store, grabbing, punching, climbing on shoulders. Alongside Cosgrove on the floor, an old woman clearly in her seventies, in lace shoes that had gaps at the soles, was crouched over the basket of sweet potatoes. An arthritic hand put one potato into the pocket of her raincoat and she was reaching for another when a little boy, ten years old, perhaps, with a lazy right eye, slipped in front of her and picked up the basket. The old woman tried to stop him. The boy spat in the old lady's face. Wordlessly, she reached for the sweet potatoes. The boy took one hand off the basket and got it onto the old lady's face and began scratching and tearing. He caught her eyes with his fingers and she made the first sound, a low moan. The kid shrieked at her, "Why you ol' lady in Baby Lee's way? I be takin' this to my woman."

Cosgrove, furious, scrambled to his feet and grabbed the little villain by the shoulder and was about to shake the very life out of him when the old lady, whimpering hurt, dropped her old arthritic hand and grabbed the front of the kid's pants. She intended to squeeze him to agony come, but instead all she got was a handful of Levi's. "You got a woman? Y'all belong in a crib!"

Cosgrove was mortified by this and could not move. The old lady instantly gathered much heart and her hand — stumpy, bumpy old fingers but with a couple of good long nails — went for the kid's face and she was going to get to him good, maybe, when the kid rocked his shaved head back, and now he brought his little shaved head flying forward into the old lady's face. It made a loud smacking sound and when the old lady put her hands to her face, he raced out with the basket of sweet potatoes.

Cosgrove put an arm around the old woman and was trying to push his way out, against a new wave of kids, this time babies, knee-highs, who scrambled determinedly into the store. There were about a dozen older kids, the ten- and eleven-year-olds, fighting for the last thing standing in the store, the glass-globe gum machine, and in the middle of the crowd came a loud report, a gun going off, and the store emptied. One of the babies, shrieking the loudest, in the most terror, was left trampled. A red snow hood was pulled tight around a cocoa face that was bunched at the openings. Cosgrove murmured to the baby, whose eyes popped open at the sight of a last, single bag of Wise potato chips lying open on the floor. "Twenty-two chips." The baby scurried through the smell of gunsmoke to the bag, picked it up, and ran out.

Cosgrove looked about. Nobody was left in the store and the store was completely bare. Not even a rubber glove left. When he walked outside, the sound of his footsteps echoed on a totally empty street. The wind was blowing potato chips along the deserted sidewalks. Great Big and Baby Rock were up at the corner, each with a huge bottle of soda and bag of potato chips. Baby Rock waved for Cosgrove to hurry.

A bus pulled up and Baby Rock jumped on it. Great Big followed and Cosgrove ran up and jumped on after them. Baby Rock slapped the change box as if paying, then went and sat down. The bus driver didn't look up. So Great Big and Cosgrove did not pay, either. "I got to go to my sister's and mother's house on account of you," Baby Rock said to Cosgrove. "I don't like where they live. But now Manslaughter gonna be lookin' for me, I got to go to my sister's and mother's."

"How wonderful!" Cosgrove said. "I can talk to your mother about you getting married. You must, you know."

The bus rocked through quite desperate streets and eventually there was a stop and Baby Rock jumped off and Cosgrove and Great Big followed him as he ran into an old, high hotel called the Flatbush Arms. The lobby was cold, dim, and crowded with adults who smoked cigarettes while children in coats and boots raced around the lobby. The lobby had no furniture.

The black curly hair of a man showed behind a Plexiglas window that had a cardboard sign taped to it. The marking pen printing on it said, THE BOILERS IS BROKE DOWN.

The head behind the Plexiglas looked up. While the man's hair was young and dark and curly, his face was seamed, and small blue eyes were almost lost in creases. He put his mouth to a metal screen in the window and spoke loudly and with great rapidity. He used a combination of *vo* and *do* for just about everything; all *w*'s became *v*'s as in *vot* for *what*, and all *th*'s became *d*'s, as in "dot's the truth." "What do you want here? The guard is supposed to stop you. That's the guard's job. Where is the guard?"

"I be goin' to my mother's house," Baby Rock said.

"Oy, a house he calls it. You're going to your mother's room, that's where you're going."

"It's my mother's house," Baby Rock said, with much stubbornness.

"Wait for the guard," the man said.

A woman in a raincoat pushed in front of Baby Rock. "When we get heat? My little girl has a flu."

"Too cold the water to make heat today. All day the water is off. First, we must fix up the boiler. You see the sign. The boiler is broke. That's the truth. Moishe doesn't lie."

"We live like dogs here." She noticed Cosgrove and turned to him. "You the crisis social worker?" Then, seeing Cosgrove's collar, she said, "Oh, you a minister."

"Priest," Cosgrove said quickly. He was irritated that the woman did not know the difference between a man of God and a Protestant.

"You here to get us some heat?"

"No, I've got something a bit more important to tend to."

"Oh. The lady on the ninth floor, she finally die?"

"I'm not here for death, thanks be to God." He clapped Baby Rock on the back. "We're here for something happy. We have to get him married. That's important."

"I'll tell you what's important. My radiator got nothing to say."

Cosgrove realized that this was all unimportant to his project, for what did it matter if in Africa people lived under too much sun and here there wasn't enough sun? Their sins obviously thrived in any climate. While heat for a baby was hardly as important as getting Baby Rock married, Cosgrove still felt an obligation to give the appearances of assistance. "Her baby must have some warmth. Have you no fireplaces?" he said to the man.

"They make the eleventh floor a fireplace six months ago," the man said. "In the middle of the summer they burn the place up. They didn't come here that day and say,

'Moishe, give us heat.' Now it's cold one day and they want heat. They should have the heat they had from the bonfire they made on the whole floor in the summer."

"You see?" the woman said. "We dogs."

"Lady, excuse me, lady, but you don't know what a dog lives like. I lived like a dog. I lived in a wooden house in Czemniki that had a floor that was the ground. The beds had no mattresses, don't worry. Straw with a cover, that's how I lived."

"I don't care how you live. I care how my baby girl live. She got the flu. We livin' raw mean."

"Moishe lived mean. In the camp where the Germans threw us, Moishe lived. Moishe saw some old lady that was reaching for a cup of soup and Moishe jumped in front of her. What do I care about you, old lady, you could die. Moishe wants to live. Moishe grabs the cup of soup. The old lady has a piece of bread, I tear it out of her hand. What do I care? Moishe lived. Moishe lived because I worked. I worked in the granites factory. You know, hand granites, what the Germans threw at the other people. What do I care who they kill? Moishe lived.

"The granites had leather straps on the cases and we pulled them off and sold them for shoes to the Polacks. They give us bread. One day I'm outside giving the Polacks straps for the shoes and come the guards and Moishe ducks inside and I say, 'What do I care what happens to the Polacks? Moishe lives.' The German had one hand and he shot all the Polacks in the head. Right there on the other side of the wall. They had a young baby Polack. Huh. What do I care? They shot the baby in the head. So what? Moishe didn't die. Let all the babies die.

"Moishe gets brought on the boat here. To Westchester

for the young boys from the concentration camp, and a woman says to me, 'Do you want to play a game?' A game, she's a nice woman and I can't tell her I want to shoot dice. I want to gamble. One day they say do you want to see the beach and I say, all right, I'll go to the beach. We're driving down this street in Queens to the beach and I see this big crowd. I say, 'What's that?' And the woman says, 'That's the racetrack.' I say to them, 'Stop the car.' I run out into the racetrack. I never came back. I meet a guy steals the purses from women. So I steal one too. What do I care, some woman cries about her purse. Moishe got her purse! I never came out. Now you want me to worry about too cold the water for heat?"

"My baby ain't no purse."

"Baby. Moishe saw babies shot in the middle of the mouth."

While the man behind the window kept talking, Cosgrove was readying a crushing answer, but then he could not feel Great Big in his presence and he became panicky and whirled around. Great Big was staring at something out the front door. "We best go, lad," he said to Baby Rock. He left the woman arguing the differences between a dead baby and a sick baby with the man behind the glass.

Baby Rock led the way to the elevator, which had a cardboard sign saying BROKE. Baby Rock swung through a brown metal door and onto a staircase and ran up eight flights of stairs, with Cosgrove panting after him and Great Big leaping two and three steps at a time. Baby Rock loped down a hallway covered with a worn tan carpet that reeked of stale urine. Chicken bones and orange soda cans and little plastic bottles over the floor. Baby Rock stopped and gathered up the plastic bottles and shoved them into his pocket. "The crack man give you ten cents apiece for them," he said.

From the last door came the sound of wildly loud music and Baby Rock banged both fists against the door many times until a young woman in her late teens, with a round face and beaming smile, opened the door. She wore a red velour cap. A crimson T-shirt stretched mightily across a tremendous bosom with lettering proclaiming her name, DISCO GIRL. Her breath showed in the cold air.

Behind her was a room with two beds and several mattresses on the floor and in a cleared space along the wall by a lone window there were stacks of cassettes, perhaps as many as a hundred and fifty of them, and on a table a cassette player so big that it could be used for a weight-lifting competition. Disco Girl began to pump her arms to the music shrieking through the room.

"Michael Jackson!"

In the doorway, Baby Rock began to sway. Great Big moved once. Disco Girl's body exploded beneath the crimson T-shirt. "You Captain Nemo!" she screamed at Great Big, who reached out and covered her breasts with one hand. Cosgrove jumped between them. Disco Girl went dancing backward, her chest moving crazily, and the sound was driving Cosgrove mad. Cosgrove stepped around the mattresses, using peripheral vision to watch Great Big, and looked for a way to turn down the sound. Cosgrove's eye fell on one of the tapes. A sticker said it cost $6.95. Clearly, the stack of tapes was worth a thousand dollars. He looked at the big complicated tape machine and decided to twist one knob, and this immediately increased the volume to an unbearable level.

Disco Girl, deliriously happy with the higher sound, danced brazenly right up to Cosgrove, placed her head alongside his, and shouted into his ear, "I thought you the person bringin' food. Man at my food place, New Opportunity Hot Line, say he gonna drop off to us."

"You have no food?" Cosgrove shouted.

She shook her head no and danced on.

"But you have this," Cosgrove screamed, pointing to the tape player.

"I pay two of my checks and my mother pay one and the man say it still not paid for," Disco Girl shouted. The tape finally ended. "We miss our face-to-face 'cause we move here and the man downstairs don't have our names right. We used to wait for the mailman every day. The day we decide to go buy the box, that's the exact day the mailman come with the face-to-face notice and the man at the desk said he didn't know us. The mailman took the face-to-face notices back and we never knew. Next thing we know, we just got knocked off the computer. We get no more checks till we have our face-to-face. Now the man in the box store say he want his money or he be takin' the box back. We got no welfare checks. Now we gonna have no musics and we already got no food."

She led them through a door and into a tiny kitchenette, which had the suggestion of warmth. Baby Rock, Disco Girl, and Cosgrove were just able to squeeze in. Great Big then barged in and the lead edge of his hip pressed everybody together tighter than a canned Polish ham. Cosgrove was smack up against a heavy woman who sat on a tin folding chair directly in front of a stove, an old stove, small and rusting. Her face was stuck into the open stove door. She smoked a cigarette slowly with her eyes closed. "Mama," Baby Rock called. The woman nodded. "She be Mother Agnes. She be me and Baby Rock's mother," Disco Girl said. The mother looked sleepily at Cosgrove. "I be Agnes O'Dwyer. You from what social office?"

Cosgrove said delightedly, "An O'Dwyer! Why, you're Irish someplace! I'm from no social office. I'm from the Mother Church. Irish! I was born in West Cork. Where are your people from in Ireland?"

"Island of Bimini."

"You've nobody from Ireland?"

"Not that I know of. 'Less some ol' cop messed around sometime. All cops be Irish, right?"

Mother Agnes wore a gray leather cap perched on a high pile of dyed blond hair and a green basketball jacket zipped up to her neck. There was a large nick in her right eyelid that had been there for some time, perhaps years. She seemed uninterested in Cosgrove, particularly after learning he was not a social worker. Nor did she bother to inspect Great Big.

Mother Agnes looked down. On the floor at her feet was a baby who was asleep on his back and smelled from need of change. Beside the baby was a black dog with fur stuck in clumps all over his body. The small amount of warm air coming out of the old oven had a foul smell that immediately took the air out of Cosgrove's nose. The four jets on the stove were also lit. Jammed in the far corner of the tiny space was a young man who wore a robe and an earring and smoked a cigarette with an elaborate feminine motion. On top of the stove was an old black and white television set on which was a rerun of "Hawaii Five-O."

"At least it get a little warm in here," Agnes said. The

"I don't make no baby?" Disco Girl said.

"Never!"

"You say I don't make no baby?"

"No."

She left the room and just as quickly bulled her way back in with her arms filled with manila envelopes. "All my business. My official records." She began to look inside one envelope that was particularly bulging.

"You little man tellin' me I don't make no baby?"

"God makes babies."

She pulled a picture of a black baby out of the envelope.

"This be my youngest son, Kuaran," she said. "He be black."

Cosgrove, who had no idea of what to say, went to the basics. "Where is the father of the child?"

"Lives way down on Tenth Street."

She pulled another picture out. "This be my next son. You know his name? He be Junior José. His father's Spanish. See the baby? Don't he look Spanish? I make me a Spanish baby!"

Cosgrove spoke calmly, for he was forming a vision. "Where is the father of that child?"

"Father's name be José Ríos. He work in a gas station on Southern Boulevard."

Now Disco Girl, with a huge smile, pulled out another picture. She clapped it to her bosom. "Now guess what else I be makin'?"

Cosgrove said nothing.

Disco Girl flashed a picture of a small dark baby girl with Oriental eyes.

"Chinee baby!"

The mother cackled.

"Made me a Chinee baby," Disco Girl said.

"She sure do," the mother said. "I call the baby 'Mi Ma.'"

Disco Girl laughed uproariously. "Her name be Latasha Yee. That's her father's name. Yee."

"You simply go around and make babies?" Cosgrove said incredulously.

Disco Girl chortled. "You know what I make next time?"

Cosgrove was unable to answer.

"White baby!"

Everybody in the room shrieked wildly and Cosgrove, smiling, waited for the noise to subside. He said that he realized that of course they were lying to him. Disco Girl took this as a challenge.

"I make one with you."

The mention of the greatest of sins, the tempting of a priest, even the slightest banter about a matter of such gravity, caused Cosgrove to seek some way out of the conversation. For he had no way to turn this upside down and say how marvelous it was. Therefore, he asked, "Where are the babies? I'd love to see them."

"They got taken away."

"By whom?"

"The BCW come last June."

"What's the BCW?"

"You don't know BCW? Bureau of Child Welfare. You never heard of that? The BCW come in here and they say my little girl was sexually abused. They take her to Cumberland Hospital and they shove Q-Tips and all up her and they say she sexually abused."

Cosgrove held himself together and said nothing.

Agnes shook her head. "I catch her playin' with herself. Any scratches and that they find inside, I say she do that to herself."

Cosgrove said quietly, "I think these things are best said in the secrecy of the confessional."

"No secret," Disco Girl said. "The BCW say it right out loud."

"They come in here with the cops and they call my nephew a faggot," Agnes said. The young man in the corner was running his fingers through his hair.

"Then they take all the kids," Disco Girl said.

"They take my youngest daughter, too," Mother Agnes said. "She the only one I had at home. They took her and they would've took Baby Rock except he don't live here now. He got his own place to live. There was no reason be takin' the one baby I had here except when they take away a child for sexual abuse, they take all the other children out of the house."

"How many children did you say you had?" Cosgrove asked her.

"Seven. One got killed. He got stabbed to death on Washington and Myrtle. They didn't find the murderer yet."

"He got stabbed thirty-two times front and back. It was on the radio," Disco Girl said.

While Cosgrove found he was much more comfortable dealing with murder and he asked many questions about this, including the present state of the investigation, he reminded himself that he had an issue to discuss with them that was far more important. "Where is your husband?" Cosgrove asked.

Mother Agnes took a drag on her cigarette. "Men don't be stayin' around. They can't get good jobs, so they be usin' that as an excuse to run away from their own child. They got to be makin' a baby. Make them feel strong. But they don't want to stay and help the woman with the baby. I sure do know that. I was with four different men and had babies with all of them. First thing they do, they wait till you turn around to fix the baby and then they be runnin'."

"How old could you be to have all these children?" Cosgrove asked.

"Thirty-four," Agnes said.

"And you're a grandmother?"

"Sure am. I be makin' babies since I be sixteen goin' on seventeen. When I was workin' at the man's hardware store on Fulton Street, he say to me that I'm too stupid to make change right. I went home from that man's store and made me a baby."

"At sixteen? You didn't know what you were doing," Cosgrove said.

"Sure did."

Disco Girl clapped her hands. "We all know that. I knew when I was eleven. Had an abortion when I was fourteen."

"I don't like abortions," her mother said.

"Thank God! That is the worst sin. The murder of a baby! A baby is human from the moment the sperm reaches the egg." He patted Agnes on the shoulder. "You give me hope."

Agnes nodded. "I told her, Disco Girl, don't you be havin' no more abortions. You be havin' all the babies you want. I don't want to hear nothin' about abortions."

"So I be havin' babies," Disco Girl said. "I waited to have a baby until I was fifteen. That's a long time. From eleven to fifteen waitin' to have a baby. Then one day the teacher in school say to me, 'You can't take typin'. You too dumb even to spell right on a typewriter.' I went home and never did go back there. Then I read in the supermarket paper that comes out with all the great stories in it that if a lady don't have a baby by a certain age, she gonna be deformed by havin' the baby. I read that and I say, Disco Girl's not gonna be deformed. Disco Girl gonna have herself a baby right now. And I did."

"And you don't practice any birth control," Cosgrove said.

"Wha'?"

Now Cosgrove leaped in with his vision. "To give an anchor," he said, voice rising, "a solid base. A cornerstone." He made a fist and shook it. "To do this, and allow a whole community to see your example, I think that we should have everybody here who has children get married on the same day that the boy here gets married."

"You mean Baby Rock? Why him? He got no babies of his own."

"I found this . . . urchin! . . . sleeping with a young woman of perhaps childbearing age."

"You mean Baby Rock fuck some girl?"

Cosgrove could not answer.

"Make it sound like he strangle somebody. They sure don't put you in jail for that. Fuckin' some little lady ain't like stranglin' somebody."

Baby Rock giggled.

"What good marryin' gonna do us at dinnertime?" Mother Agnes said. "We get more food if we get married? The social worker don't say that."

"To be perfectly truthful with you, it's the soul I worry

about. But, dear God, if there is an ounce of sanity in this universe, somebody will hear God and take care of you, I should certainly think."

"Food don't think," Mother Agnes said. "Food be makin' you growlin' when you ain't got it."

She looked at him suspiciously. "We sittin' here hungry and you want Baby Rock get married, too?"

"Yes. Think of it. You and your two children, Disco Girl, Baby Rock. Three of you married at the same time. Think of the message that will give to this entire community."

"You get the food and get all our babies back from the BCW and for sure we get married for you," Mother Agnes said.

"Of course," Cosgrove said. He jumped to his feet. "I'll be at this first off tomorrow." He was elated, and also apprehensive as he saw that Great Big had his hand on Disco Girl's behind. Cosgrove decreed that it was time to leave. Disco Girl said she would escort them all out of the building, which Cosgrove appreciated, but with wariness. He walked between Great Big and Disco Girl.

Disco Girl walked them down the hall and looked in a door that was partly open. "Excuse me, Lydia, can you buy chicken wings?"

Inside, Lydia sat in a blue robe and snowboots. She had a white wool hat pulled down to her eyes. She sat on a broken couch that had originally been used in an office someplace. A yellow sheet covered the window. On her lap was a baby about two years old. Lydia's middle showed a bulge; she was obviously pregnant.

"Chicken wings?" Lydia said. "All I have is change."

"Where you keep it?" Disco Girl said.

"In the envelope with the papers in the closet."

Disco Girl opened the closet door and reached up. She took change out of an envelope. "We got about sixty-five cents. I was thinkin' of goin' out and buyin' three dollars' worth."

"What kind of chicken?" Lydia said.

"Chicken that you fry," Disco Girl said.

"We're going to have to wait," Lydia said. "I called the New Opportunity Hot Line and they said somebody was coming over here anyway so they would stop off here. Leave us a few cans of something, I suppose." She yawned and patted her baby.

"What time did they say they'd come?" Disco Girl asked.

"Anytime now," Lydia said. "My son is outside waiting for them."

"Let me see," Cosgrove said, smiling, "you have a wee one here, a son outside, and —"

"And one right here," Lydia said, patting her middle.

"And no food," Cosgrove said. "Is your husband out looking?"

"Husband?"

"The father of the children."

Lydia looked at him in wonderment. "I'm nineteen now. I had my first baby when I was fourteen. The father is Carl Sutton. He was seventeen. He's away in the Army someplace now. I met him at hip-hop parties. The fast life. I didn't know what I was doing. I had a baby. His name is Dwayne Edward Reed. He has my mother's maiden name. I was using my father's name then and my mother said I was too young to give the baby a name so she had the baby use her name. That's why my first child is named Dwayne Edward Reed and my name is Lydia Moore. This is my daughter Yolanda." She patted the sleeping baby in her lap.

"I didn't want her. I wanted to do something about her. But then it was too late so I had her. Her father is Leon Smith. I don't know where he is. He's home someplace, I guess. I didn't want Yolanda because my social worker had me going to school and I was doing very well. You might not believe this, but I was doing very well in languages. But I had this baby and I thought that would be it and I would just try and make it through with my two children. And then look what happens to me."

"What happens is that you have been living an essentially immoral life," Cosgrove said. "You have been fornicating. The only thing you can say for yourself is that you have not used abortion or birth control."

"I sure haven't," she said. "Because this baby here —" she patted her middle — "is one I really want."

"You planned an illegitimate baby?" Cosgrove said. "That was very foolish of you because if you gave it such sufficient reflection and full consent of the will, then there is damnable gravity to the sin."

"I just wanted the baby. They wouldn't let me go to school, so I decided I better do something big."

"Make her a baby!" Disco Girl shouted.

"Third year in high school, I left the day before I had my daughter, this one here, Yolanda, and I came right back to school the next week and I passed everything. My social worker said that if I didn't have any more babies I could go to a college and he would get welfare to pay for day care. So I worked hard all through the last year in school. I took tests and I did very well. One day I went on the BMT to Brooklyn College. They saw my marks there. I was very good in languages. French, Spanish. I thought Brooklyn College would be great for me. It was only one subway to-

ken each way. I could save my money and get to school. So
then I got a letter. They said I couldn't go."

"What was the reason?" Cosgrove said.

"Because of my babies."

"They would not give you a chance to redeem yourself
because of your illegitimate children? Was that an order
from the bishop?"

"Bishop? Bishop doesn't run that school. I got an order
from the state DSS." Lydia handed the baby to Disco Girl
and went to an old dresser and opened the top drawer. Pa-
pers were crammed into it and she went through envelopes
and folded papers and wrinkled mimeographed forms until
she pulled out a letter. "The man in the registrar's office at
the college told me that he would get welfare to pay for day
care for my children. He said the welfare should pay dou-
ble. They were not only helping my children but I was going
to go to school and get out of what they call the cycle of
dependency. I remember I was so happy. I could get to
Brooklyn College for one token each way. Two dollars a
day. It was hard. Ten dollars a week, maybe I'd walk home
Fridays. That was all right. Then look. Last April, I get this
letter."

She handed it to Cosgrove. The letter said:

Under Section 131-a (6) (d) of the New York State Social Ser-
vices Law, day care in a day-care center, in a family home or
in an approved "in-home day care" is provided if the home-
maker is receiving occupational training. As attendance at a
four-year institution that grants degrees is not the prescribed
occupational training, you are not entitled to day care for your
children while you attend classes at Brooklyn College. This is,
we must stress, a New York State Social Services Law and is
not a college regulation.

The regulation states that if you attend a full-time college, you have relinquished your role as the primary caretaker of the children and are no longer a full-time parent. Therefore, your children, rather than being eligible for day care, should be placed in a foster home program. As previously you stated that you are unable to attend classes at Brooklyn College because of your need for day care, we suggest to you that you enroll in a school that gives occupational training and thus enables you to be eligible for day-care benefits.

A four-year course at Brooklyn College, with a romance language major, simply is not occupational training. It is our feeling that you should seek enrollment at the Institute of Human Resources, where there are many courses for Hospital Dieticians, Nursing Care Specialists, and Teacher's Aides. You then would be covered under the New York State Social Services Law as one undergoing approved occupational training and thus your children could be placed in day care, and funded for such, while you go on to a richly satisfying career. Thank you very much for thinking of Brooklyn College.

Lydia sighed and got up. "When I got that letter, I saw they had a law against me attempting to make anything out of my life. So I said, 'Well, let me just make something that no law can stop me from making. Let me make it all by myself.'"

"You didn't make that by yourself," Cosgrove said. "You committed a sin against the Sixth Commandment by fornicating with a man."

"Any man can help you start," Lydia said. "But I make the baby. Where is it such a sin for me to make a baby?"

"Without a man to whom you are married in the eyes of God?"

"Never mind the father."

"Where is this man?"

"Supposed to be home with his wife and children. But he thinks a video game store is his real address."

She stood up and proudly showed her bulging midsection. "Wherever the father is, we sure know where the baby is. This is the real human resources administration."

"You are using some clerical error as the reason for committing sin," Cosgrove said.

"It's no error. It's the law. They don't help you through school unless you promise to become only a beautician or a fry cook in a hospital."

"But these are only temporal matters. The Lord said that the poor always shall be with us. It is sin that is the eternal matter. Because of some temporal matter, some grubby school or some such, you decided to go out and risk your soul for all eternity and defied God."

Lydia grabbed her baby from Disco Girl. She looked at Cosgrove and saw insanity. He looked at her and saw all the reasons he was in America.

~~~~~~~

Out on the sidewalk, children in snowsuits ran in the dullness and one of them, about four years old, held a small bag of potato chips. When all the hands grabbed at the potato chips, he ran out into the street, shouting into the cold air, and Baby Rock ran after him and grabbed him just as a blue van stopped short.

"Watch your little brother better than that," Bushwick Taylor called from the van.

"He be Lydia's kid," Baby Rock said.

In the van, Sarah said that was probably one of the people they had on their emergency delivery list and she had Bushwick pull the van to the curb. As Bushwick was getting out, people were starting to run from all parts of the block.

Food riot! Then Bushwick saw that they were all looking up. Across the street, a woman threw open a window at the top of a five-story building and screamed, "Stop him from jumpin'."

A young man in a checkered cap and coat stood on the roof. Cosgrove, running out into the street like a fast crab, called to the mother, "Who is he? What can I say to him?"

"He's my son. He be all beamed up," the mother said.

"Beam me up, Scotty," Baby Rock said.

"He mean crack," Disco Girl said. "All beamed up on crack."

"Crack?" Cosgrove said.

"Crack is whack," somebody yelled.

"Crack-a-Jack! Crack a bridge take you over the moat to the castle," somebody else called.

Cosgrove cupped his hands and shouted up, "Do not jump. You will lose your immortal soul."

The woman in the window leaned far out and twisted around and yelled to the young guy on the roof. He swung his hands in great irritation and jumped out into the air about three feet and landed on a fire escape jutting out from the fifth floor.

"Now he got to jump again," Baby Rock said.

"Baby Rock, you makin' jokes again," Disco Girl shrieked.

Cosgrove ran out into the middle of the street and called up. "You must come to your senses," Cosgrove said. "If you jump again, then it is with sufficient reflection and you will be damned forever. Suicide is despair and despair is a loss of hope in God's mercy. There can be no forgiveness for suicide. You don't even have time to make a perfect Act of Contrition, one in which you truly are sorry for hurting God and are not saying the Act of Contrition merely because you are afraid of going to Hell."

"Where's Hell?" the young guy on the fire escape called.

"You must come down here and I will talk to you," Cosgrove said.

"People been talkin' to me all my life and look where it got me. Ain't no motherfucker be talkin' to me again."

"That is disrespectful to the Lord to talk to me like this!" Cosgrove bellowed. Of course he felt comfortable saying this, for it was obvious to him that as long as the man was engaging in conversation with him, the man had no intention of jumping to his death and therefore, no matter what the situation, Cosgrove felt that there had to be some decorum in speaking to a priest.

On the fire escape, the young guy in the checkered cap and coat turned his back to Cosgrove, dropped his pants, and bent his knees so that his rear end observed Cosgrove.

"More disrespect!" Cosgrove bawled.

The young guy now bent his knees even more and flung himself backward out into the air and zipped to the sidewalk.

"Jumped twice," Baby Rock said.

Immediately a large crowd of people ran to the scene and Cosgrove had to fight his way through them and drop to his knees, and while the crowd around him cavorted and shouted, he gave the man the last rites. At the edge of the crowd, Bushwick Taylor and Sarah stood for a moment and, as the priest finished his task and was replaced by an emergency medical crew, one of whom carried a body bag, Bush-

wick thanked the priest. Suicide was not mentioned in his
job description, but he thought that as a representative of
New Opportunity, and one with ambitions, he should thank
the priest.

"The man is in Hell," Cosgrove said sadly.

Bushwick answered this with dead silence. He and Sarah
went to the van and took out three industrial-size cans of
corned beef hash and beef stew and gave them to Disco
Girl, instructing her to give one can to Lydia. Then Bush-
wick and Sarah drove to the Redeemer Salvation Church
basement, a few blocks away. There had been many phone
complaints about the food center's never having any food
at all, yet the New Opportunity Hot Line computer print-
outs said this was an impossibility, that there never had
been an absolute shortage at the center, which was open for
only one meal a day, the dinner meal, and was staffed with
professional soup kitchen workers, who understood that
portion control would ensure that the end of the line, too,
receives something.

Oh, yes, there was now a job classification of Soup
Kitchen Worker in New York, for the first time in the city's
history, too. Quite often, those so classified were reformed
derelicts who had undergone health tests and training. New
Opportunity had placed a couple, Jerry and Ellen Doherty,
in the Redeemer Salvation soup kitchen to serve the meals.
A fine couple, working for $3.65 an hour, two of them work-
ing three hours a day, giving them an income of almost
twenty-two dollars a day. Bushwick could not understand
why the center was in such continual trouble.

Driving up the street, he happened to glance out the win-
dow and on the sidewalk he saw Jerry Doherty, his knees
bent as he carried a heavy cardboard box into Santiago's

bodega. Behind Jerry was his wife, Ellen, lean and mean after a lifetime of ravaging her body on cheap wine. And on his knees, Santiago, the bodega owner, was removing sixty-ounce industrial cans of corned beef hash from a New Opportunity Hot Line box and putting them on the shelf of his bodega.

The moment Jerry Doherty saw Bushwick, he ripped the top off a bottle of wine and began draining it.

"Why do you hurry now?" Bushwick said.

"Because I'm afraid you'll take it from me."

Sarah Carter took out her clipboard and wrote a note saying that both Dohertys were officially discharged. She and Bushwick then grabbed the boxes from Santiago, who frothed at the mouth and screamed that he had purchased them legally. Bushwick showed him the New Opportunity Hot Line stencil on the boxes and said that he would be prosecuted by every prosecutor alive. Bushwick and Sarah carried the boxes out. Santiago smacked Jerry Doherty in the mouth.

At the Redeemer Salvation Church soup kitchen, the noise from the basement exploded onto the sidewalk. Inside, perhaps a hundred people thumped the empty tables. "All cramped up. Can't wait no more, can't wait no more."

Bushwick and Sarah carried the boxes into the kitchen, turned on the lights, and set to work immediately, Bushwick opening the cans and Sarah Carter spooning the hash, chili, and beef stew into pans and warming them. The table pounding stopped and a line formed and Bushwick slapped food onto the plates and handed out rye bread. All the clients had a worn identification card stating that they were needy and assigned to eat dinner only in this particular soup kitchen. At meal's end, Bushwick impressed a couple of the hungry to come into the kitchen and wash off the paper plates for use again; the cost of new paper plates for each meal was not included in the New Opportunity Hot Line service.

As Bushwick and Sarah drove back along Fulton Street on the way to the bridge, there was Disco Girl, dancing and shouting happily in front of the hotel. A little girl who clutched a shopping bag stood beside her. Cosgrove, Baby Rock, and Great Big were with her, too.

"Drive me to the city. Got me a job!" Disco Girl said.

"What kind of job at this hour?" Bushwick asked her.

"Traveling job. You know the lady whose son just jumped out the window? She just pay me to take the little girl — this is the lady's little girl right here, this be Roberta, you say hello, Roberta — we goin' to see her father and tell him what happened to the son. The father in Clinton."

By Clinton, Bushwick knew, she meant Clinton Correctional Facility at Dannemora, New York, which was closer to the Arctic Circle than to Brooklyn.

"I've been talking to her about what she should say," Cosgrove said.

"I say the truth. His son jump off the roof."

"Jump twice," Baby Rock said.

Cosgrove shook his head. "I am prepared to go with them to the prison and see the man myself."

Bushwick explained to Cosgrove that Clinton was an eight-and-a-half-hour ride on a big old tour bus that was filled with women and children going to visit their men. He would of course take Disco Girl to Columbus Circle in Manhattan, where tour buses leave at night for the long ride to upstate prisons. They all piled in and Bushwick drove over the Brooklyn Bridge and into lower Manhattan, which was silent and dark; the streets turned bright as he moved uptown. He had to stop once because Great Big became carsick. At Columbus Circle, tour buses sat in the darkness in front of the Coliseum. The fountain in the middle of the circle was unlighted. But uptown, toward Lincoln Center, the street was an inferno of lights.

Disco Girl got out and ran up to an old toothless man in a shapeless gray overcoat with a badge pinned to it. He wore a policeman's cap with a badge that said, BUS DISPATCHER.

"Which one is Clinton?" she asked.

He pointed to a cluster of women with children who carried shopping bags and waited in front of an old red intercity tour bus whose door was open. Inside, the driver's cigarette glowed in the dark. The drivers never let the people on the bus until departure time, for they are going to live with the people for far too many hours and the later they all get together, the better.

"It cold," a child on the line said.

"Soon," the mother said.

Disco Girl and the little girl Roberta got on the line.

"Do you have your money?" Bushwick said.

"The lady gave me a hundred dollars. Cost sixty-four dollars for the bus. Then the bus stop twice on the way up and back."

"Stop three times each way," the woman in front of her said.

"Three times, then," Disco Girl said. "We stop three times for Burger Kings. That's three Burger Kings goin' up and three Burger Kings goin' down. That takes all the

money, don't it? How'm I goin' to make any money then?"
She thought. "Maybe I eat Burger Kings only twice." She
looked at the little girl. "No, Roberta, she be wantin'
Burger Kings every time, I know that. Roberta, you got
your change bag?"

Solemnly, Roberta held out a small paper bag filled with
change. "I buy my daddy a cheeseburger!" she said.

"Roberta, you little liar. You buy yourself a cheeseburg-
er. You see this child? She knows only a visitor can use the
cheeseburger machine in the visit room. The man in prison
isn't allowed to go to the machine. The guard, he can't make
change. So you got to bring your own change for the ma-
chine. If the man in prison want something only the visitor
can get it for him. You see today, Roberta, she go to the
machine for her father, then she stand by the cheeseburger
machine and eat it all up right in his face."

"Let's talk about what you are going to say to the man,"
Cosgrove said. "What is he in this accursed prison for, any-
way?"

"What else do you go to prison for? Drugs."

"How long does he have to serve?"

"A nice cool six year."

"And what is it you are going to say to him?"

"Tell him his boy die." She thought for a moment. "Tell
him his boy jump off the roof."

"Jump twice," Baby Rock said.

Now, from up the street at Lincoln Center, people were
walking from the opera, the men in tailor-made clothes and
the women in fur coats and diamond earrings and just as
they came to the women waiting on line to go to the prisons,
many of the operagoers turned into a door leading down to
the building's parking garage. In doing this, they had to pass

through a couple of lines, one waiting for the bus to Elmira, the other for the trip to Attica Prison. The men coming from the opera held an arm out to guide their women through the prison lines and the women, as a reflex, held their hands out, showing fine leather gloves. Their ears were ablaze with diamonds, which now had as a backdrop the snow jackets of the women on the line for Attica.

Octavia Ripley Havermeyer was one of those walking. The opera, a benefit performance for the New Opportunity Soup Kitchen, was attended, as usual, mostly by New York builders, not a precise description because they are men who by sneakery and bribery get valuable land and have designed for them the most grotesque structures. Legitimate workingmen do the building. She was on her way to a gala dinner party with these "builders." Upon leaving the opera up at Lincoln Center, Octavia walked with builder Golden's wife who, at twenty-five, was about half of Golden's age, Octavia surmised. Golden's wife had hair that was much lighter than her antecedents ever had, and she also had not listened to more than a few bars of the entire opera.

Octavia knew that because, rather than listen herself, she had studied the faces around her and seen Golden's wife ready to expire from boredom. Outside of one or two popular arias, Octavia hated every opera she had ever attended. As did, she knew, Golden's wife and about eighty-five percent of the people at the benefit. Octavia and Golden's wife walked together because they were in matching sable coats. They passed a long line of limousines, all with smoked-glass windows, but they did not feel deprived because they knew that they were going only a short distance. As Octavia Ripley Havermeyer and Golden's wife walked out of the Lincoln Center plaza in front of the opera house, a man and woman with rags wrapped around their heads stood with a baby in a shopping cart that was filled with newspapers and rags. "Help us!" the man screamed. "We are homeless. Help us!"

His bellowing made the people coming from the opera walk more erectly, the better to look over his head as they passed the bawling man.

"My husband says it's a shame," Golden's wife said.

"It is just horrible," Octavia said. She was digging into her purse, trying to find a single dollar.

"That's why my husband says we always have to do things for them," Golden's wife said.

"That's gracious of him," Octavia said.

"That's why he said we got to go to this dinner. To help the others."

Octavia Ripley Havermeyer went into her purse and brought out a dollar, which she pushed into the man's hand. "Help! Help!" the man screamed at the next people.

Golden's wife, embarrassed that she had given nothing, went into her small purse and brought out a dollar, which she gave to the man. "Now just a minute, I must do one thing with you," she said. She produced a small notepad, ripped off a sheet, and handed the slip and a pen to the hungry man.

"You have to write a receipt for me. My husband told me never to give anything unless I get a receipt for the taxes."

The hungry man looked at her with half-shut eyes. "You want a receipt."

"My husband told me to get one."

He nodded numbly. "You want a receipt for a dollar."

"Oh, just put down anything," Golden's wife said.

The hungry man nodded. He handed the dollar to his wife. He put the slip of paper on top of the newspapers in the cart and carefully and in big letters printed his receipt. He handed her the receipt and pen and turned and again bawled at the crowd, "We're starving!"

Golden's wife glanced at the receipt and her eyes widened. "Oh! That louse!"

Octavia read the receipt, whose big bold letters said, THE BEARER IS A DIRTY CUNT!

Octavia took Golden's wife by the arm and hurried her away. "What are we going to do about these people?" Golden's wife said.

"They are just going to wait until we do everything for them," Octavia Ripley Havermeyer said.

To evade beggars, Octavia and Golden's wife went across Broadway. A block down, a man had an old upright piano placed smack on the sidewalk, against a fence, and he sat on a stool and pounded a fast tune into the cold air. He played with his nose close to the keys and his back to the people passing on the sidewalk. As Octavia and Golden's wife got close, Octavia recognized the tune as "Everything's Coming Up Roses." The piano player had a washtub on the sidewalk alongside him and people walking past threw coins into it. As the coins clanged into the tub, the piano player threw one hand in the air in thanks and kept pounding away. When a man and woman walked past and did not throw in anything, the piano player half spun on his stool, to check his washtub, then threw a middle finger into the air at the two people walking away.

A little man in his fifties, wearing a sleeveless down jacket and a head as bare as a doorknob, he began to swing into the start of the song again, the music to the lines "You'll be swell, you'll be great . . . ," as a man in rags came up to the piano. Obviously, the bum was only pretending to listen to the music, for his eyes were fixed on the coins, which caused his head to lower and the shoulders were following the head and soon he would be in a full stoop over the tub of money.

The piano player's head was down close to the keys, and he pounded with his right hand and reached out with the left, feeling until he had his hand on the bum's chest. He had his elbow bent. He spread his fingers against the bum's chest for leverage and then with a great jerk the elbow straightened stiff and the bum went quickly backward and up on his toes and nearly off his feet and out into the traffic. Quickly the piano player brought his left hand back to the keys and his nose went lower and lower to the keys and he was pounding, pounding, pounding, and he heard the bum making a comeback at the tub of money. The piano player was at "Curtain up!" when he lifted both hands high and spun around on the piano stool and kicked with his right foot. Kicked with much effort showing in his lined face. He was wearing big tan lace-up winter boots and he caught the bum right full in the face and it was a beauty, a clout in the face on a freezing night. The bum clapped both hands to his long, shaggy face in pain and stumbled away.

"I only needed something to eat," the bum said.

The piano player now had his nose almost to the keys and he raced through "Roses."

The bum, his face still contorted with pain, started to tiptoe back toward the bucket of money.

"Watch out!" the piano player suddenly called out.

The bum kept coming toward the tub of money.

The piano player held one foot out. "You'll be eating this halfway down your throat!"

Averting her eyes, Octavia looked across the street and saw this line of women and children in the dimness in front of the Coliseum. Thank the Lord, she thought, for she didn't know what she would do if the piano player attacked the poor street man once more. "Oh, look," she said to Golden's wife. "They're going on a skiing trip."

She and Golden's wife strolled back across Broadway toward the gay young people on line. Abruptly, a young boy with a scarf wrapped around his face ran off and a woman in white sneakers turned around and shouted, "José! *Ven acá!*"

Which caught Octavia and Golden's wife in midstride, and they saw that the lines were all black or Hispanic. In the entrance to one bus, in the dim light, a black woman in an army overcoat stood on the step and ate a sandwich.

Golden's wife said, "Oh, there he is. Look at where my husband is. All the way over there." She pointed at her husband a full block ahead and followed her finger away from this pack of blacks and Hispanics. Octavia Ripley Havermeyer knew she would feel far better if she, too, got away from all this, but as she walked through the lines of women and children waiting to get on the buses, she felt a little twinge. Yes, she said to herself, the heart does go out. And she knew that this was the thing that set her apart from the others, who were so glazed that they felt nothing. She could feel the pain of others. Of course, she knew that nothing really could be done tonight about the reasons for the pain, but that was not the point. She told herself that she did care.

She stopped alongside a little girl and said, "And where are you going, dear?"

"To see my daddy," Roberta said.

"Clinton Correctional, baby," Disco Girl said.

"And how long do you stay at this . . . institution?"

"Eight hours to get there. Visit lasts eight hours," Disco Girl said. "Then we get on the bus, come right back down here. Be here midnight tomorrow night."

"What does this poor child do all day?"

"Sits on a chair across from her daddy."

Octavia, speaking in a little voice, said to Roberta, "And what did you bring with you to read?"

Roberta became bashful. "Nothing."

"My word," Octavia said. Turning to Disco Girl she said, "Do you have something for the little girl to read?"

"Lights be out in this bus all the way to mornin'," Disco Girl said.

"But certainly the little girl will become restless in the morning," Octavia said. "Then she will spend all day in this one room. The little girl absolutely must have a book with which to occupy herself."

"Not allowed to buy books," Disco Girl said.

Octavia looked at her in puzzlement.

"Bureau of Labor Statistics welfare grant say that people receive no money to buy things to read," Disco Girl said.

At first Octavia was going to remark that this was insane, but she stopped herself, for her memory told her that the statement was true. Yes, this young woman was right, the basic welfare grant did note that, on the one hand, the poor did not have to pay any income taxes on their checks, and therefore, on the other, they could not expect to have money included in their payments to buy such things as books.

Here, on the dim sidewalk by the bus, it seemed unfair and absurd to Octavia, but she reminded herself that all these rules must be examined dispassionately, in an office far removed from squalling children, and only then did they begin to make sense, and almost always very good sense, too. In this case, there must be a good reason for their not receiving money for books, she thought. She remembered the other rule she had read, the one about day care being disallowed for any mother attempting to go to a four-year college and earn a degree. That one had been devised by somebody in a different social assistance office, in a different city to be exact. She remembered that, for she had read about the man who devised the day-care rule, for which he was the recipient of a government employee service award for the idea of withholding aid to these cheap frauds.

If you listen to some of these . . . street leaders, they would have everybody believe that there was a conspiracy to keep these people down, Octavia said to herself. And out here, if you were to tell this to people, they would probably believe it. Why, most of the time when I first hear one of these silly charges, I believe what I'm told, Octavia admitted to herself. I must never say anything until I am back in my office and have it explained to me . . . reasonably. She smiled, for she was comforted by knowledge this time. Here we had two people who drew up two rules and the people were in different cities and did not even know each other. They had never spoken to each other. Why, this absolutely proves that there is no conspiracy to stop these people at all. Things just always work out this way.

With this, she patted little Roberta on the head and walked off to catch up with those going to the supper party. When she looked back into the doorway of the Coliseum and saw Cosgrove huddled with Great Big, sharing a cigarette, she hurried off the curb and crossed the street. There is the biggest drug addict I have ever seen, she said to herself.

6

WHEN THE BUS to Clinton pulled out of Colum-
bus Circle that night, Cosgrove, Great Big, and
Baby Rock stood on the sidewalk and waved,
and Disco Girl and Roberta waved back and
the bus was gone. Baby Rock ran down the up escalator
into the subway at Columbus Circle and came racing back
up the down escalator and reported that there were too
many policemen on the platform. The three then walked
over to Seventh Avenue and went downstairs and there
were no police and they took the train back out to East New
York. Baby Rock, who said he was tired, stepped into his
storefront and fell on his couch. Cosgrove and Great Big
walked to the church. On one block the sidewalk was en-
tirely covered with garbage and the two stepped out into the
street. Suddenly, a Lincoln town car rushed at them and
stopped with a scream.

The young hood from the Chief's restaurant, gold chains,
chewing gum, called from the car to Cosgrove, "If you want
to walk with niggers, do it on the sidewalk."

Cosgrove stepped out of the way. Great Big did not move quickly enough for the Chief's man, who stepped on the gas and aimed the Lincoln town car directly at Great Big. This caused Great Big to jump away. But as the car passed him, Great Big brought both hands high into the air, locked them, and then brought them down with a tremendous crash onto the roof of the Lincoln town car. Great Big's hands punctured the roof and caused the Chief's man to swerve almost out of control. Halfway down the block, the car stopped and the Chief's man shouted something that Cosgrove couldn't hear.

"That was the hand of God," Cosgrove shouted back.

The car pulled away and Cosgrove walked back to the church with Great Big. It is good that not too many people challenge him, Cosgrove thought. He remembered how Great Big had reacted when it counted in Africa.

~~~~~~

At dawn, the French priest who was being replaced by Cosgrove drove him in the Land Rover to the mission. They traveled on a dirt road, a path really. Sunlight blazing off the tin roofs of huts caused him to blink. Soon there were no tin roofs, only round mud huts with thatched, conical roofs. People were naked or did not wear enough clothes to matter. Cosgrove looked at the people, but they did not look at him. The heat and expanse and people everywhere on parched ground gave him the feeling that the African centuries would leave him covered by dry grass.

His mission was a cinder-block church raised from the ground on rocks in a place where the bush country sat in the heat on the edge of loneliness. He found that the sun never set. Much of the time it was somewhere at the top of the sky, the heat wrapped around it like gauze, scalding the eyes of all who dared to stare. The sun appeared to allow the day to become night, but it did so by fakery, crouching to create shadows and darkness, yet never allowing its great flame to as much as flicker. The sun's flame burned through the day and burned through the night as Cosgrove, raised in the madness of the rain, now lived in so much heat that he awoke each day with the thought that he was sleeping on a bed of ashes.

That first Sunday he was a little unsure of what the reaction would be to his French in an area where the natives spoke Yoruba, a language that had existed before the Romans. But it was the vastness of the place, as it sat in constant heat, that was unsettling. Outside, a woman walked in the steaming morning with wood for cooking fires strapped to her back. Bent over, she could have walked forty miles for this wood. Upon putting it down, she probably would not be able to stand erect. What was she — thirty? — and her back had collapsed forever from hauling so much wood over so many miles. Defeating herself and everyone around her, God bless her, Cosgrove thought. He came from land where tens of thousands had starved to death because the rains had drenched a soil so that only leaf diseases grew. And here in the sun in the bush, desertification was the enemy. The bush had little jungle and no rain forests. As rainfall usually originates in the area where it rains, and forests usually provide the standing water crop out of which rain is formed, each tree hacked down in the bush caused a death in the air around it. The sun baked the land until the soil lost its structure. Somewhere at the edges, where the grass turns yellow and becomes as thin as an old man's hair, the land is claimed by monotonous sand, which is a tan blanket smothering the earth from bush in Africa to sea at the northern edge of the continent, thousands of miles away. The wind causes the sand to swirl, but this is only a rearranging of grains; the sand is there until the day God commands the earth to be gone.

On Sunday, the white cassock, which came down to his ankles, was sticking to him and it had been over his body for only a few moments.

"You can say Mass in an undershirt here," the old French priest he was replacing said.

Cosgrove went through his suitcase for the white surplice with a gold cross on the back. He dropped it over his head, arranged it at his shoulders, and draped a stole around his neck, giving him three layers of starched cloth.

"You will boil to death," the Frenchman said.

As Cosgrove's foot hit the altar, his shoulders squared and his chin rose and he cared not about language or the number of people in the church; he was a man following his calling. He turned around to face the congregation and the heat dealt him a glancing blow. He held on to the altar for support. He was in the middle of the Confiteor when he and his three layers of heavy vestments went down like an accident victim. They got his clothes off, threw a bucket of water over his head, and put him under a tree where he looked out at women with bare breasts and tried to ignore them as he immediately swung into his sermon. "Celibacy is the calling of Christ until you become married."

One woman, her arms folded under her breasts, causing Cosgrove's startled eyes to look at the ground, then the sky, said to him, "Celibacy?"

"By that I mean not fornicating," Cosgrove said.

"What do I do if I sleep with my man every night?"

A man said to him, "How do you expect me to marry my woman until she has shown me she can give me a son?"

"It is a sin to sleep with her before you are married," Cosgrove said.

"It is a greater sin for me to marry her and she does not have a son for me," the man said.

When Cosgrove finished, one huge man at the rear of the crowd applauded. Cosgrove saw that the man might be as tall as eight feet. When Cosgrove gave out communion under the tree, the man opened a mouth so wide that Cosgrove felt he would lose his hand to the wrist if the mouth snapped shut.

Later the French priest drank a bottle of beer and said to Cosgrove, "Are you usually this insane?"

"I know, to dress like that," Cosgrove said.

"Not what you wore. What you said."

"Sins of the flesh," Cosgrove said.

"You are deteriorating already in this heat," the Frenchman said. "I will tell you what is an important sin in this country. A broken sprocket is a great sin. If you have a broken sprocket, then you cannot use your bike to get food. Let them chew themselves to shreds in their beds! God understands. It is our duty to pray that their sprockets do not break. The priest who can protect sprockets, and fix them, will be the true patron saint of Africa."

"I did not come here to negotiate my religion," Cosgrove said.

"I can assure you, dear man, that if you persist like this, you shall be sent home in a cage."

One day following this, Cosgrove walked through dirt al-

leys between huts in search of a woman whose middle was
so filled with fluid that death, too, was around looking for
her. From off to the right came a hollow sound of people
beating on trees. It was the sign that death had found her,
and the people were trying to chase death away.

Cosgrove went to the hut, anointed the woman's body,
and, feeling ill, went to the last hut of the village and start-
ed across a field of grass so dry that it crackled underfoot.
The path went in the direction of Idjebo, the witchcraft vil-
lage whose saying has been the same through the centuries:
"The stranger who arrives here in the morning becomes the
sacrifice by sunset." Nearly everybody uses a circle route
to bypass Idjebo. Cosgrove started across the field, in the
middle of which rose the large man who had clapped so hard
in church. He rose from the hot ground like a spire. Cos-
grove walked through grass so stiff that it sounded against
his ankles. The huge man called out in Yoruba, which Cos-
grove did not understand, and then in French, which Cos-
grove did understand, that the grass was a stockyard for
snakes. Cosgrove retreated.

The man walked barefoot through the grass to Cosgrove.
He had shoulders of such width that to fit through a door-
way he would have to go on the oblique. Underneath his
shoulders, his body fell away, and his ribs hung like vene-
tian blinds. Evidence of how often he had been forced to
live on himself, like an old bear in a tree stump, while the
ground around him produced nothing but dust. His face,
too, was hollow under cheekbones that sat in his face like
iron bars.

He gave an initial appearance of great meanness, but this
dissolved as he came closer and Cosgrove could see that his
eyes were sad as he listened to the wooden death sound

coming from the woman's hut. He told Cosgrove his name, which in English turned out to be Great Big. He took Cosgrove to a mud hut that was a long walk through fields and bushes with dead leaves and in the midst of a clump of trees that somehow had been chopped down. In the fields around the trees was Great Big's cash crop, peanuts, most of whose plants were withered. Great Big produced a goatskin bag that had first been used in the African sun when persons in places like England and France lived by the spear. Great Big held up the goatskin bag to the hot sky and let a clear liquid run into his mouth.

"Good water," he said.

Now he put the spout to Cosgrove's mouth. Cosgrove had been raised around poteen, homemade whiskey, and felt that an African home brew such as this one would be nothing more than a soft drink. Great Big stood over Cosgrove and tipped the goatskin. "Good water," Great Big said, insisting that Cosgrove have more.

The elation that comes with drinking came and passed so quickly that Cosgrove was wondering what had happened to it, and after one particular swallow Cosgrove noticed that some of the alcohol dribbled from the corner of his mouth and he wiped his chin to prevent the pure alcohol from dribbling onto the thick, precious rug that he suddenly saw under his feet. Cosgrove pointed to the rug and told Great Big to be careful of spilling on it. Great Big said he could see no rug. A long bare foot stamped on the ground to prove this. Cosgrove said of course there was a rug and as he said this, a hand wriggled out from under the rug and smacked him in the face.

When he woke up hours later, Cosgrove found himself naked inside Great Big's hut. He reached out and felt his clothes, which were in a damp bundle beside him. For some reason he did not want to pick himself up. He stretched his legs, his hips swiveling his front against a mat over the dirt floor. A delicious feeling came through him. He saw nipples of lovely breasts. Not the black breasts from church. Those he saw now were white and pink and above them was the face of the lovely young woman from the courtyard of the school in Toome. Cosgrove suddenly lifted his head. The Devil had followed him to Africa.

Streaming past the mission at all times were silent groups of people who looked like toothpicks and swayed from all the miles they had walked from their homes in bushland that was becoming desert. Some of the refugees wanted nothing more than a place to die with some order. When Cosgrove found that most of these people had never been baptized, he baptized all who would agree and even kidnapped some: a child with glazed eyes and a potbelly squalled with the little strength it had left as Cosgrove carried him into the church, where he splashed water and prayed fervently. When he was finished he turned around and found there were no hands to accept the child. Cosgrove carried the baby into his cubicle and put him on the mattress on the floor. Like everybody else, Cosgrove was eating once a week, his meal consisting of rice and tomatoes and tiny shreds of chicken, which he fed to the child who, drugged with food, fell asleep.

"This is not an orphanage," Cosgrove scolded himself. "You must think of a thousand souls and you cannot be tied down to one."

Returning to the mission church one day several weeks later, Cosgrove found that the postal service had delivered two large cardboard cartons from Dunboy Bay. The first box held a crackling new, handmade quilt thick enough to keep out a thick blizzard. Pinned to it was a note that said the Rosary Altar Confraternity Society had made this quilt and would continue to send articles for the black babies of Africa. The second contained a wonderful hand-knit Irish fisherman's sweater, the cable stitching of such thickness that a full drenching by a cold wave would not be enough to soak through to the body inside the sweater. The sweater was baby-sized. The note inside said it was from the Dunboy Bay Men's Catholic Club. The envelope contained many pound notes, which, when stuffed into his pocket, produced in Cosgrove a feeling of exhilaration.

Shortly thereafter he was on a folding chair in the bar on the second floor of the hotel in the capital city, drinking an oversized bottle of strong beer. Over these big bottles of beer, Cosgrove decided to attack the British educational system. As supervisors of the missionary schools, the British were truly disappointed each time a student learned to read. "This is a plot against these people," Cosgrove said. "And this is the only place on the earth where such a thing could be allowed to happen. It is the act of savages not to help children learn to read." The few textbooks in the mission school were over forty years old and the printing in them was so small that even young eyes watered. Therefore, he was astonished at the language capabilities of the students, most of whom wore no shoes and came from families in which nobody could read or write in any language, yet these barefoot students knew Yoruba, passable English, and those who had been exposed to the French priests were able to get along in that tongue, too. Cosgrove felt that great strides could be taken by his students if they could ever get as much as a few grammar and literature textbooks to pass around.

After consuming several more bottles of beer, which led him to see himself as Africa's savior, Cosgrove drove over to the British education office, which was on the second floor of a government building. The school overseer, a lanky man with a pasty face, sat in a yellow swivel chair that squeaked loudly. The desk in front of him was bare. There was no other furniture in the room. A telephone sat on the windowsill behind the man.

"A requisition such as this requires a special order," the man said.

"May I make one?" Cosgrove asked.

"We need a special form for the special order," the man said.

"May I have one and I'll fill it out?"

"Oh, dear boy, we don't have those forms here. We never have had a call for them in the past. I must send to Liverpool for such a form."

"Wouldn't one letter saying what we wanted —"

"Oh no. Proper form always. I'll just get on to Liverpool for our special forms."

"How long will this take?"

"Oh, dear boy, time is precisely what these people have. They have centuries to waste."

The yellow wooden chair squeaked as he leaned back, spun around slowly, and reached for the telephone on the windowsill. Cosgrove coughed.

"Oh yes," the man said, looking back over his shoulder and seeing Cosgrove with his hand filled with pound notes. "Just leave your message on the desk, thank you," the man said.

Cosgrove threw the bribe on the desk. The overseer's head turned and, looking out the window, the man placed a phone call.

When he returned to the village, Cosgrove told the mission school pupils that soon there would be the first new textbooks they had ever seen, and those who worked hardest at their lessons now would be the first to receive a new book. The black faces smiled sarcastically. One boy, Joof, laughed aloud. Rather than causing happiness, Cosgrove's promise of textbooks only reminded the students of the hopelessness of expecting anything from whites. A notice then arrived from the British office in the capital, saying the request made by Cosgrove had arrived. Cosgrove pointed a finger at the most skeptical, Joof, and announced that he would travel to the capital in the Land Rover as a special assistant in charge of carrying books.

"There will be no books there," Joof said.

"Of course there will."

When he arrived at the second-floor office, Cosgrove found a new man sitting at the desk. The man was just as thin and his face just as pasty and idle as the previous man's. That person had returned to London, the new man said as he inspected Cosgrove's notice.

"Of course," the man said, "no matter who is at this desk, our system and our people in Liverpool are quite efficient." He reached into a manila envelope for a thick form. "Fill out all six copies, please."

Cosgrove looked about for a seat.

"Why don't you just get it back to me at your convenience?" the British man said.

"Yes, but you see, I'd like to take the books with me now."

"The books? Oh, dear boy, I have no books. Not now. These are the forms you must fill out. When the forms are processed and approved, they'll hunt up the books for you. If, as a matter of actual fact, the books are even available."

"How long will this be?" Cosgrove said.

"Oh, we'll hear."

Cosgrove turned with the forms in his hand, and as he started to explain them to Joof, he saw weariness and disappointment cross the boy's face.

Cosgrove sent Joof out of the room and then he stepped up to the desk and threw down pound notes.

"Yes," the clerk said, nodding as he saw the money. The chair squeaked as he spun around to reach for the phone. "All the best."

Over the hours on the way back to the mission, with the sun turning the Land Rover into a hot plate, Cosgrove regarded himself as truly defeated.

Suddenly of a sullen morning, a printed notice arrived stating that the British, as preparation for departing from the country, were placing several departments, including banking and education, under local jurisdiction. This meant black. As the boy Joof had been present at defeat, Cosgrove had him accompany him once more to the capital, this time to see that the enemy had been vanquished.

Once there, he passed two bank buildings with two long lines in front of them. At the old British building he found the education offices locked and silent. He waited with Joof in the hall until three o'clock, when a short black man in a crisp white shirt came along and opened the door to the education office. Inside, the man sat at the desk once occupied by the hated British overseer. He patted the breast pocket of his shirt.

He explained that this was a bank deposit slip. "Tomorrow the color of all the money of the country will be changed from green to gold. It has not been announced yet because there is a great deal of black market money being held by unscrupulous persons. The first act of our new treasury will be to change the money and leave these people with their pockets filled with worthless paper. My friend is part of the group that takes over the treasury today, the same as I am in charge of education. We will be one of the few with correct currency." The white shirt smiled. When Cosgrove told his story, the clerk made proper faces and wrote boldly on a pad. "This is excellent that I have this information, for if you did not tell me, then I would not have it," the man said. "We will act on this once we get ourselves in good order here. Thank you."

The yellow chair squeaked as he spun in it and reached for the phone on the windowsill.

Cosgrove pulled out pound notes and, coughing, placed them on the desk.

One day Cosgrove sat in his village and began to draw up charts of his baptized Catholics and where they lived. Using his students to provide family information, Cosgrove drew elaborate charts, and Cosgrove became alarmed at the similarity of family bloodlines. Cosgrove discovered that, even from his preliminary charts, the number of baptized Catholics in his mission district who were living within the third degree of kindred was so high as to freeze his breath.

He had always questioned the Book of Genesis, which begins with Adam and Eve destroying world peace by having intercourse and producing Cain and Abel. In the Book of Genesis, the paragraphs after Adam and Eve all deal with Cain as the murderer of Abel. A following paragraph ends with Cain going off to the land of Nod. Abruptly, the next paragraph says, "Then Cain's wife conceived and presented him with a baby . . ." If you were to believe Genesis, Cosgrove always thought, you either suspended credibility or you assumed that for the human race to start, there had to be several generations of incest. Perhaps covering as long as a full half century. This had to lead to a world population strewn with mongoloid children or hemophiliacs. One prominently placed thorn bush, Cosgrove thought, could have killed a significant part of the world's population.

Now, perhaps a million years later, Cosgrove felt that nothing had changed. The lines on his family charts, rather than going up and out to the tops and bottoms of the paper, kept coming together in horizontal V's. Sisters and brothers seemed reasonably safe. But each time the chart got to nephews and nieces, the lines simply joined and refused to leave. No outcrosses. Cousins, the lines showed clearly, apparently never got out of the same beds; Cosgrove's charts showed that anyone past a first cousin was a complete stranger.

Cosgrove went out with a lantern, much as Redemptorist priests had once patrolled the lovers' lanes about Limerick Junction. At the hut of a man named Robinson, who lived with his first cousin Rig, Cosgrove patiently lectured about bloodlines.

"You must live your lives outside the third degree of kindred," he said.

Robinson appeared to be listening.

"Otherwise it makes people crazy."

Robinson hugged his first cousin while he listened.

Cosgrove then tried to get Great Big's lineage. Great Big said he had been born in Idjebo. Happily, he began to name people in his family and their marriages and children. Cosgrove stopped writing. Great Big's family rarely got past an uncle and niece. "You cannot marry within the third degree of kindred," Cosgrove told Great Big, who yawned.

Cosgrove grabbed the goatskin and drank home brew which, mixed with the sun on his head, clouted him out. That night he heard a noise outside the building and on looking out saw Great Big standing in the hot night with a young woman who had a face so round and pleasant that his instinct was to reach out and pinch her cheeks. The young woman looked directly at Cosgrove and giggled. For some reason, he found this disturbing. Great Big then announced that the woman wanted to be baptized. Cosgrove walked to the corner of the room, picked up a bucket of water, and threw it out the open window onto Great Big and the young woman while calling out, "I baptize you in the name of the Father, Son, and Holy Ghost." Great Big and the woman with the happy cheeks stood outside, dripping and laughing. Cosgrove flopped on his pallet. He was suddenly tormented by sex and spent the night praying against temptation.

At this time, the nation had a civil war, whose first objective seemed to be the total starving and maiming of all the helpless and isolated in the nation, particularly those with children. Cosgrove offered his own pain to God on behalf of the persistent hunger. Once Cosgrove went nine days without anything to eat and finally a government truck delivered a sack of rice. Cosgrove sat in his church and slowly ate a small bowl of it. Great Big grabbed the bowl and licked it clean. Cosgrove lectured him on his manners.

"Manners," Great Big repeated.

But a short time later, Great Big scooped up a milk goat that was important to the women of the village and walked off into the bush with it. The women shrieked and the goat bleated, although not as loudly as the goat did when Great Big, in a hurry to eat, simply threw the goat into a cooking fire without bothering to choke him to death first. Later, Great Big walked into Cosgrove's church and threw a leg on the table. The leg had some burned meat at the top and Cosgrove had an overwhelming desire to jam it into his mouth. This was a temptation he could resist, however, and he refused to touch the leg bone. He lectured Great Big on the sin of stealing the goat.

As he was listening, Great Big picked up the goat's leg and began to chew on it. "I got hungry and forgot my manners," Great Big said.

～～～～～

Perhaps it was the next day or the one after that — by then Cosgrove couldn't tell — he heard a crackle in the yellow grass. Sparks shot into the air from the brush fire that devoured the dry thatch of the village. He and Great Big walked all the way to the city, drinking water from the copper streams. At one stop, as Cosgrove looked up at a sky colorless with too much heat, his teeth worked on a bitter long stalk of grass that was impossible to chew. He had suffered, Cosgrove told himself, but he had learned the depth and tenacity of the Devil, and beyond this he now knew well the one sin, the only sin on earth available to most people, Sin of the Flesh. Immediately after this came the good fortune to serve on the Pope's African tour. Cosgrove regarded the subsequent assignment to America as a challenge worthy of a saint. On the plane to America, he had visions of the canonization ceremony in Rome and the resultant celebration in his town in Ireland.

7

EARLY ONE MORNING, Cosgrove left Great Big asleep in their bedroom in the rectory and by whim decided to cross the marshes to Howard Beach. Cold water welled up in the mud and Cosgrove rolled up his pants. He thrashed his way through the bullrushes, forded a stream of cold salt water in the middle, and came up on the last street in Howard Beach, Seventy-fifth Street, in front of the last house on the block, a large yellow-brick house with a back yard made entirely of marble.

Parked at the curb on the far side of the house was a Lincoln town car with a punctured roof. "The Chief's car," Cosgrove said. Quickly he walked to it. He glanced down the driveway running alongside the house and saw an assembly of burly men, all wearing Persian lamb hats and trench coats. They jumped into a line of Lincoln town cars in the driveway. The first car filled up and pulled away. Cosgrove saw the Chief in the front seat. He waved furiously at the Chief because he wanted to apologize to him for the punctured roof, but the Chief did not see him.

A second town car pulled away and a third was about to go when a voice inside screamed to Cosgrove, "Come on! How could you be late!" Cosgrove got in the back with two others. The man next to Cosgrove, whose fur hat was tipped down over his eyes, shoved a black revolver into Cosgrove's belt. "The gun don't miss. The man better not." Cosgrove was about to talk when suddenly everybody in the car displayed hand-held radios. Over the radios came the Chief's voice: "One voice only from now on."

The man next to Cosgrove scolded him. "You're supposed to have a radio."

The Chief's voice came over all the hand radios in the car: "What do we got at the courthouse?"

Now another voice came over the radios: "I just come out of the courtroom. The judge says he folds at four-thirty today. I heard Big Paul say he stops at Milton the lawyer's office right after that, but then he got an important meet at the restaurant on East Forty-sixth Street at five-thirty."

"He got some date," the Chief's voice said. "Big Paul got somebody with him?"

"Tony the Driver, like always."

"Does Tony think something is going on?"

"He's like edgy. He just said to me, 'What do you really think of me?' I told him I think plenty of him. I say the truth, I'll tell you that. I dream of this fucking rat Tony being dead so many times that I got a whole cemetery filled. Big Paul thinks he's God, so he can't see anything happening to him like it's going to. We follow them from the court to the lawyer's, we wait, and then we follow them uptown and keep calling you. They turn onto Forty-sixth Street, we disappear. Unless you want us to do something else. Go inside the restaurant first or something."

The Chief's voice exploded. "Nothing changes! Three in the restaurant. Frank LaCarva's son Frankie sits there crying. Jimmy Brown and Larry Salerno sit and hold Frankie's hand. Sit and cry and wait."

Now the thug next to Cosgrove seemed perplexed. "Three in the restaurant? The Chief got that wrong." The thug looked at Cosgrove. "You make a fourth in the restaurant, right?" Cosgrove, bewildered, did not answer. The thug frowned. "Maybe I better tell the Chief he made a mistake. No, I better not. He gets mad at mistakes." He looked at Cosgrove carefully. "Boy, you sure look like a priest. They got you comforting the family, right?"

"Family?" Cosgrove said.

"LaCarva's son Frankie. His father just died. Big Paul never got to pay his respects to the family, even go to the funeral on account of he's on trial all the time. We asked Big Paul to come pay his respects to LaCarva's son. Five-thirty. Big Paul got diabetes. He can't eat nothing Italian. We tell him, come to the joint on Forty-sixth Street for a piece of fish. You probably get to eat his fish for him. Anything goes wrong on the sidewalk and Big Paul makes it to the restaurant, he sees you, Big Paul don't get nervous. He says 'Good afternoon, Father.' You take your piece out and shoot him right between his fucking eyes. You get a good payday. Where are you from, anyway?"

The last question was the only part of the conversation that Cosgrove understood and he was pleased to answer quickly, "Africa."

"So I ask a silly fucking question," the hoodlum mustache said.

"Before that, Ireland," Cosgrove said.

"All right, forget about it," the guy said. "At least I'll tell you where I'm from. They brought me in from Cleveland."

A man in the front seat said, "What kind of animal could this Paulie be, lettin' a wolf get into the police station and eat up Buster?"

"That's what they say Big Paulie done, sneak a big wolf into the cell with poor Buster."

"Where Big Paulie's going, he could explain to Buster in person."

Everybody laughed and Cosgrove, who caught the name Buster, was about to ask a question when the car rushed onto a wide boulevard and nobody in the car uttered a word as they whistled through a tunnel and stopped in Manhattan on a late winter afternoon. When everybody piled out, Cosgrove took the gun out of his pants and said to the nearest thug, "What is th —"

"You crazy?" The thug shoved Cosgrove's hand and the gun it held into his pants.

The Chief was barreling through the rush hour on Third Avenue. Cosgrove tried to run after the Chief to apologize for the car roof and to give him this dreadful gun. He also wanted to ask the Chief about Buster.

"Walk," one of the thugs said to Cosgrove. "You give it away by running."

They turned onto East Forty-sixth Street. In the cold shadows of high buildings at the front of the restaurant, the Chief intently inspected three men.

"Frankie, will you put a sad look on your face?" the Chief said to one of them. "Your father just died. You're acting like you're happy."

"I am so happy that we are going to kill that rat Big Paul,

I forgot my father just died." It was obvious to Cosgrove that this was the poor deceased LaCarva's son. Pretending to cry, LaCarva's son and the two with him went into the restaurant. The Chief wheeled and walked away. Cosgrove pulled out the gun and started to chase the Chief. He was almost yanked off his feet by one of the thugs.

"No! You don't shoot him. You shoot Big Paul. You're so fucking dumb! Where did they get you from?"

Several pairs of hands pushed the gun back into Cosgrove's belt. People streamed by on both sides, but nobody even looked at the struggle to hide the priest's gun. Hands gripped Cosgrove firmly. "Stay here. You get mixed up." The Chief walked up a few yards to a construction site for a new office building. When workmen, dawdling at the end of the day, saw the Chief they fled. The Chief hid under a scaffolding. Now over all the hand radios, including that of the thug who was holding Cosgrove, came the Chief's command: "Get ready. They're out of the lawyer's office. Just two in the car. They're at Twenty-eighth Street already."

Cosgrove saw men in fur hats and trench coats in doorways, one hand in the trench coat pocket and the other clutching the radio. Crowds hurrying by took no notice of the hand radios. Suddenly, the thug holding Cosgrove shoved him into the restaurant. Inside, a bartender crouching in apprehension relaxed as he saw the clerical garb. LaCarva's son and the other two sat in the back directly alongside the kitchen door. All the tables near them were empty. The kitchen door opened slightly and a waiter's hand came out and put menus on the table. The waiter's hand quickly disappeared. Cosgrove went right to the table. "I am sorry for your trouble," he said to Frankie LaCarva.

LaCarva's son became angry. "Get out of the way. I can't see through you."

"I thought that as long as I am here I would offer my condolences. It must be very difficult to lose a father. I lost my mother and I never really got over it. Is your mother living?"

"Yes," LaCarva said absently.

"That is one blessing, anyway."

The two at the table with LaCarva said at once, "We don't need no acting. We need to see. Get out of the way. Where do you belong, anyway? You're not supposed to be in here."

"How old is the dear mother?" Cosgrove said.

"I don't know, she must be seventy-one, seventy-two," LaCarva said.

"The dear women shade a year now and then," Cosgrove said.

"I'm going to fucking shoot you," one of them said.

Cosgrove went outside, where the sidewalk was packed with crowds hurrying in the winter darkness. He intended to walk directly up to see the Chief at the construction site and apologize for Great Big's breaking the roof of the car. Looking up to the construction site, Cosgrove saw, over the heads of all the people hurrying home from work, the fur hat of the Chief bobbing frantically and out of the corner of his eye Cosgrove saw gray Persian lamb hats moving out of all the doorways. A gray Lincoln town car nearly grazed Cosgrove's knee as it pulled up in front of the restaurant. The man on the passenger's side was a large man with a prominent nose and heavy glasses. He smiled at Cosgrove and opened the door.

"Are you here for the LaCarva family, Father?" the man said.

"You mean the man whose father died?"

"That's him. That's nice of you to come, Father. We could pray over the bread for poor Frank. You got no idea of the respect I had for this here man."

The driver looked up and said to Cosgrove, "I got respect, too."

Big Paul started to get out of the car. At this moment, all the men in gray Persian lamb hats and trench coats rushed out of the doorways up and down the block and the first three men jumped out of a crowd, knocked Cosgrove out of the way, and began firing point-blank into Big Paul. Cosgrove fell to the sidewalk in terror. He sensed people rushing away and screaming and the men kept firing guns so much that it seemed they would never stop.

Big Paul was halfway out of the car with blood coming from the sides and front of his head. He tumbled into the sudden silence of empty guns. His head on the sidewalk, his feet in the car. Now there were new screams, shrieks, the slapping of shoes as people ran off, and Cosgrove opened his eyes to see Big Paul's dead body and he knew instantly that he was to cease cowering and to accept — no, grab! — this opportunity to serve God. He crawled across the sidewalk and once again on his short visit to America he prayed over the body of a deceased. Running past him was the Chief, who looked at Cosgrove, and Cosgrove glanced up in the middle of his prayer and looked at the Chief, who skidded to a stop and began to tug his gun out of his trench coat.

Immediately, Cosgrove stopped praying and pulled the gun out of his belt and said, "Take this." The Chief, color draining from his gaunt face, jumped back and into a swift moving crowd that had been inside office buildings when the shooting occurred and knew nothing of it. A man whistling merrily and walking briskly nearly bowled the Chief over. The Chief took off for Third Avenue, where the twelve men in identical hats and coats already had melted into the crowds, which is what the Chief proceeded to do.

Cosgrove noticed that Big Paul's driver had been blown up, too, dropped the gun, and crawled over Big Paul's body to pray for the dead driver. A policeman pounded up and ordered Cosgrove not to put his hands on anything. A detective appeared, took one look at the famous dead, and said, "Hey, Father, say a prayer for the phone pole ahead of these guys."

"All men need prayer," Cosgrove said.

"And all police need witnesses." An officer with gold braid had appeared. "Let's get some men interviewing the crowd right away. If you get a witness, put them into a patrol car with a blanket over their head. Anybody who saw this stands a chance of getting choked to death. Excuse me, Father, but you got to move now."

Cosgrove found himself pushed back through the crowd and into the stream of people walking along the building wall, and, numb, praying for the dead men, he was carried down to Third Avenue. Right away, he thought of the tremendous fortune that had come his way. For now he truly had specific work in Howard Beach. I must go directly to the Chief's house and save his soul, Cosgrove told himself. He also wanted to ask him about Buster the Cabdriver.

8

T THIS POINT, we see the magnitude of the betrayal of Cosgrove by the Papal delegate to America. The man was so small of mind that even the vaguest and most unfounded suspicion that cash money would go anywhere but to him caused the Papal delegate to act treacherously and leave Cosgrove virtually penniless in a deserted parish.

On this particular morning in Saint Lucy's, the pastor said he had a meeting to attend with the diocesan money changers, as he called them. As it was the last few days of the month, things could happen quickly, he said. "Pray with your bags packed," he said. He left. Immediately, Cosgrove ransacked the rectory for a bottle of anything that would make him feel great. As we have seen from observing him closely, Cosgrove had been drinking nil since his arrival in America, but now idleness, truly the Devil's workshop, attacked him throat-first. He became very agitated when he could find nothing to drink in the entire rectory. Cosgrove waited for the mailman, for as he was basically a person of tremendous faith, he was sure that at any moment he would receive his special orders from the Papal delegate. When no such mail arrived, Cosgrove woke up Great Big and left the place in thirst and in rapidly increasing anger at his desertion by the local representative of Rome.

While looking for a liquor store on the dilapidated avenue, they found Baby Rock and the little girl Seneca arguing on the sidewalk. Baby Rock complained that, earlier, Manslaughter had been around looking for his gun and that he, Baby Rock, had been forced to flee. He blamed Cosgrove for throwing the gun away and Seneca for bringing Manslaughter around. Seneca denied this vigorously, stating that now Manslaughter was mad at her, too. "I don't be bringin' Manslaughter here. He be comin' here himself. Him and his big gun." Her feet beat on the sidewalk in a dance. Baby Rock played the drums against his thighs. Seneca shrieked. "I be dancin' like this and Manslaughter pull out his big gun. He say, 'Freeze!' I go like this. 'Freeze.'" Seneca was a little statue with cornrowed hair. She stopped, pouting. "I can't go to school because I got to pass by Manslaughter. I want to go to school. I think I'm going to get me E for excellent in school."

"Do you now?" Cosgrove said.

"Sure do. You could ask my teacher. I want to be a judge or a lawyer. Lawyer's good. Get people out of trouble. My teacher say I should sure come to school every day. Get me another E for excellent." She looked around the corner and pointed down the block, where three teenagers in white sneakers stood in a doorway. "Blocking my way." Right behind the teenagers, a sign hung from one of the few stores open on the block: LIQUOR.

"Well, I'll just go and talk to him," Cosgrove said.

Seneca shrieked. "You make Manslaughter mad."

Baby Rock said, "He vic you."

"Utter nonsense. Why, he's only a young lad," Cosgrove said. "Furthermore, if he is so angry about losing his gun, why doesn't he just come up here right now?"

Seneca laughed. "Because he think Baby Rock got his gun and he could shoot back. If Manslaughter knows you don't have a gun, he be shootin' you right away."

Cosgrove thrust his chin out and walked determinedly up the street. His eyes were fixed on the liquor store sign. He had thirty-four dollars in his pocket, the last of that breed, but he needed drink. As he approached the three in white sneakers, he heard them growl. One, his eyes hooded, stepped out and faced Cosgrove.

"Good day to you, my dear lad."

The hooded eyes said nothing.

Cosgrove said, "You are Manslaughter, are you not? When I'm through with my errands here, I'd like to have a little chat with you."

"You strapped?" the one on the stoop said.

"Am I what?"

"Strapped. You carryin' a piece?"

"You mean a gun? Oh, good Lord, no. I wouldn't dare carry a gun."

Manslaughter now spoke. "Freeze!"

Manslaughter put the gun inches from Cosgrove's chest and pulled the trigger. There was a click as loud as a building collapse. Manslaughter screamed, "Jesus Christ!" This brought Cosgrove back to life. "My good lad, you're not supposed to take the name of the Lord in vain. Look, lad, a sprightly lad you are, too, and you've had your good fun with me, but now I must ask you, what have you got in front of you for the rest of the day? Do you intend to stand here and waste your life playing with a toy gun all day?"

"You call this motherfucker a toy?" Manslaughter crouched and banged the gun on the sidewalk.

Obviously, I am not getting through to this lad, and I know that I certainly could if I had time, Cosgrove told himself. Besides, he had this real good urge for a drink. Cosgrove went into the liquor store and bought a fifth of Scotch, leaving himself with twenty-four dollars. Emerging, he saw Manslaughter pounding the gun on the sidewalk, first with one hand and then the other. He couldn't seem to make up his mind which to use.

"I'll bet you have dyslexia," Cosgrove said. "Lad, have you ever been tested? You know, dyslexia is more than seeing letters backwards. It involves the difficulty of knowing which han —"

The sidewalk exploded. The second time Manslaughter's gun went off, the shot splintered a wood window frame right above Cosgrove's head as he tore past empty stores, his arms wrapped around the bottle as though it was a baby. The noise caused Great Big to come loping and Manslaughter, even with a gun in his hand, felt inadequate against somebody of this size. He and the two with him disappeared into an empty store.

Great Big started to pursue but was distracted by the bottle of Scotch, which he snatched from Cosgrove, opened, and took a huge swallow. "Good water!" Great Big shouted. He took one more swallow and Cosgrove had to grapple for the bottle, which Great Big was about to empty right there. Cosgrove stepped into the store — after all, it

would do no good for him to be seen drinking on a street —
and had his first drink in quite a while. Oh boy, it tasted
good.

Looking around, Cosgrove saw little Seneca running off
toward school. She was a full block away by now and he
felt exhilarated; he had opened the way for her.

Baby Rock saw it another way. "We better leave the land-
scape," he said. He led them onto the bus, where, again,
they didn't pay. Cosgrove held the bottle, but not for long.
Great Big snatched it at a red light and the bottle never saw
the light turn green.

At the Flatbush Arms, a security guard in a baggy uni-
form and with a red bandana wrapped tightly around his
head waved a nightstick to keep a crowd at bay. All
clutched yellow tickets. Disco Girl, wearing a cranberry-
colored knit hat and shivering in her red Disco Girl T-shirt,
was yelling, "I got a low number, I got number fifty-six."

"Number fifty-six is too high," the guard said. "You got
to be one of the first forty-five or you miss."

"I'm not missin'," Disco Girl said.

At the curb was the special truck of the New Opportunity
Hot Line, its back doors open and Bushwick Taylor stand-
ing on the truck with cardboard boxes of food. The guard
tried to make the people form a line. A woman in a black
raincoat and red pants ran out from the right side of the
lobby doorway and when the guard tried to grab her, a little
girl shivering in a green summer blouse darted past on the
other side. Three women went by the guard at once. "I'm
not missin'," Disco Girl yelled. She bolted for the truck.
Quickly a crowd was clutching at food boxes and just as
quickly the crowd was gone.

"I missed the meat," Disco Girl cried.

Mother Agnes emerged with her arms full of the family papers. Her long brown down coat was fastened with a large safety pin. She grew angry when she saw that Disco Girl had no food. "You missed the meat! Told you to stop listenin' to that music. Child, there was meat to be had and you be too busy dancin'."

"I like the music," Disco Girl said.

"That damn old music takes up your mind."

"The music is the only thing that makes me forget," Disco Girl said.

She smiled brightly and danced in circles all over the sidewalk. Baby Rock beat his hands on his thighs. Mother Agnes walked toward the subway kiosk in anger. "She's going to welfare to reapply," Disco Girl said. "I go next. She got the coat today!"

Mother Agnes started to cross the street but had to pull back as fire trucks rushed by.

On the top floor of a rooming house some blocks away, the first piece of plaster hit James Woods down by his ankles. Under the blanket, his cat, High Yellow, jumped. "Damn old rat!" James Woods said. James Woods kept his eyes closed; he couldn't start the day watching High Yellow eat a rat right in his bed.

Not after what he'd seen the other night. James smoked a chunk of crack while Don Johnson of "Miami Vice" drove his Porsche right at James Woods. James, in his Bentley, decapitated Don Johnson. Watched Don Johnson's head bounce right out of the television set. "Next time stop for the red light."

Another piece of plaster fell right smack between James

Woods's eyes. He found he was looking straight up to the sky. "They stole my roof!"

Georgie Larson in his fire hat looked through the hole in the roof at James Woods. "Hey, I lost the last one who didn't stay out of the building like he was told. What are you doing there? Somebody didn't tell you?" James Woods didn't answer. "You didn't hear the fire? Woman end of the hall had a hot plate on the dresser. Took a while for it to burn through, but when it did it must have hit the socks. Five o'clock in the morning."

"I was in the emergency room with Don Johnson," James Woods said. He glanced at his bureau, on which sat his personal holdings, one welfare check. Another fireman kicked his way into James Woods's room. He stomped right through the debris, grabbed the dresser, and pulled it away from the bedroom wall. "Look at this!" The back of the dresser was charred and rippled and smoke swirled from it. Suddenly a tiny flame showed on the top of the dresser. The flame licked at James Woods's welfare check.

"My case money is smokin'!" James screamed, trying to jump out of bed.

The check burst into flames. The fireman pushed the dresser out the window.

"I don't even have money for a bun," James cried.

"You got your life," the fireman said. "If you were asleep another two, three minutes, the dresser goes up like a Christmas tree and takes you with it."

James took clothes and a towel from a chair and went into the rooming house hallway. Fire hoses ran the length of the hall and the floor was covered with freezing water. The smell of an old fire, giving the instant feeling of desolation and nakedness, hung in the air. He turned on the icy water, dipped in the tips of his index fingers, and ran them over his eyes. Then he stepped back from the sink, spread his legs, braced himself, and put his right hand into the cold water and splashed his left armpit. His body cringed as the cold water hit him. He swung his body and cupped his left hand under the water and splashed the right armpit. Now he braced himself further. "Test your ticker." Woods threw ice water against his chest. The water nearly knocked him down. He went back to his room and threw on last night's clothes, smelling like it, too, and left. At the corner phone booth, he dialed the courthouse and counted the rings. Twenty-six. He stamped his feet in the cold. Finally, a woman clerk answered.

"Just go to the courtroom to which you are assigned."

"I told you I had a fire."

"Tell it to the jury."

"That's what I am."

"Then go to the courtroom where you're supposed to be."

Once, Woods tried to make it on marginal jobs, but he was roundly defeated. Now he took the long walk to the East New York Income Maintenance Center, which services people who have no income. Along one wall was a row of phones, with a list of extension numbers of caseworkers, including his caseworker, M. Singer. He dialed her number, 5347, which phone rang in one of the offices upstairs. Welfare caseworkers don't appear in these huge crowded rooms; the only reason to do that would be if you were on welfare yourself and didn't care about getting punched around in a waiting room. Therefore, the clients communicate by phone, much as people visiting jails speak to prisoners through telephones.

James Woods waited half an hour on the phone. Finally somebody picked up upstairs.

"Case number?"

"Ms. Singer, this is James Woods. I talk to you all the time."

"Case number, please."

"I don't have it with me. My check and papers got burned alive in a fire."

"Woods? Let me see." He stood for fifteen minutes. Ms. Singer returned. "I have your name. But I have nothing else. The last notation says you have been removed from the computer because you have not appeared for your PWP job."

"I couldn't do my public works program job because they got me on jury duty. I showed you my jury duty notice. I be in jury all day long."

"You could not have given me a completed jury duty notice or you would not have been taken off the computer," she said.

"How could I show you a completed notice? I didn't finish my jury duty."

"If you didn't finish your jury duty then you did not have a completed jury duty notice. And a completed jury duty notice is the only excuse for not appearing for your PWP duty. So you are off the computer."

"I got to start all over again?"

"Are you applying for emergency funds?"

"I got burned out last night."

"Oh, then of course you must start at the very start of the process."

"That takes a month," James Woods said. "If I don't go back to jury duty, the judge puts me under the jail."

"Without a completed jury duty notice, you are a new applicant," Ms. Singer said.

James Woods hung up and sat down next to Mother Agnes on a tin folding chair. Both knew they had a long way to go.

Many blocks away, people also sat at Kings County Supreme Court, Part 24, People versus Francis Anthony Teretola, a.k.a. Frankie Five Hundred. He was called Frankie Five Hundred because he had once kidnapped the mother of a man delinquent with his loan-shark payments of $500. In his present case, he was charged with violation of 110/120.5, which is attempted assault, the use of such a word, *attempt,* bothering Frankie Five Hundred greatly, for Frankie Five Hundred felt this indicated a failure at crime. Which he knew he was not, for on the day before this case started, he had been a shining star in the assassination of that arrogant bum Big Paulie, who happened to be coming from a courtroom himself. "He thought he was in the witness box, but we put him in a pine box."

Here in this case, Mr. Frankie Five Hundred also was charged with "at the time and place of this crime, the defendant did display a loaded gun and threaten serious physical injury." The method Frankie Five Hundred used to display the gun was to nestle it into somebody's ear. Most prosecution witnesses against Frankie Five Hundred failed to show up. "They all got ears and they don't want nothin' stickin' in them," Frankie Five Hundred enthused to himself.

One juror's mother died and the juror was replaced by an alternate, who suddenly became ill and that left exactly only twelve people in the jury room. And now, in court on this morning, Frankie Five Hundred sat with his lawyer and heard a clerk muttering, "Missing one juror." Later, a door opened and the judge called out, "Has anybody heard from him?" The clerk said, "He never called." The lawyer whispered to Frankie Five Hundred, "You got a mistrial. Your prayers are answered."

Frankie Five Hundred thought using the word *prayers* was funny; he had a contract from the Chief to find and blow away that little priest who somehow rode in the car to Big Paulie's thing. Frankie Five Hundred still couldn't figure out how the priest winds up sitting right next to him in the car. But the Chief blamed Frankie Five Hundred for this, and therefore it became his job to find the priest and shoot him. Too bad it was a priest, but he was a witness to the whole thing. What a witness! He was right there and he saw the Chief in person holding a gun over Big Paulie. "They shoot the Pope, I could shoot a priest," Frankie Five Hundred told himself.

Next, the judge looked out and told the clerk to draw a contempt warrant against juror James Woods.

~~~~~~

On this same cold morning, back in front of the Flatbush Arms, the normal small food riot ended, Bushwick had a cigarette with Sarah. When Cosgrove walked over, Bushwick explained, "I told them I'd run out. Last week I figured that we could keep food right in each welfare hotel so they could give it out easier. What do they tell me? The supervisor says the children would get hungry and steal the food. He tells me to put it in a storage room in Bayview, the women's prison over by the river. I go there to pick up some food this morning, I know I don't have half enough, and wouldn't you know it, the guard doesn't open the door for me. I have to tell you, I tried to kick the door in. You know what the guard does? Excuse me, Father, but I got to tell you exactly what he does. He calls out over the loudspeaker system in the prison, 'Man be tryin' to come in and fuck our ladies!'"

Bushwick got out of the truck. "Drives me crazy that I know most of these kids. I'm sorry, but I'm going to get a drink." Cosgrove asked him where he was going and Bushwick pointed to the bodega across the street and said that there was a liquor store right around the corner from it. Bushwick now remembered Cosgrove's scrawny face. "You were here when the kid went off the roof across the street. What agency do you work for?"

"For Jesus Christ."

Bushwick held up his hands. "All right. I'm sorry."

"And for whom do you work?" Cosgrove asked.

"B. B. King," Bushwick said.

Bushwick had only a ten-dollar bill and he asked Cosgrove about money, and Cosgrove said he certainly could help buy something good in a bottle. They started for the liquor store. Seeing Disco Girl hugging herself in the doorway while chattering to Great Big, Cosgrove said, "Can I get you something?"

Everybody in front of the hotel heard this. All bolted for the bodega. Right away, a girl ran in front of Disco Girl in the cold day. She was wearing a frayed red coat with a hood that had no string and when she ran it fell from her head. She was tall, with cornrowed hair, and looked older than the others, but when she turned her head, Cosgrove could see that she was only about nine. She was dressed in scraps, with no socks and summer shoes of frayed red cloth. Her yellow flowered summer pants did not look clean. There were four other young girls running through the traffic and after them, a couple of boys.

At the bodega, Bushwick, being thin, was able to wedge himself through the crowd to the counter. Cosgrove was squeezed against a bin of dusty roots. He held up a ten-dollar bill and Bushwick reached over heads and snatched it from him. "We'll split whatever it comes to." At this, the sight of sure money, hands grabbed at a shelf of honey buns, white icing showing through packaged cake. The tall girl with cornrowed hair cried out, "Toast and butter and jelly." She burrowed through the dusty winter jackets, grabbed at a shelf, and held up two jars of baby food. "Something for my baby sister." As she was standing at the counter with her jars of baby food, all the others hit her.

She smiled in embarrassment but did not hit back. "Leave Dawn alone," Disco Girl said. "People in the hotel always smackin' her. She never does anythin' back. She just walks in the hall and they smack her. They used to do it to me. I sure stopped them. Had me a baby. That's what you have to do, girl. Make you feel better. You won't go around lettin' people smack you. Soon as you're able, you have yourself a baby, Dawn." Baby Rock said, "I help you." Dawn giggled and tried to hide her face inside her jacket. When she did this, the top of a soiled blouse showed. She fell to the floor, trying to hide. Disco Girl hit Baby Rock on the head. "Baby Rock, you be crackin' jokes."

Cosgrove could not contain himself. He called from the corner of the store. "That is no joke. That's the mortaler!"

Everybody burst out of the store at once. Dawn remained. She leaned on the counter and chewed on a piece of toast with jelly. She pointed at pads of paper on a bottom shelf. Cosgrove said, "Good girl yourself. Taking that to school with you, are you?" Dawn stuffed the other piece of jelly toast into her mouth.

Bushwick said, "They get embarrassed in school. They got to give a welfare hotel as an address. That's worse than giving a prison as an address. A lot of them lie when the teacher asks them where they live. Some like Dawn here don't even go."

"What do you need the pad for?" Cosgrove asked Dawn.
"Draw."

"Draw you shall." Cosgrove took a pad and pen, paid the counterman with the ten, told himself that God would provide, and gave the change to Bushwick, who went to buy a fifth of Scotch.

Sarah Carter waited with paper cups and now everybody went into the hotel, where Great Big stood holding hands with Disco Girl while the guard with the red bandana gripped his club and had his feet in position to flee Great Big, but upon seeing Bushwick and Sarah, he exhaled. Sarah headed for the soda machine on one side of the dim lobby and Bushwick went to the opposite side and yanked on an old wooden door until it opened to a big dark barren place that in the past, when the Flatbush Arms was a regular hotel, had been a barroom.

The sound of Bushwick's feet caused a rat to leap from a mound of empty soda cans and crushed cigarette packs. The rat climbed a steam pipe and disappeared into the torn ceiling. The dusty bar was along one wall and Cosgrove went to it most eagerly, slapped his belly full into the wood, and put one foot up for the bar rail but found nothing there, brass being highly perishable. Bushwick put the Scotch and paper cups on the bar and Sarah came in with cans of ginger ale. Whether ginger ale was good or bad as a chaser didn't interest Cosgrove, who drank the Scotch straight and warm out of a paper cup and immediately wanted more, which he grabbed.

Not until then did he notice that Great Big was missing. Dawn was seated on the floor, her back against the far wall and her knees pulled up as she drew pictures on the pad. He inquired of Dawn, who reported that Great Big had gone upstairs with Disco Girl. Fair enough, Cosgrove told himself. I'll just have a wee drink or two and go collect him. He reached for the bottle. The garbage dump of a room had taken on the proper glow of a real barroom.

When she had her second drink and lit another cigarette, Sarah hummed and then broke into a rousing hymn:

> A Mighty Fortress is our God,
> A bulwark never failing;
> Our helper He amid the flood
> Of mortal ills prevailing;
> For still our ancient foe
> Doth seek to work us woe;
> His craft and pow'r are great . . .

Cosgrove raised his voice and joined her in the final line:

> And arm'd with cruel hate,
> On earth is not his equal.

Cosgrove was quite pleased with his rendition. "Marvelous hymn. Notwithstanding that the words are Martin Luther's."

"He wrote both the words and the music," Sarah said.

"Imagine such music flowing from such an evil man," Cosgrove said.

When Sarah laughed, Cosgrove frowned. "I say that as a matter of actual fact. By my lights he was. He preached the promulgation of sex from the pulpit."

Sarah's eyes widened. "How in the name of God did he do that?"

"By advocating artificial birth control from the pulpit, that's what he did. Funny thing, a man can be exalted for committing a sin of that magnitude."

"I met a nun the other day you might be interested in," Sarah said. "She told me she was on an 'erotic' schedule. I said to her, 'Oh, it must keep you busy.' She said, 'It sure does. It has me going around crazy.' I said to her, 'Boy, do I know the feeling.'"

"Please don't talk to a member of the clergy like that," Cosgrove said.

"I'm in a better religion," Sarah said.

"There is only one true religion," Cosgrove said.

"Methodists are better than Catholics because we have better music," Sarah said.

When Cosgrove chuckled patronizingly, Sarah said, "I'm in a very active church. I'm going out to Las Vegas to get arrested at the nuclear testing site. They told me yesterday the best honor was to have a nuclear arrest on my record. My commitment gets a little shaky when I think of jail toilets. They have no door on them. Maybe I'll weaken and sell my soul as a prostitute if the guards give me a toilet with a door."

"Now your humor fades," Cosgrove said.

"What have you done about nuclear war?" she asked him.

"I think of the eternal soul, not some temporal explosion."

"When that thing goes off, it takes temporal with it," Sarah said. "Where do you come from, anyway?"

"I am a member of the Holy See's African missions."

"No."

"Absolutely."

"If that's so, then why do you talk like such a hot-eyed little man about irrelevant things?"

"In Africa it is a shame that the true message of the faith is difficult for many to receive. But in a civilized land like this, one can demand that people adhere to rule. Rule of Rome."

"Isn't it interesting that you call this a civilization?" Sarah said. "I have a notion that at least in Africa you can starve to death without being despised. Here, if you're black, they hate you while you die."

"What nonsense," Cosgrove said. "Looking at it from Rome, with fantastic objectivity, it was plain for all to see, from the Pope to the lowest clerk, that the trouble with America is wanton sex."

"We were in bed with each other all last night." Sarah kissed Bushwick.

"You speak like some brazen hussy."

"What did she do, kill somebody?" Bushwick asked.

"You spent the night in bed with a man to whom you are not married in the eyes of God?"

"Of course."

"That's the mortaler."

Sarah laughed and Cosgrove, in utter confusion, let Scotch splash full to the lip of the cup and threw it down, and to break the religious tension, which was going to split his heart, he roared into song:

> The wheel fell off of the hearse,
> The coffin fell out on the road.
> The mourner looks out of the windows
> And remarks: "Well I'll be blowed."
> The widow goes up to the driver,
> With tears in her eyes and she says:
> "What's my poor Henry done to you,
> That you muck him about when he's dead?"

Sarah was surprised that this man, whom she obviously regarded as being insane, could sing with such charm. She laughed so delightedly that her head rocked almost into Cosgrove's chest. There was just enough of a smell, not full perfume but certainly sweet soap, to cause Cosgrove's prick to leap into life. He had another drink to drown it, but of course that only made his lust so rampant that he trembled from the insides of his shoes to his ears. He held out his arms to embrace Sarah, but she knew well enough to pull away. Cosgrove did not know enough to stop and he kept moving toward her, arms out, and she retreated along the bar and finally said, "Oh, I know you Irish priests! The first man into the house to comfort the widow!" This caused him pain and embarrassment and he said that he had to retrieve Great Big.

On the way out, he stopped to ask Dawn what she was drawing. She showed him rough drawings of Bushwick, Sarah, and himself at the bar. All had wide flat noses and thick lips and the dress on Sarah had the word *Love* going down the front like buttons. Bushwick's shirt had a sign across it with the word *Love*. And Cosgrove had a crucifix on a chain which was made of the word *Love*.

Cosgrove and Dawn walked up staircases where men stood lighting their glass crack pipes. Up on the ninth floor, the hallway was filled with kids screaming and running around playing tag. They stopped playing and all turned and hit Dawn. "Your clothes stink!" they yelled. She hid her face. "Your mother makes you wear stinky clothes."

Cosgrove paid no attention to this silliness. "Which room?" Cosgrove demanded. Dawn pointed to one, and Cosgrove pounded on the door until it was answered by a woman with a wrinkled sheet around her. Behind her, a man wearing nothing held the collar of a large yellow dog with a mean mouth, who struggled to get at Cosgrove. The room had a bed with no sheet on the stained mattress. On the windowsill, a hot plate sat on cardboard whose edges were black from a fire of some sort. Directly over the hot plate was an old paper shade. The window, lined with rags, looked out onto a brick wall. The floor was covered with scraps of clothes. The woman glared at Dawn. "Go play, child."

"I want something," the girl said.

"What do you want?"

"Clean shirt. They say my clothes stink."

"Who says that?"

"Everybody."

The mother stepped out into the hall naked and screamed at the kids, "Who says her clothes stink?"

Nobody answered. "You better not say anything about my daughter!

"Go play," she said to her daughter. She slammed the

door and all the kids fell on her daughter and began hitting her. "Clothes stink!"

Cosgrove, looking for Great Big, banged on the next door, and a man in a baseball cap looked out. He saw Cosgrove, but then his mouth broke into a great smile, revealing one tooth in the top of his head. "Come in here, see me," he said.

Dawn hid her face again.

"She will do nothing of the sort."

"Girl! I said to you to come in here, see me," the guy with one tooth said.

Dawn obeyed the man. Cosgrove grabbed her by the arm and was about to lead her away when the man with one tooth reached out with a bat of some sort. Cosgrove never saw it coming, but it sure did arrive. When Cosgrove came out of it, the kids in the hallway were standing over him and passing a glass crack pipe around to each other. Crack smoke streamed from a little girl's nostrils.

Cosgrove pulled himself up, pushed the kids smoking crack out of his way, and went from door to door, banging hard, and finally, one was answered by Disco Girl, who was wearing her Disco Girl shirt but not much underneath that, and only some sort of panties. Cosgrove of course would not look at them. Disco Girl beamed. Behind her, barechested, was a grinning Great Big. The music was so loud that Cosgrove could only see Disco Girl's lips move. She stepped forward, right into the hallway, and Disco Girl said proudly, "We make a basketball player." Cosgrove's finger pointed at Great Big. "That's the mortaler!" he screamed in French. Great Big was too happy to be contrite. "You might end up living in Hell," Cosgrove said to

Disco Girl. "As for you" — he addressed Great Big — "come with me."

~~~~~~~

The church was dark by the time they got back there. A note was tacked to the front door and he read it in the faint light from the streetlight. The note, from the pastor, said that the money changers, as he called them, at diocesan level had closed the church and reassigned him and that Cosgrove could give the keys to the old caretaker who, as his last act, was going to padlock the church and fill in the front door with cinder blocks. Those at diocesan headquarters also knew nothing about Cosgrove's claimed assignment from Rome and were unamused and suspicious about the story he had told. "All concerned think it best that you return to Ireland," the pastor concluded. Cosgrove shuddered. "Go back to Ireland! I'll drown." He went inside and pulled the light cord in the front hall. The bulb went on, for which he was thankful.

In the morning, he said Mass for himself in the empty church, made bacon and eggs, noticing it was the last of the eggs, and was listening to the radio when it abruptly went off. There was a sound outdoors and he rushed to the door to find a fat man, carrying a flashlight and clipboard of the utility worker, walking to his van. "Lights out!" the utility man said.

It was Friday, and Great Big, hungry as Hell, began to prowl through the empty rectory, ripping open cabinets one after another. The man no longer had patience, Cosgrove said to himself. There also was no mail.

On Saturday afternoon, the lone woman on the block, the

old one across the street, told them to be over in an hour sharp for a full meal. When he and Great Big arrived, she met them at the door with one hand clutching an old blue robe. She led them past a small kitchen and into a dining room that had a linoleum floor, two stuffed chairs, a couch with a plastic cover, and a television. She had them sit while she became engrossed in a television show, a rerun of a family comedy. When the show ended, she said, "Wasn't that a good dinner we had? I'm stuffed. Come tomorrow if you want." She showed them out and Cosgrove spent the night listening to Great Big prowl and mutter in the dark.

On Sunday morning, Cosgrove threw vestments over his arms and led Great Big out through the weeds, and they emerged in the silence of sleeping homes in Howard Beach. Cosgrove thought of ringing the Chief's doorbell to speak to him about the condition of his soul, but he would do that later, and he walked the streets until he found the big brick Catholic church, with its school across the street, and the place had a reasonable crowd for the first Mass of a Sunday, a fine well-dressed white crowd, and Cosgrove, in vestments, went down the center aisle before Mass started and Great Big followed him on the altar and went to the door of the sacristy from which the regular parish priest was about to emerge to say Mass.

On the altar, Cosgrove opened Mass. Great Big kept the frantic parish priest trapped in the sacristy. Cosgrove said Mass fervently, but with a certain speed of prayer. He told the worshipers, "The collection today is to assist the African missionaries." As this was no lie, Cosgrove had no qualms about walking down the aisle with the collection basket himself. On this morning, he did handsomely for such an early hour — almost fifty dollars — and when he came to the last pew, which he knew was a signal for Great Big to go out the side door so both could start the getaway phase of the Mass, he was facing an old lady wearing black and with her gray hair pulled into a bun. She sat with a powerful, dark-haired man, undoubtedly her son.

The dark-haired man was sleeping soundly. His expensive blue shirt was open to reveal a chest laden with gold chains. Cosgrove held the basket in front of him. The old lady poked her son, Mr. Frankie Five Hundred, who had performed the Sunday morning ritual of coming directly home from his night out, collecting his mother from the basement apartment of his house, and taking her to first Mass. Bleary-eyed, but still able to see well enough, Frankie Five Hundred reached into the collection basket and grabbed two fives and the lone ten.

Cosgrove dived into the pew and tried to snatch the money back from this man. Who now looked up and, seeing Cosgrove, let out a yelp. "You the guy!"

Cosgrove instantly knew Frankie Five Hundred as the man who had been alongside him for the whole day when the poor man Big Paulie was killed on the sidewalk in front of the nice restaurant in Manhattan. "I must speak to you," Cosgrove said. "Excuse me, ma'am, but God bless you." He patted her hand and the old lady nodded. "I must speak to your son."

The old lady said, "I won't let him sleep no more during Mass, I promise."

And Cosgrove said, "No, I have something more important. We must speak. Can we go outside?"

Frankie Five Hundred looked about wildly. How do you

kill a priest right in church? At this point, his mother grabbed him by the arm. "You stay awake and pay attention in church."

Frankie Five Hundred said, "I got to go outside with this guy."

And the mother dug her old nails into Frankie Five Hundred's arms. "You stay." Cosgrove tried one last snatch at the money in Frankie Five Hundred's hands but he couldn't get it. Great Big was coming down the aisle and Cosgrove was pointing at Frankie Five Hundred and he was sure Great Big would be able to get the money. Up on the altar now, the parish priest was shouting for police and nobody quite knew why except for Cosgrove, who led Great Big out the door. Cosgrove threw the vestments over his arm as they walked.

Upon approaching the last street, Cosgrove felt compelled as a priest to tell the Chief that he must save his soul immediately, to point out most vigorously that the Chief could drop dead ten minutes from now, expire without the chance to say an Act of Contrition, and for killing Mr. Big Paulie, the Chief would burn forever in the eternal fires of Hell. He turned the corner and strode right up to the Chief's house and rang the bell. He did this many times before a heavy, middle-aged woman, auburn covering her gray hair, clutching a robe, opened the inside door, looked out through the storm door, disappeared, and came back carrying her purse. She opened the storm door partway and her hand came out holding a bill.

"Thank you, but I came here to speak to the Chief."

"Who speaks to him?" the woman said, instantly withdrawing the hand offering the money. "You listen to him.

That's one good thing about being with him. You never say the wrong thing. That's because you never got nothing to say."

"I'm familiar with protocol. I worked directly under the Pope."

"Then you know."

"Let's say I'd like an audience."

"Come back at noon when he gets up."

"My dear woman, you don't understand. I must speak to him now."

"Forget it, Father."

"Now you just wait a minute." Cosgrove fumed. "I am here to save your husband's soul."

"Who told you that it needs to be saved? My husband is a good man. He umpires Little League baseball games."

"I believe I have the right to say that a man's soul needs saving."

"Who told you to come to a man's door, say a thing like that?"

"I did," Cosgrove snapped.

"Are you trying to put the bull on me?" the woman said. "What am I supposed to do, be afraid of your collar? Say, how do I know what you are? I don't think you're a priest at all." Suddenly, she looked past him and saw Great Big on the sidewalk.

And now Mrs. Chief shrieked. "Oh, Chief! It's a setup!"

She slammed the door in Cosgrove's face.

Cosgrove walked off. "The woman doesn't understand," he said to Great Big. He led Great Big into the marshes. As they pushed through the grass, it crackled and waved. And there was a squeal of tires as a car rushed up to the Chief's house and Mr. Frankie Five Hundred, bundled in a beautiful pearl gray overcoat, jumped out. He was halfway up the walk to the Chief's house when the door opened and a voice snarled from inside and Mr. Frankie Five Hundred spun around, his hand going inside his beautiful pearl gray overcoat for his gun, and he stood on tiptoes to see into the marshes. He saw the weeds waving. Mr. Frankie Five Hundred, crouching, his gun straight out, went into the weeds and followed the crackling sound.

He did this until the noise stopped. Uncertainly, Frankie Five Hundred forged ahead. He felt the first of a cold winter rainfall. He looked down and saw that his wonderful pearl gray coat was getting wet. More drops fell on the coat. Mr. Frankie Five Hundred looked up at the sky. "I am getting wet in the rain."

He was so intent on the sky that he did not notice the immense hands reaching through the bullrushes.

Mr. Frankie Five Hundred woke up bound and gagged in a place he had never seen before. A basement somewhere. He looked about. In the flickering light of a tall ivory candle he saw a black man sitting on the floor in the corner. The huge black man stared at Frankie Five Hundred.

9

I N THE MORNING Cosgrove prayed with an untroubled
conscience because clearly they had snatched this
Frankie Five Hundred out of the weeds in self-defense.
Although the matter did present problems: they had to
free the man, yet remain safe from retaliation, and if every-
thing went wrong, if Cosgrove did not provide food, the
doctrine of *quisquis agit, agit propter finem* — extreme
measures in extreme times — would start to come into play.
Frankie Five Hundred undoubtedly could turn into at least
the near occasion of sin for Great Big and perhaps tran-
scend sin and become a necessity. Cosgrove thought that
somehow God would provide an answer. Then, in a won-
derful sign, the old lady across the street actually tottered
over to them and brought a platter of baked ziti covered
with a white linen napkin for breakfast. They fed the bound
man and Cosgrove alertly let Great Big eat all but a few
forkfuls.

At this point, while Cosgrove was wrestling with prob-
lems but still enjoying the morning, there was noise at the

door. At first Cosgrove thought the gangsters had descended upon them, but he realized there had been no sound of cars. He then thought it was the old lady returning for her platter and the cloth napkin, but then he heard the mailbox sound. Rather than the clang of metal, there was the sound of a breeze blowing glass chimes and Cosgrove felt great hope surge through him. When he pulled out the mail there was a letter in shaky handwriting, from an old parishioner undoubtedly, and a second letter, whose envelope carried the yellow seal of the Vatican. Inside was a sheet of paper, no seal on it, which disappointed him immediately, and when he glanced at the bottom and saw that no secretary had typed it, indicating no carbons were distributed around the offices in Rome, his expectations dropped slightly more. Still, his hand trembled.

The note was from the monsignor in Rome and it expressed sorrow and apprehension that he had not made proper arrangements for Cosgrove and that he was horrified to be in receipt of a note from the Americans asking who Cosgrove was and what he was about. The monsignor said that while he was not personally to blame for this deep error, he still would accept responsibility. He said that the speech-writing group working on the Pope's upcoming American tour would, for the first time, go out and do actual research, rather than write learnedly in Rome. The team would find Cosgrove's observations, on Howard Beach and sex, as originally contracted for, extremely valuable, particularly for the Pope's Detroit speech. The monsignor said he could well imagine Cosgrove's plight, all alone and with no resources in Queens and Brooklyn. Therefore, he personally and officially had contacted the only religious residence in the United States owned and run directly by the Vatican, the seminary of Saint Josephinus in Delaware, Ohio. Cosgrove was to pack up and go to the seminary, where he would find the superior not only awaiting him, but under full orders to provide both for Cosgrove and for this large man accompanying him. The monsignor in Rome listed the phone number and address in Delaware, Ohio. He ended the letter.

No wonder he indicated no copies going to anyone, Cosgrove thought. The monsignor, such a brilliant man, had made a mistake and in order to gain authority to provide funds and direct help right here in New York, he would have to admit to such a mistake and ask a superior in the Vatican to rectify this. But how could a man have a successful career if he were to admit a mistake? The monsignor would make the best arrangements he could, Delaware, Ohio, but had no means or authority to send a check or tickets.

Cosgrove, however, decided that, surely, the speech-writing team would be able to handle expenses and the like summarily. Therefore, he told Great Big in the most glowing tones of what would happen to them, and he said that all they had to do was guard this Frankie Five Hundred until he, Cosgrove, found a way for them to flee the area and go to the magnificence of Delaware, Ohio. He left the rectory and walked the streets until he found the post office. A clerk showed him on a map that Delaware, Ohio, was just outside of Columbus. Cosgrove used a precious quarter to call American Airlines and was shocked when told that the fare for two people, one way, was $212.

He thought of the return tickets to Rome that he had back in the rectory. Never would he risk them on any plan, he told himself. Why, he could cash in the tickets, use some of the money to fly to Ohio, and get to the Vatican seminary and find the Papal delegate there and in charge and Cosgrove would be in Ohio with Great Big and with no way ever to return to Rome or anywhere else. Even to Africa. For a fleeting moment, Cosgrove experienced the feeling that he had never really left Africa. So far, things in East New York seemed as close to Africa as humans could make them. Then his mind, so active when in trouble, seized on a wonderful idea. He would get the airfare from public assistance, just as Disco Girl and the others were doing at this precise moment. Good boy, Cosgrove!

Later, enthusiastic because he had found the place on his own, Cosgrove arrived at the four-story East New York Income Maintenance Center, whose title only serves to further confuse thirty-two thousand people in the immediate area who have no income to maintain. In front of the center was a hot dog truck, a wide woman with a shopping cart filled with empty soft drink bottles, and a repairman trying to fix an outdoor phone that had been ripped out. Standing directly against the doors, two silent women were holding babies.

The waiting room, which had five windows in it, was thick with cigarette smoke and had a tile floor and ashstands and hundreds of women on lines, with as many more sitting on many rows of folding chairs, children climbing on and off their laps. The women smacked quarter bags of Wise 22 percent more potato chips, the added percentage being at least reluctant to appear. Cosgrove saw Disco Girl waving to him. She said that she had the use of the coat today. A baby in rubber pants slid off the chair next to Disco Girl's and Cosgrove settled into it, right into a puddle. He jumped up. Disco Girl clapped her hands. "You should never sit by the baby. They pee all over."

Disco Girl pointed excitedly. "The girl and her man got silver fox coats."

On one of the long lines waiting at the windows was a young couple, each with silver, bushy short fur jackets and fur hats with earflaps.

"They cost a hundred dollars," Disco Girl said. "They fly people. Fly girls. Go around with gold hanging out of their ass — excuse me for talkin' like this — but that's what fly girls are."

The fly girl was chewing gum and smoking a cigarette. Disco Girl watched the fly girl carefully as she took a last drag on her cigarette and bent over to put it in the ashstand. Disco Girl was off the chair and over to the fly girl and snatched the butt and began smoking it.

"How much that coat cost?" she said to the fly girl.

Because of the thick fur flaps the fly girl couldn't hear what she was saying.

Disco Girl shouted. The fly girl pulled up an earflap and listened to the question. "Two fifty."

"You hear that?" Disco Girl said. "Two hundred fifty dollars each. They homeless. They know how to do it. Me and my mother be wearin' the same coat the last two years."

"How do you get the coats?" Cosgrove said.

"Sell," the man said.

"Sell what?"

"Sell her pussy."

"How can you say such a thing? That is the Devil's bargain. A fur coat for prostitution."

"Sellin' her pussy keeps us warm in the snow."

The curtains on all five windows suddenly were pulled back and clerks appeared. Cosgrove started for the first window and found himself reeling to the rear of a line that went from window to wall. There wasn't even room on the second line to fit against the wall. He settled on the third line. Cosgrove counted: he was number 63. He was bumped from behind.

"Excuse me," a woman said. Her gray eyes, a beautiful contrast to smooth dark brown skin, displayed amazement. "You the first white person I ever saw on this line." She laughed loud. She said her name was Elise Mabrey. "I spend my life copyin' white people and now look at you copyin' me. You be findin' out that it's hard work. You got to spend at least forty hours a week bein' poor."

Cosgrove grunted. "I have had experience with the worst human beings on earth, British bureaucrats in Africa. I'll move these people along."

"Maybe you do better because you're white," Elise Mabrey said. "I tried copyin' white people but it didn't work. Had me a job, just like all the white women, doin' computers for a Jew lawyer. Kornbluth and Kornbluth. I worked midnight to seven in the mornin'. I ask my supervisor to change my shift and my supervisor got mad. You're entitled to twelve days' sick leave. I took all my time. Just sat home for twelve days. My supervisor had me suspended. I had a hearing and I won. But they put me on nights again. I was gettin' four hundred dollars and cabfare home to Brooklyn. If I worked overtime, I got breakfast money. I had to stay up all day watchin' my little girl. I go to work at night, I wind up noddin' on the computer. Sometimes I didn't go to work at all.

"One night my daughter was at her grandmother's house and she called me up at nine o'clock and said she felt sick.

I said to her, 'Child, it's just a tummyache. You go to sleep and if you don't feel well after a while, you just call me. I called up my office and said I had a sick daughter. Turned on the television and got to watchin'. My daughter woke up in the middle of the night with all cramps and she called her mommy at work instead of where I was, at home. The supervisor made a great big thing. I said, 'Well, let me just do this exactly like the white people do. I'll just stop work for a while and take out unemployment.' I went to work when I was seventeen. I deserved a rest. Had me a vacation. I got up at eleven, had coffee with the blanket wrapped around me, and watched 'Love Boat.' I watch all the people carryin' on out on the ocean. I drew unemployment for six months.

"When it ended, I said, 'Woman, you better go out and get something to make the landlord sing.' All I could get was temp work. All I needed from welfare was a hundred eighty dollars a month to help my rent. But to get my rent check I had to come here every fourteen days. That's the rule. They make out a two-party check, your name and the landlord's name. You got to come here and get the check right away and take the check right to the landlord at the hotel. You can be late for dinner, but you can't be late payin' the landlord. Temp work only give me an hour at lunch. You come here every two weeks, you be standin' on line three, four hours, you miss work. I confided in my supervisor. She said, 'We both do our best.' But with me missin' afternoons every other week, she couldn't save my job. So I got evicted. From then on it was about stayin' in the Flatbush Arms. No more temp work. Nobody hires you if you're stayin' in a welfare hotel. Hire a prisoner from jail before somebody from a welfare hotel. Oh! Look at this!"

She stamped her foot. The curtain was pulled across the window and a woman with her chin out, her body stuffed into a bright purple dress, appeared from a door.

"She's goin' for coffee right in my face!"

"Goin' for coffee in my face!" somebody else said.

On another line, Disco Girl, holding a blue slurpy to her lips, said, "Goin' for coffee in my face!"

The large woman in the purple dress, chin out, a chin as strong as a radiator, sauntered out of the waiting room.

Then the fly girl flounced off the line and headed for the door with her boyfriend right after her. "She goin' for coffee, I'm goin' to the G Building," the fly girl called out.

"You gamblin' girl," Disco Girl called out.

"I be foolin' them at the G Building while you be standin' on your feet so long they disintegrate." With a wave of disdain, the fly girl walked out.

When Cosgrove asked what the G Building was, Elise Mabrey and Disco Girl clapped their hands. "That's where some crazy doctors are. The G Building is at Kings County Hospital. They got another one on the eleventh floor, Brookdale Hospital. If you go there and act crazy enough, one of them signs you up for checks right there just to get rid of you."

"Why doesn't everybody just go there?" Cosgrove said.

"Because if you overact, you get too crazy, they got another one throws you in a padded cell. Sometimes you go there to get a check, you don't come back for thirty days."

"I'll have to think about that," Cosgrove said. Which he did. It was one bloody act to pull, for he had lost a mother to a mental institution. *Quisquis agit, agit propter finem.* The doctrine of extreme measures in extreme times. He would have to think about this more. But then he decided that he would merely wait, like everyone else. Certainly he could afford the time. He was definitely certain that he had left Great Big in reasonable comfort. If Cosgrove had had a mere suspicion, the least inkling, the smallest worry, that Great Big would be unhappy, he never would have left Great Big alone with Mr. Frankie Five Hundred. The rectory, while cold, was palatial compared to Africa.

The welfare worker with the powerful chin returned, the curtain was thrown back, and the line moved painfully slowly. From her line, Disco Girl hollered to Cosgrove, "You step ahead now. Baby Rock's here. He be bringin' you your papers." Cosgrove saw Baby Rock burrow into a line. "Get out from my front!" an old woman squawked as Baby Rock scooted ahead of her. It took him only fifteen minutes and he returned with two New York State Department of Special Services applications for: public assistance, medical assistance, food stamps, services. Cosgrove left his line and stood alongside Disco Girl and Baby Rock. Baby Rock had Hostess cream cakes, orange soda, and Wise 22 percent more potato chips.

Cosgrove took out his reading glasses and looked at the applications. He had seen papers such as these when he had gone over his final university honors-level tests. On the welfare application, in two places, in large letters, there was the warning "Do Not Write in Shaded Areas." But at the same time in the shaded area, there were forty-eight boxes to be filled in and there were blue shaded lines all over the page. In the first white area there were so many blanks to fill in that Cosgrove ran a hand over his brow. Upon turning the page, he was dazzled by a centerfold of both blue and white and of so many blanks to fill in that he quickly shut the booklet.

Seeing this, Disco Girl screamed, "You no better than we are. I be afraid every time I open that thing. It's just like a Burger King application, you fill in the blanks." She waved her pen and made a couple of quick strokes on her paper.

"Is that what you say?" the woman behind her on the line said. "You say it's the same as Burger King? Just like signing up for hamburgers? That's what you say."

"That's exactly what I be sayin'."

"Then why did you write here!" The woman snatched the application and held it up triumphantly. Immediately over the sign that said, "Do Not Write in Shaded Areas" was Disco Girl's writing, right through the shading.

"She signed in the shaded area," Elise Mabrey, standing on line, said.

"That gets you no food," a woman on line said.

"She signed in the shaded area," Elise Mabrey, standing on line, said. Her gray eyes were amused.

"That gets you no food," a woman on line said.

"They pay the rent to the wrong place. The place where you don't live."

Disco Girl, mortified, had a hand clapped to her mouth. Then she began laughing. "When I got my job in Burger King they had me sign in the shade. I kept thinkin' I was writin' down for Burger King."

Cosgrove looked at his form. There was a blue box saying, "Check which programs you are applying for." The boxes were for (a) cash assistance, (b) medical assistance, (c) food stamps, (d) services, (e) expedited food stamps. Disco Girl told Cosgrove to check each. There was a sixth box, with no name to it, sitting in blue shading. Disco Girl held the pen directly over the box. The woman on line laughed. "Don't you touch that, child!"

Disco Girl held the pen directly over the box. "This be double or nothin'. Come on. We go for everything. We either gets nothin' or we gets a house."

Baby Rock clapped his hands. "We go for a house!"

"Indulging in nonsense," Cosgrove said.

"My girlfriend Braithwaite won herself a house last year. She be checkin' the all-or-nothin' box sixteen straight times. She be gettin' nothin' sixteen straight months. She be hurtin' and hungry. Then they have the drawing and she be winnin' a new house. The house be so low to the ground that it didn't even have a fire exit! When she move in, her stomach sure was growlin'. But she be movin' into a new house."

Happily, Disco Girl checked the all-or-nothing box. Whereupon Baby Rock raced across the room and banged on a door marked SPECIAL SUPERVISOR. It was opened by a small man with curly hair and full, surly lips. His face was mostly covered by large thick eyeglasses. He wore a wrinkled white shirt that was several sizes too large for him. A plastic identification card was pinned over the breast pocket. Cosgrove saw that the name was Harold Feinberg. Sticking out of the pocket was an eyeglass case and several pencils and pens.

"This is for the housing lottery only. Otherwise, you must wait out there on line."

"We be goin' for the house," Baby Rock said.

"Goin' for the house," Disco Girl said, waving the paper.

Feinberg's hand whipped the paper from Disco Girl. "Why, this is only your application! Before you even receive your first check, you will be thrown off the computer because you are in the lottery."

"We lucky," Baby Rock said.

Feinberg's mouth tightened in skepticism. "This could break your heart."

"How it do that?" Disco Girl said.

"By just the losing."

"My heart don't know any feelin' but losin'," Disco Girl said.

"And winning guarantees nothing. Look at the woman who won in November. This perfectly ignorant woman moved straight into the house at night and we didn't even see all her papers and she isn't in the house a half hour and her boyfriend stabs her to death."

"The difference between me and her is that I be dead long before I be winnin'," Disco Girl said. "But I be a gamblin' girl. Put me down for the all-or-nothin'."

Feinberg ripped along a perforated line and took the house lottery coupon from the application form. He held it over a drum that stood beside him. "You're sure you know exactly the risk you are taking?"

"Sure do," Disco Girl said.

"And you?" Feinberg said to Baby Rock. "You're on this application as a dependent."

"Double or nothin' for Baby Rock."

"Excuse me," Cosgrove said, "but why do these people have to risk all their benefits on the chance that they could get a house?"

"I told you, it's a lottery."

"But why must impoverished people lose all their benefits because they dare hope?" Cosgrove asked. "Why cannot they receive their benefits and still be a part of the lottery?"

"Because what if they won the house before the computer knew it and we still sent the rent check each month?" Feinberg said. "We need that rent check for someone else. We want to be sure. We cut off their rent the moment they enter the lottery. Make good and sure we have no severe mistakes. Nobody wins a house from the city still gets a rent check while I'm here."

"But then what happens when you lose a lottery?" Cosgrove said.

"You lose the meat," Disco Girl said.

"Lose the meat," Baby Rock said.

Feinberg became impatient. "Sometimes after a drawing it is true that many names of entrants get lost in the computer and it takes some time to get them back on the computer. We do lose whole blocks for a time."

"You lose the meat file, too," Disco Girl said.

"Oh, sometimes the restaurant allotment for welfare hotel residents gets lost in the computer, but we find it after a couple of months or so. But this is not a severe mistake. A severe mistake would mean we kept the winner on the rent rolls. But that won't happen with me. I have won awards for cutting the number of checks issued by this entire center. One month, we issued 1311 fewer checks than at any time in the past three years. We had the special mother-and-daughter house for the lottery prize and we had double the number of poor souls trying for it. So we did lose double the usual number of files in the computer. But it certainly looked great on the books. I was given two municipal service awards. However, Reverend, I assure you, we do correct the computer. And in the meantime, your charge here can dream."

"We be goin' hungry while they fixin' their computer," Disco Girl said.

"Then why enter this infernal trial?" Cosgrove said.

"Because it's the only thing they got that I can enter," Disco Girl said.

Feinberg made a note of Disco Girl's application number and said to Cosgrove, "I'll try to take special care that her file doesn't get lost in the computer. By the way, you're new, aren't you? How long have you been with Catholic Charities?"

"Oh, I'm not there," Cosgrove said.

Feinberg's eyes boiled. "You're not in Brooklyn Catholic Charities?"

"I just said no."

"You're just a common priest?"

"I am proud to say yes."

"Who do you know in the Brooklyn Democratic organization?"

"Nobody."

"Of course you do. That's the only reason I'm talking to you. You didn't just walk in here. You're connected to somebody. Who is your district leader?"

Cosgrove said nothing.

Feinberg became excited. "You're a thief."

"Of course I'm not," Cosgrove said.

"Yes, you are. You're not even a priest. You're a thief. You're here to steal. Give it back, you filthy thief."

On one of the lines, Elise Mabrey leaped happily as she heard her name. A caseworker, a small woman with half-glasses and wearing no makeup, appeared with an application form. She told Elise Mabrey that she must have proof that she was ineligible for Social Security Income, for all possible sources of income must be exhausted before the state and city social services can give relief. Elise Mabrey showed that she already had filled in that she was ineligible for Social Security because she was not sixty-five and not disabled. The caseworker said that only the Social Security people could say that. "But I am saying the truth right here," Elise Mabrey said. The caseworker made a face. "You must go to the Social Security people."

"What floor is that?"

The caseworker smiled. "Oh, they are not in this building. Here is the address." She gave Elise Mabrey a slip of paper.

"That's a whole hour from here!" Elise Mabrey said. The caseworker didn't answer. "Take me two hours there and back. Make me wait there, who knows how long? All day probably. What if it's too late for me to get there by four o'clock?"

"Then you must come back tomorrow."

"But what happens to me on the computer at four o'clock?"

"Whatever the computer does at four o'clock is what happens to you," the caseworker said.

Two lines over, James Woods jumped up and down as if playing basketball. "Goin' to lunch in my face!" The windows were curtained and caseworkers walked brazenly out of the waiting room.

"Goin' to lunch right in my face!" James Woods screamed.

Throughout the large room, seeing caseworkers going to lunch, women jumped up and down. Two security guards, positioned to quell disorders, rushed up to James Woods because he obviously was at the vortex. The first security guard held a club in both hands and swung it like a baseball bat at James Woods. Who skipped out of the way as the security guard missed by so much that he spun in a circle.

James Woods now skipped back with a really nice right-hand punch, particularly for a person who didn't do this for a living. The security guard went down on his face and a woman grabbed the club and proceeded to give him the beating of his life. When the security guard folded his arms over his head, the woman beat his fingers back. The other security guard ran for the exit sign.

Cosgrove felt it was his duty to assist the security guard, and he was in the middle of the crowd, frantically pushing women away from the fallen security guard, who rolled like a barrel out of the crowd just as police rushed in from the street and the first club hit Cosgrove, who was thrown out of the crowd like a rag. The cops had James Woods against the wall, and a woman in a business suit, who seemed to be in charge, spoke to James Woods and led him down a hall-way.

The people had to wait for several hours until the police felt the atmosphere was calm enough for business to re-sume. The frilly curtains flew back and the crowds rushed forward. Cosgrove was buffeted about and wound up stand-ing through the afternoon until his legs wobbled and at ten minutes to four, a woman got up from her chair and ran out to the center of the room with her hand swinging back and she hit her baby a tremendous whack on the backside. On the line next to Cosgrove a woman holding a child who was fretting hit the infant atop the head. One baby darted for the front doors. Quickly others followed. Mothers ran after them, hands flying. Babies screamed.

At 4:00 P.M., the computer terminals in the building, as did all other computer terminals in every welfare office in the city, sent swiftly back to the main computer center all names, payments, dispositions. And, as in all of life where the sins of omission are the worst, the names the computer did not send back were the ones in trouble. The machine was programmed for a notice to be sent to a person, and if that person did not appear within fourteen days, the machine, at 4:00 P.M. on the fourteenth day, rubbed out the name as it shot information to the center in Manhattan. The person could be standing on line in the waiting room, and it would be of no avail; he or she would be off the computer, and thus penniless, for all the months that it took to get back on.

In the moaning and squalling of babies being hit, a wall phone rang with an emergency cadence and security guards raced upstairs. As quickly as it had erupted, the vast first-floor waiting room became quiet. At 4:01, mothers picked up their sobbing children.

"They done," Disco Girl said.

"Sure is," the other woman said. "They either sent me in or sent me out. Four o'clock make me nervous."

"If they make a mistake on you, you got yourself a new name," Disco Girl said. "You be 'Official Mistake.'"

A window on the other side of the room opened and Baby Rock jumped to it, put his hands against the wall, and pushed back hard to make room for Disco Girl, who shouted into the window, "Carfare home, me and my little brother."

"I have 719-G forms," the woman said.

Disco Girl grabbed, looked, and snapped, "Where's the carfare?"

"This is only carfare authorization," the woman behind the window said. "It's got to be signed by two people."

"We need emergency, too," Disco Girl said.

"Oh, then you need an E check," the woman said. "That is Form W661-A and that requires three signatures and of course I must take this upstairs and they must interview you so that we can see if you are eligible for emergency funds and if you are and we have the three signatures you may wait for your E check. You must do all that tomorrow." She disappeared. They stood for some time. The woman returned and pushed two tokens onto the counter for Disco Girl. "What do I use to get back here tomorrow?" Disco Girl asked.

"When you come here tomorrow we will give you more carfare," the woman said.

"I don't have the carfare to get here to get the carfare," Disco Girl said.

"That is your business, I am sure."

When she pushed a token at Cosgrove, he, too, complained and the clerk said, "I cannot give you two tokens because if you do not use the token to come back here tomorrow, it means that you are a welfare fraud and cheat. In order to protect the public against such fraud, we can only give you carfare when you return tomorrow."

Cosgrove smiled amiably. "My dear woman, I truly think tha —"

The curtain swung over the window, and in the waiting room Disco Girl screamed, "She went home in his face!"

"She went home in my face!" Cosgrove shouted.

Later, as Cosgrove, exhausted and nervous, came down the street to the rectory, he heard a window opening and the old woman from across the street looked through her grillwork and said, "I got oxtail soup. I got leftover. You want?"

The old lady gave him a caldron and Cosgrove rushed to the rectory with it. He took only the smallest amount for himself and filled two large bowls and brought them down to the basement that ran beneath both church and rectory. There Great Big sat with Mr. Frankie Five Hundred, who was writhing. His bound hands reflected a lack of circulation. The gag in his mouth had him on the edge of insanity. His pants were sopping; Great Big didn't care if the man drowned in his own urine. Great Big pulled out the gag and held the bowl to Frankie Five Hundred's mouth and poured until Frankie choked. Great Big replaced the gag.

Cosgrove, watching Great Big eat, thought that his friend was becoming rank. In solitary confinement, with only a gagged man in a dim, cold, damp basement, with the candles burning low, Great Big took the passing of a few hours as if they constituted a month. Cosgrove was surprised at how even the outskirts of civilization had caused Great Big's patience to deteriorate. "Once we had to wait a whole year for rain," he said to Great Big. "And now you cannot sit here for two days." Cosgrove decided that there was something about taking Great Big out of a natural landscape, even one as barren as the bush, and suddenly placing him in a concrete room that might well be a jail.

In the morning, he finally decided over prayers that the doctrine of *quisquis agit, agit propter finem* was vital. He had been deserted by his superiors, yet he had a mission to fulfill. He would attempt the welfare lines for another day or so, but then he clearly would have to move. Therefore, he would develop an option.

He went directly to Baby Rock's corner, where he found

Seneca, schoolbooks in the crook of one arm, talking to Baby Rock, who was on his couch, staring at the fire in the oil drum. Cosgrove asked Seneca for a sheet of paper out of the looseleaf book. He walked down to the bodega for the address, came back, and, using the building wall near Seneca, printed a note. The rough surface under the paper caused the printing to be uneven, which he felt was good because it made it impossible to trace. He wrote a note, which said:

> To the Chief:
>
> We have your friend. The name in his wallet says that he answers to the name of Frankie Five Hundred. We need more than that of course if you are to see him again. If you want Frankie Five Hundred back, go to the telephone pole in front of the bodega at 177 Delta Street at nine P.M. and there will be a note telling you what to do on the next step.

Cosgrove thought for a moment. He wrote a second note:

> To the Chief:
>
> You have shown interest in getting Frankie Five Hundred back. My gang has Frankie Five Hundred in its clutches. We will let him out of our clutches for the sum of fifteen thousand dollars. That is not a great amount of money for the Mafia. But we are a benevolent gang. Frankie Five Hundred will attest to that upon his return. Leave fifteen thousand in an envelope on this very same telephone pole by midnight. Also, do not let us catch you hanging around this telephone pole or we will kidnap you, too.

Seneca lost interest in watching him and left for school. Baby Rock yawned and closed his eyes. Cosgrove went to the bodega and bought Scotch tape with one of the last two dollars in his pocket, taped the second note outside onto the telephone pole, and began walking quickly through the morning-empty streets to the Chief's restaurant.

A delivery of several large paper bags of bread, greatest bread, giant loaves of semolina bread with seeds, sat in the doorway. In the middle of a starving neighborhood, they could leave bread in front of the Chief's door; real fast capital punishment deters all crime. Cosgrove put the first note, announcing the kidnapping, in the top of one of the bags of bread. The presence of two notes would indicate some planning to the Chief, who would act with care as he would feel he was in against professionals.

Cosgrove went back to the storefront, shook Baby Rock awake, and the two jumped aboard the bus, Cosgrove with great spirit and disdain for the fare box. He considered himself on the way up. Between the ransom note for Frankie Five Hundred and the application for welfare emergency funds, the path would soon soften. If he didn't get the ransom for Frankie Five Hundred, at the least he and Great Big would have the welfare funds. Arriving at the Flatbush Arms, they saw Mother Agnes on the sidewalk. She was holding a low number, 23, for the morning food.

"You just missed Disco Girl. They come this mornin' and say she could have her babies back. They make a mistake with the test. Remember I told you that nobody sex-molested Disco Girl's baby. That baby play with herself."

"And now she must stop doing that."

"Tell that to the child. She the one does the playin' with herself. I sure don't."

"Where is that Disco Girl? I'll certainly tell her."

Mother Agnes shrugged. "She's out ridin' in the van for apartments. They take you to three places. The rule is, you got to take one of the three apartments they show you or they put you back at the bottom, they put you in a shelter, and you got to wait your turn to get back here."

"When is the all-or-nothin' drawing for the house Disco Girl gonna get?" Baby Rock asked.

"Child, nobody gonna be winnin' a house."

"Disco Girl win! I know she does."

His exuberance touched Cosgrove and caused inspiration. "What was the last school you attended?" he asked Baby Rock.

"School be I.S. 234. Why?"

"I'd like to see it."

"It be on the way to the welfare center. It be a good walk."

"How wonderful. A morning constitutional. We both can use it this morning." Cosgrove took Baby Rock by the elbow and they walked until they arrived at the old gloomy five-story red-brick school, which sat behind a black metal picket fence and had graffiti scrawled on its double metal doors. "Show me inside," Cosgrove said, holding Baby Rock's arm. The boy said no.

A woman leaning against the fence said, "I sure wish they would just let me sit inside. I leave the hotel with my little daughter at seven-thirty. I stay here all day. I go up to the Lutheran church up there on the avenue for lunch, that's when I can get in. They only gave me food money once at the welfare center. I stay here and pick up my little daughter at three o'clock and we walk home. They haven't given me any carfare for school yet. My asthma's acting up and I don't have any Medicaid. I sure wish they'd let me inside. I can't even go in. You can and you don't even want to go in."

"Do you see how lucky you are?" Cosgrove said to Baby

Rock. He pulled Baby Rock inside, where security guards nodded agreeably at the priest and student. Baby Rock took Cosgrove up to the empty hallway outside a third-floor classroom. "In you go," Cosgrove said.

Alarm flushed onto Baby Rock's face. "I can't.

"You've come this far," Cosgrove said. "Clutch at the opportunity, lad. Off you go now, there's a good lad."

"English class," Baby Rock murmured.

"How splendid. Verb conjugations. We must get you in the correct tense. First person, I am."

"I be late," Baby Rock murmured. He stood on his tiptoes and looked in the small glass window in the door.

"You haven't been here in weeks. Actually, they'll be delighted to see you."

"I be late today. Everybody in there."

"Then get in there yourself," Cosgrove said.

Baby Rock shook his head. Cosgrove put a hand on his back and Baby Rock began to lean backward again. Cosgrove reached for the doorknob and Baby Rock twisted to get away. "They look at me," Baby Rock said.

"Is that what you're afraid of?"

"I walk in, they all look at me. That's why I don't be goin' to school. Bus get me here late, they all look at me."

"Then I shall accompany you." Baby Rock twisted violently. "That would embarrass you more, will it? Well, you'll just have to do this on your own."

Tears formed in Baby Rock's eyes. Suddenly, he grabbed the doorknob and pushed the door open and barreled into the classroom. Every face looked at him. Baby Rock stood alone in total silence in the room. He was alone in their glare. The teacher stood in front and she, too, glared, and the silence lasted and now Baby Rock, alone in everybody's stare, shouted, "Fuck you!"

The teacher's mouth opened in exasperation and her eyes became hooded as she regarded the urchin in front of her. "It's bad enough that you live in a hotel and don't care about school, but now you disturb the entire class."

Baby Rock exploded and the teacher dismissed him with a wave and turned her back and the class was laughing at Baby Rock. Who whirled in the front of the room, looking for something, and his hand went for the woman's purse, which sat in a bottom desk drawer that the teacher carelessly had not fully closed. His fingers came out with her red wallet.

Baby Rock was out of the classroom and down the hall, almost to the staircase, when the teacher let out her first howl. And came running. Cosgrove was amazed at her speed. She had on a loose dress and eyeglasses on a chain around her neck. She was about forty-five, with the first little bits of gray showing in her light brown, but she had young energy, plenty of it. Baby Rock, sensing her speed, shouted to Cosgrove to hurry, and Cosgrove did.

Baby Rock and Cosgrove flew past the security desk on the first floor and the guards jumped up and when the teacher came screaming past them the guards joined the chase. It was some run. After two blocks, the guards quit the chase. The teacher did not. Baby Rock tore down the sidewalk in his white sneakers and Cosgrove ran out of sheer fear. Behind them, grim, determined, persistent, came the schoolteacher. When Cosgrove looked back once and saw that the schoolteacher was running with her elbows tight to her body and her knees high, pushing like pistons, he understood that at least he was going to get grabbed. He let out a strangled call to Baby Rock, who spun, saw the problem, held the wallet high over his head for all to see, primarily the gaining schoolteacher, flipped it high into the sky, turned, and kept running. Cosgrove followed. Behind them, feet slapping the sidewalk, the schoolteacher veered off and went for her wallet, which was in the gutter. As she did this, she was screeching for police. Baby Rock was around a corner and saw a doorway in the back of a row of one-story attached buildings and went flying into it, with Cosgrove right behind him. Three Chinese were bent over pots in a narrow restaurant kitchen. One looked up and said, "You late."

Baby Rock, trying to catch his breath, said nothing.

"You Cat-lick Cha'ties?" the older man said to Cosgrove. He didn't wait for an answer. "I tell them have boy here at ten-thirty A.M. Now it's ten-fifty." He shook a finger at Baby Rock. "Tomorrow, be here on time."

"You've got a job!" Cosgrove exulted. He asked the Chinese man, "How often does he work?"

"All day every day."

"And he can eat?"

The restaurant man shrugged. What else do you do in a restaurant?

"Good boy yourself," Cosgrove said, clapping Baby Rock on the shoulder.

The Chinese man pointed to a garbage bucket. "That go outside," he said. Baby Rock seemed almost cheerful as he picked it up, his first task on his first day of work.

Cosgrove walked warily. There was, however, no sign of the schoolteacher. Soon he walked jauntily and ripped off

his Roman collar, so that when he reached the welfare cen-
ter he would appear to be just another in emergency need.
He thought of how the day's events had helped Baby Rock
and perhaps this same good fortune would assist him today.
Cosgrove felt he had the basis for luck. If he could get emer-
gency welfare assistance, there would be no need for Mr.
Frankie Five Hundred's ransom. And surely, it was going
to be easier to get emergency welfare than it would be to
gain ransom for a Mafia gangster.

When he arrived at the income maintenance center, he
bought a bag of Wise potato chips for a quarter and ate them
by the water fountain. When the potato chips ran out, he
smacked the bag in hopes of getting the 22 percent more. A
woman next to him did the same thing. "They forgot to put
in my percents!" the woman said, finding nothing more in
her bag.

On line with his application blanks, Cosgrove stood be-
hind a woman who kept patting her hair with one hand. Cos-
grove saw baldness showing through the dark hair. She held
her papers with the other. "I'm on chemo," the woman said
to Cosgrove. "Chemotherapy. I've got leukemia. I feel mis-
erable. I shake. I took the bus here. I had to get off sick."
Cosgrove asked the people in front of the woman if they
would let her through and everybody pretended not to hear.
Finally the woman reached the window. She fumbled with
her papers and the clerk looked up and said, "We're busy
here." The woman said, "I've had so much medicine that I
get confused." The clerk in the window snarled. "Get off
the medicine so you'll know what you're doing." With that,
she pulled the curtain in front of the window.

Cosgrove leaped to the closed window and banged on it.

He turned and placed a hand on the woman. "I am heart-sick."

The woman shook her head. "I don't want sympathy. I just want people to be nice to me."

By noon, Cosgrove found himself slipping into a daze, not unlike that of one who spends a long time in hospital hallways, and he shuffled forward rather than stepped and lost track of time and sometime in the afternoon found himself at the window and the clerk took his application blank, sniffed, and told him to take a seat. He sat somnolently and a young woman in a black beret sat next to him. She fingered a quarter and spoke to herself. "In case I got to call whoever. Nobody, I guess."

A shouting Disco Girl brought Cosgrove's head up. She ran into the big room, threw open her brown down coat and made her body shake. "I get my babies back!"

"Where are you going to put them?" Cosgrove asked.

"My new house." When she saw that Cosgrove was skeptical, Disco Girl said, "I win the roof today. You don't think I be winnin' a new house today? Little man, I be mad at you. You be uninvited."

"I guess anything can happen today. You got your children back and Baby Rock got a job."

"Where he be?"

"Working in a Chinese restaurant."

"Baby Rock get his belly full of rice. One time he went fifteen places, nobody give him a job so he quit lookin'. And you get Baby Rock that job? You did? Then you be invited to the house." Disco Girl spun around and clapped her hands. "I be bringin' my baby Latasha Yee to visit Baby Rock at work in the Chinee. You know what I say when I walk in? I be sayin', 'Mi Ma'!"

"When are you supposed to get this new house of yours?" Cosgrove smirked.

"In the three o'clock drawin'."

"Where?"

"Right here. Comes in on the computer machine three o'clock. You be here. You see Disco Girl win the roof."

"Oh, I hope so. I also hope you know what you'll do if you don't win," Cosgrove said.

"I be ridin' around in the van for apartments since yesterday." The admission took away some of Disco Girl's buoyancy.

She handed Cosgrove a sheaf of paper to do with her housing. The rent at the Flatbush Arms was $2100 a month, but that was emergency housing funds, the form said in bold letters. The federal regulations allowed emergency housing funds at such rates for years, but once a welfare woman was moved out of emergency housing and into regular housing she was under strict rates, and the form showed that in Disco Girl's case, a family of four, she was allowed no more than $425 a month. The writing on one carbon said that Disco Girl had turned down the first two apartments she was shown. One had no front door and the building had no heat. The other was without a toilet. The form said, "Recipients should regard apartment seeking as similar to baseball. Only three apartments are shown to a client. If all three are turned down, then that is strike three. You are out. Client then must go back to the city shelter (dugout). Remember baseball when you see apartments. For it's one, two, three strikes you're out at the old ball game."

"The apartment van don't come tomorrow. It come the day after tomorrow. The man say it my last ride. What if I don't know whether to take it or not?"

"I'm sure it will be fine," Cosgrove said in all lameness.

"You come with me, little man, and help me decide?"

"Of course."

"You promise? They take me out day after tomorrow," she said.

"Of course."

She sighed. "I never be havin' an apartment. You know that? I always live in a shelter or a welfare hotel. My whole life. I see an apartment all empty and I say, 'What do I put in it?' and the man say I get a furniture allowance. I never bought furniture. How do you say to the man what chair you want? Then what do you do? Does he box it up and hand it to you? I can't be carryin' no couch home in a big box." She thought. "Maybe it be fun except it has me scared. Don't know anythin' about apartments and furniture. All I know how to be doin' is dancin'."

She jumped up and danced all over the space in front of the row of chairs, her summer shoes skipping across the cigarette-covered floor. "I be worryin' about furniture for an apartment. I should be worryin' about furnishin' my whole new house. Look at me. I be the winner today." She laughed and made the women sitting near them burst into laughter, too. Abruptly, she sat down.

"Now just supposin' I don't win, I'm goin' to apply," she said.

"For what?" Cosgrove said.

"For everything. I studied all night for my face-to-face. I got to know all the answers. Ask me something. Ask me mortgage."

"A mortgage?"

"Got no mortgage. I sure know I don't. That's one question I'll answer for sure."

One of the women said, "Bonds."

Disco Girl closed her eyes. She shouted, "Got no bonds!"

"Other investments," another woman said.

"Got no investments. Got no any other investments. And . . . and I got a new part of the answer that's goin' to make the woman laugh. I'm not tellin' you. Tell you after I tell it to her."

Disco Girl stopped dead as she heard her name called over the loudspeaker and she ran around a partition and disappeared. Cosgrove sat and became drowsy, heard Elise Mabrey's name being called but didn't arouse himself to look for her, and then he heard his own name called. The security guard directed him around the partition to a large room with bare metal desks, where welfare workers sat and interviewed clients without looking at them. When Cosgrove walked in, he saw Disco Girl over in the far corner. A clerk directed him to an empty desk next to the one where Elise Mabrey was going over her application with the clerk. The Social Security clerk had written, right under where Elise Mabrey had written the same thing, that she was under sixty-five and not disabled. The clerk was very happy. Elise Mabrey said to her, "I didn't get knocked off the computer?" The clerk said, "When was your deadline?"

"Yesterday."

"Then you are off the computer."

"You sent me out!"

"That is no business of mine. If your deadline was yesterday, and you were not here, you are automatically off. But when you fill in a new application you do not have to go to the Social Security." Elise Mabrey said, to the air in the room, for the clerk wasn't looking at her and hardly seemed to hear what she was saying, "It'll take weeks." The clerk said nothing. "How does my child eat while I sit here for weeks?" The clerk still said nothing.

At the next desk from Elise Mabrey, another clerk told a heavy woman in a blue raincoat that her rent allowance had been increased from $375 a month to $425, that this must go to the landlord, and that this adjustment also meant that she would receive $15 a month less in food stamps. "That is the regulation."

"My children got a regulation, too. They got to eat."

The clerk became angry. "Here is the pamphlet from the secretary of agriculture himself. Read what it says. 'An American must be willing to sacrifice in order to have a good roof over his or her head.'"

A clerk with a high-pitched West Indian accent appeared across the desk from Cosgrove and began to read his application.

"Just for emergency funding," Cosgrove said. "I am not a long-term person."

"I am reading this application that you have given to me," the woman said coldly.

He decided to go over and watch Disco Girl, who, biting her lips, was answering questions for her face-to-face hearing.

"In the past six months, have you had any relatives die?"

"My mother's cousin be killed by a train in Virginia."

"Did he leave any inheritance?"

"His picture."

"Do you have any mortgages?"

"No, ma'am!" Disco Girl shouted.

"Do you have any bonds?"

"Sure no!"

"Do you own any municipal debentures?" the woman asked.

"Wha'?"

"You do not know what municipal debentures are?"

Disco Girl shook her head.

"You must be sure. I cannot fill in the form if you do not know whether you have them or not. There is a line here for municipal debentures. If you had even one municipal debenture in your house and you said no on this form, you could go to federal prison."

"What do they look like?"

"I don't know these things. I know only that the question is on the sheet. You didn't even bother to study for it. This will cause your application to be rejected. You will see that this will happen to you. You were told to study all the questions."

Disco Girl was silent. The clerk went back to the form. "Do you have investments in the stock market?"

"I can't even go to the food market."

"Any other investments?"

"I got no investments. I got no other investments. And . . . and I got no vest!"

The clerk's face did not change. Her eyes remained on the application. She became irritated. "You have no first name on the birth certificate of your third child."

"She be Latasha Yee. You talk to her. She say to you, 'Mi Ma.'"

"You don't have the first name filled out on the official birth certificate. All I see here is baby, female."

When Disco Girl said she would just fill in the name now, the clerk shook her head. She said that Disco Girl had to go to the Board of Health and get a proper birth certificate for the baby. Disco Girl said that for several months the baby had been held by the Bureau of Child Welfare.

"They never ask her name when they come take her away from me," Disco Girl said.

"Well, I must have the proper first name," the clerk said.

Disco Girl said it would take hours to go to the Board of Health and the clerk said it was no matter of hers. Cosgrove turned and called, "You are being unreasonable over a simple form." At this, his own clerk looked up and called across the room to him crankily. "Look at this. You filled in all the blue blanks. You are the only person today who has not been sent back for writing in the blue blanks."

"What do I do now?" Cosgrove said.

"Come back tomorrow."

"Why do I have to wait?"

"Why? You should thank us for giving you something to look forward to."

Outside in the lobby, Cosgrove, Disco Girl, and Elise Mabrey stood moodily. It was drawing close to three o'clock. Disco Girl bit her lip. Now a small group of women gathered at the last window, a few steps across from the doorway to the special supervisor's office. At the last window, the curtain was pulled back and the women pushed around it. Disco Girl, who was forced to stand in the second row, got up on her tiptoes, saw that wasn't good enough, and pulled up a tin folding chair. She got up on the chair, hunched over with her hands on her knees, and watched through the window to where a clerk sat stonily at a computer screen.

"One more minute!" Disco Girl called to Cosgrove.

Everybody in front of the window took out social assistance identification cards and studied the numbers. "Mine be seven two six seven," Disco Girl said, reading it aloud as if reciting in class. She concentrated on the window and there was the sound of breath being sucked in and held and the computer screen was blank and dark. The screen flashed and everybody writhed and looked at their cards. Peering between shoulders, Cosgrove saw the computer screen blink and all the women exhaled in disappointment. Disco Girl jumped off the chair. She jumped high and screamed and threw her legs straight out. She landed on the dance.

"I win the roof!"

At the counter, the woman held her hand out and demanded Disco Girl's card and Disco Girl gave it to her and kept dancing and the clerk checked the card against the computer and came out and knocked on the special supervisor's door. Harold Feinberg stood in the door with his head down, to show deep thought as he listened to the clerk. His head flew up when he saw Disco Girl, with Cosgrove alongside her. He shrieked, "Stop celebrating! You win nothing! You are disqualified!"

Disco Girl turned into a statue.

"You see, you are not married. I distinctly told you the last woman who won a house was killed in it that very night by her boyfriend. That caused us to change the rules. I told you so! This lottery is pro-family. You must have a legal husband before we can let you have the house. We can't allow transients to be killing each other all over the place in our houses."

"I won fair and square. I won the roof!"

"You can appeal it to the Central Welfare Board. I can do nothing for you here."

Cosgrove rushed forward to protest and immediately

Harold Feinberg pointed at him and said, "You are a thief. You probably found a way to fix the lottery. You are a no-body thief. You don't even know a district leader. If she had a chance to appeal my ruling, you cost her that chance. Who would listen to her with you around?"

He slammed the door shut and Disco Girl pounded on it for several minutes, but Harold Feinberg never came out.

Disco Girl pouted. Then she snarled. "I'm goin' to the G Building. I'll act up so much they'll give me two checks just to get out of there."

Elise Mabrey shook her head. "I got to get home to my little girl. If I overact in the G Building, who takes care of her?"

"I don't know about you, but I be at the 'G,'" Disco Girl said. Disco Girl left, with Cosgrove walking rapidly in an attempt to keep up with her because in her anger she was taking huge strides toward the bus stop.

The G Building at Kings County Hospital was one of many high, gloomy buildings that glowered down on the two-story neighborhood. In front of the G Building, cars were double-parked, and the sidewalk was crowded with people who appeared to be on drugs or had had too much to drink or, it occurred to Cosgrove, were simply nuts.

Disco Girl walked up the steps and into the lobby, which was covered with cardboard signs handwritten in English and Spanish. People waited on lines, but much shorter lines than those at the income maintenance center.

A male in a security uniform looked up from a desk and waited for Disco Girl to announce herself, but rather than speak, she pulled her coat off. Then swiftly, so swiftly that Cosgrove could only stand in shock, she removed all her clothes. She stood with her back to Cosgrove, the ceiling lights glaring on her ebony bottom, and her last motion was to grab her Disco Girl T-shirt and pull it off and stand there in her bra, which she got off and now, naked, she started to dance in the lobby, but the people on the lines didn't bother to turn and watch. Suddenly she spun around and here she was, facing Cosgrove full-on, facing him with all she had, two big black breasts and, far worse, this great black bush wavering in front of him as her hips swung all over the room.

"Come on, little man!"

"You lewd woman!" Cosgrove screamed.

He was red as a rose and had spittle flecking his lips and he rushed at Disco Girl and, like a matador, she danced away from him, this black bush of hers clearly driving Cosgrove into a frenzy. He put his head down and ran with tremendous initial speed right across the lobby at the waving bush and Disco Girl shrieked, "He be dancin'."

A man in a white jacket, holding a clipboard, emerged from an office and the security guard, regarding this as a sign of concern, stood up, but the man with the clipboard seemed unconcerned until he looked at Cosgrove. His brow then furrowed.

Cosgrove made a low rush at Disco Girl and she stopped dead, clapped both hands behind his neck, and pulled his face into her bush.

There was a primal scream and an upheaval and Cosgrove, with superhuman strength, flipped Disco Girl up into the air. "You will be consigned to Hell and you will have darkness inside your mind and the exterior will be fires in darkness forever!"

The man with the clipboard made a move on Cosgrove, who found himself surrounded by security guards.

"Put your clothes on," the man with the clipboard said to Disco Girl.

"I'm starvin'. I be dancin' here till I get back on welfare."

"Go into the office and they'll help you fill out all the emergency forms right now. We'll see you get aid before you leave here," the doctor said.

Disco Girl, calmed, walked over to her clothes and began putting them on. "It work," she called to Cosgrove as he was being taken into an office by the doctor and one big black security guard. "How dare you talk to me, you lascivious woman!"

"Are you all right?" the man with the clipboard said, slipping behind a desk. "My name is Eric Gross. I'm a doctor here." The black security guard left and a new one slipped in. The security guard was a strong-looking young white guy with a thick neck. He chewed gum confidently.

"I am to be about my Lord's business," Cosgrove said.

"And what is that?" Gross said.

"I just followed my calling outside here," Cosgrove said. "And you people followed yours. The Devil's."

"Why do you say that I follow the Devil?"

"Because you permitted that filthy lewd sin."

"What would you say if I told you that we had people in this building who cut heads off and tried to eat them?"

"I would say that does not change what just occurred."

"It means nothing to you? A head cut off?"

"Of course not. I've seen it all before."

"Where?"

"In Africa."

"Oh, you were in Africa."

"Yes, and when people are hungry they can be expected to do anything. It is all right. You know the theory. *Quisquis agit, agit propter finem.*"

"I see," the doctor said.

"But there was just an extraordinary occurrence there. The presence of the Devil in your very room. That woman, and I know her well, was clearly possessed of the Devil for the moment. And you chose his side."

"How did I do that?"

"By allowing that woman to sink into sin in front of your eyes."

"Was she doing something as bad as cutting somebody's head off and eating it in Africa?"

"Africa. Don't be smug. I have seen that done right here in New York."

"You have?"

"Of course. I didn't feed Great Big properly and therefore he got hungry and forgot his manners."

"I see."

"No you don't. You are a man who sees nothing. You just stood in front of sin, sin in your very eyes, and you talk to me of utter nonsense."

"Eating somebody is nonsense?"

"That is something done for hunger. Sin is done for the Devil."

The doctor stared at a pencil in his hand. He looked up at the security guard. "Why don't you just wait here a moment," the doctor said. He went out a door in the office that led into the hallways somewhere.

Twenty minutes later, sitting in silence, listening to each other breathe, Cosgrove and the security guard looked at each other. "Do you have a cigarette?" Cosgrove asked.

"Sure do," the guard said. He held out a pack and carefully lit Cosgrove's cigarette for him.

Cosgrove inhaled and closed his eyes. "When is your man returning?"

"He said he was coming back," the guard said.

"I heard him say no such thing," Cosgrove said.

The guard did not move.

"He didn't go to get me welfare?"

"No, I know he didn't," the guard said.

"Then I believe I shall leave."

"He asked you to wait."

Cosgrove opened his eyes, fixed them like headlights on the security guard, sat erect, and was about to say something when the guard said, "You were fooling with the doctor, you tell him you got somebody eats people?"

"I never speak anything but the truth."

"You got a cannibal with you?"

"If that's what you care to call it. Actually, it isn't that simple."

The security guard took out a key and unlocked the door and looked out into the lobby. The guard was trying to watch Cosgrove and still attract the attention of somebody in the lobby. "You'll have to wait," the guard said.

Cosgrove was breathing onto the guard's neck and the guard tried to hold him in.

"There's the little man!"

Disco Girl came bounding through the lobby, her brown down coat held together with the big safety pin, and the guard trembled as Disco Girl kept coming.

"Is she with you?"

"Of course."

The security guard tried to shut the door, couldn't, and simply ran out into the lobby in the late afternoon and tried to find somebody.

Disco Girl and Cosgrove walked out of the building and into the crowds heading for the bus. Disco Girl grimly held her emergency check. When Cosgrove mentioned her behavior in the G Building, Disco Girl exploded. "You the reason I can't even appeal the ruling on my house. You worried how I act? What about how you act? You lost the appeal on my new roof!"

"I'll try to rectify this tomorrow," he said.

Disco Girl snorted in annoyance. "You don't even take care of yourself yet."

"I will tomorrow," Cosgrove said. "Then I'll get you that house."

10

O N THE NEXT DAY, Cosgrove stood for hours in the East New York center and finally, when the four o'clock eruption subsided, a clerk asked Cosgrove for his name and after carefully writing it on a form, she gave him a mimeographed slip of paper with an address on East Sixteenth Street in Manhattan. He was to present this slip of paper before five and would be sent to a job training place and at the job training place a man would sign the slip of paper, which, when brought back to her, the clerk, would be an initial qualification for getting emergency funds. She gave him a second slip of paper, which entitled him to get $9.30 carfare for job hunting.

He went downstairs, waited twenty minutes on the carfare line, ran to the subway, going over the turnstile without touching this time. He found the address on East Sixteenth Street, a shabby building with Puerto Ricans clustered in the narrow doorway. He walked up one flight and into a barren room with harsh fluorescent ceiling lights where at a desk was a man in a shirt and sleeveless sweater, his head down, gray hand held out for the sheet of paper. He stamped it and returned the paper to Cosgrove without looking up. The stamp on the paper said, "Report to Evening Session Manhattan Dog Grooming School, 235 East 34th Street."

Cosgrove walked four doors and into a saloon crowded with Puerto Ricans. Cosgrove took three shots of cheap rye with two big cold beers and it all went swooshing down like a babbling brook and he had the same again and stayed there until he had three dollars and change left. He walked up to East Thirty-fourth Street dreamily, humming, taking a misstep here and there. You haven't been drinking enough, he told himself, so it hits you immediately.

He found the Manhattan Dog Grooming School, which was in a storefront next to a bar. The air inside was thick with perfume. A skinny man, talking on the phone, seemed annoyed when Cosgrove walked in. Cosgrove gave the man his paper, which the man, talking on the phone all the time, stamped, and he gave Cosgrove a form to fill out, which said, "Reimbursement for Manpower Training."

He waved a hand to direct Cosgrove to a long room in the rear, where four black women sat on high chairs and combed poodles, which sat like princes on round tables. One wall was lined with cages where more poodles sniffed through the strong wire.

A red-haired woman in a green smock directed the black women. When Cosgrove walked in, she opened a cage and brought out a black poodle. "The other students here tonight are already on their second session," she said. "We are giving you a particular lesson. See this dog's hair? You'd think the owner would know enough. See how matted his hair is? This won't do at all. You just can't wash and brush this hair. You must shampoo the dog thoroughly and shave the hair. It is matted beyond our ability to help. You must be very careful for this is an expensive job. The bill for this will be at least fifty dollars." Until now, Cosgrove had been dreaming in his alcohol. "Fifty dollars, you say?" The woman nodded. "And how much of that is mine?" She said without smiling, "Oh, you are a student. You are learning a trade. Not only do you not get paid, but the city pays us for you to be able to learn here."

"That makes it perfectly fair," Cosgrove said. He looked at the black poodle, which was perched on the round table with its nose twitching and its beady black eyes looking at Cosgrove. The student down at the end snapped at her dog, "Sit, bitch!" The red-haired teacher scolded her for this. "You must not speak to a dog like that. You can get an *F* for failure if you do that. Do you want an *F* for failure on your school record?"

Cosgrove put the black poodle under his arm and walked for the front door. He knew the woman didn't see him because she never yelled, and the man at the front desk was so busy on the phone that he never looked up as Cosgrove went out onto East Thirty-fourth Street and headed for the subway. He walked as far as a bar, which he was about to pass when he heard a gleeful shout inside. This was the same as throwing a brick wall in front of Cosgrove. He went inside with the poodle squirming under his arm. He put the poodle on a stool, and the dog sat up elegantly. A man with red cheeks and in shirtsleeves called out, "Give the man and his dog a drink."

"The dog is a teetotaler," Cosgrove said.

The red-cheeked man burst into laughter. "Let the man drink for the dog, too."

"And the man will," Cosgrove said.

He ordered two ryes and beer chasers and swallowed them rapidly and to give cheer to the bar, he held the empty beer glass up to the poodle, and the poodle gave it a tentative lick, made a face, and pulled his head back.

Cosgrove grabbed some peanuts and held his hand over the poodle's mouth. The poodle sniffed and Cosgrove dropped peanuts into the dog's mouth. The dog chewed them up.

"Peanut fed!" Cosgrove said. "That's the best feed. He'll make me a great dinner." The red-cheeked guy felt that was great and he absolutely insisted that Cosgrove have another drink, which Cosgrove did. Twice. Wiping a hand across his mouth, packing the dog under his arm, he called out, "All the best! I'm going to have a leg myself."

This had the saloon roaring as Cosgrove left with the dog. He walked until he found the subway, waited for the clerk to count change, and was through the gate and onto the train. Somewhere in Brooklyn, he wasn't too certain where, but it sure was Brooklyn — he was the only white in the car — Cosgrove got into a struggle with the poodle, who began to whine and writhe in Cosgrove's arms and Cosgrove, out of whiskey irritation, or maybe a drunken test for himself and a preview for the dog, sank his teeth into the dog's shoulder. The dog howled.

A man seated across from Cosgrove jumped up and announced to the car, "I finally seen news! The man bit the fucking dog!"

When Cosgrove got to the avenue in East New York, he clapped a hand over the poodle's mouth and stepped into Baby Rock's store, which again was empty. He peered around the corner and saw a Lincoln town car in the shadows a few yards up from the telephone pole. Sitting in front, three men, their heads apparently on axles for they were rotating so rapidly, were trying to see anything moving on the dark street. There was nothing. Cosgrove sat on the couch, held the dog, and waited. Sometime later, the car pulled away. Emboldened by alcohol, Cosgrove simply stepped out of the store, walked down to the telephone pole, and, seeing a fat envelope tacked to the pole, grabbed it, stuffed it into his pocket, and walked on.

He had no idea of the time he arrived home, but he made so much noise that Great Big, sleepy and grumpy, appeared in the hallway and opened the door. Cosgrove held the dog high. A delicate trophy. But enough to prevent starvation. "Here's a meal for us!" He carried the dog into the kitchen and put him on the table and lit a candle. The poodle sat on the kitchen table and waited for someone to comb his hair. Cosgrove waited for Great Big to take the poodle outside, run a stick through him, and start roasting. Of course there was no sin to doing this. As a dog has no immortal soul, he may be killed and eaten upon the slightest hunger.

Great Big snatched the dog, carried it to the back door, and threw the poodle out into the night.

"What was the matter with him?" Cosgrove asked. "Poodles are clean dogs. There was enough on him to eat. Aren't you hungry?" Great Big shook his head. Cosgrove pulled the envelope out of his pocket. "No mind. Look what I have for tomorrow and the days after that." Great Big paid no attention to this and walked out of the room.

Cosgrove ripped open the envelope and, bending over the candle, examined it. There was five hundred dollars in twenties and a note that said, "The man's name is not

Frankie Fifteen Thousand. It is Frankie Five Hundred. That is all you get. You better send Frankie Five Hundred back. Or we will pay you back good."

There can be no greater shock, even for one who has taken a vow of complete poverty, than to receive fourteen thousand five hundred dollars less than expected. Cosgrove sat down. Heavily. Some minutes later, the last of the alcohol in him effected a temporary rescue. Rather than being overwhelmed by defeat, he saw that the note was highly useful, for he could show it to Frankie Five Hundred, who would see how little regard these gangsters had for him. This might be invaluable, for Cosgrove had no idea of how to release Frankie Five Hundred without having him run straight to the gangsters, who immediately would kill Cosgrove. If, however, he could show Frankie Five Hundred that the gangsters thought he was virtually worthless, and intimate that perhaps they would kill him as soon as look at him, Frankie Five Hundred would go straight home rather than report to the gang.

Elated, Cosgrove, holding a low candle, clumped downstairs, where he found Great Big asleep in the doorway to the basement, as if guarding Frankie Five Hundred. Cosgrove stepped over Great Big and called into the darkness to Mr. Frankie Five Hundred. "Here! See what these creatures with whom you associate truly think of you? They say you are only worth your name. Here, look at this." Trying to adjust his eyes to the darkness, holding the small candle aloft, Cosgrove waved the envelope and money at Mr. Frankie Five Hundred, who was not there. The rope and gag were there, but not Mr. Frankie Five Hundred.

Glancing down, Cosgrove saw on the floor next to Great Big the wrapping from their last pack of Tums.

Cosgrove was distressed at this turn of developments and went back upstairs, where he sat in deep contemplation. The doctrine of necessity, as in *quisquis,* he thought, was one thing. But in introducing ransom, ugly temporal money, into the situation, he clearly had departed from that doctrine. Not even in recollections of Aquinas could he find a plausible thought, a partially open door that would get him out of this. He was so furious that the gangsters had short-changed him that he wanted to hold them responsible for the whole thing, but he could not. Nor could he affix blame on Great Big, who had lived in harm for so long that, even with constant admonishments, he had no idea of any line between good and bad in any given situation. Thinking all this over, Cosgrove saw plainly that redemption required him to face this matter squarely.

At six o'clock that night, he and Great Big walked into the Chief's small restaurant and went straight to the table where the Chief and his men sat over an early dinner. One of the gangsters scrambled to his feet. "I told you I seen a cannibal around here."

"Sit down," the Chief said quietly.

The Chief, as placid as a harbor, indicated that Cosgrove and Great Big were to take seats. Cosgrove dropped the envelope on the table. One edge touched the marinara sauce. "Pick it up," the Chief said. Cosgrove stuffed it into his pocket, the red sauce splotching the black suit. "You left this envelope for me?" he said to the Chief. The Chief nodded.

"I am here to return it," Cosgrove said. "This person of yours was no longer there when I returned last night."

The Chief nodded. "He excaped and you got the nerve to come in here like this?"

"I am a man of honor," Cosgrove said. "When you and I met on that night that Big Paulie was deceased, I attempted to speak to you directly but you left hurriedly, you might recall. By the way, we better spend time tonight talking about that. Just the two of us. You cannot go walking around with a thing like that on your soul. My dear fellow, if you were to be hit by a bus you would die in the state of mortal sin. Remember to talk about this with me before I leave here. I always face up to matters. As regards your Mr. Frankie Five Hundred, I wrote you a note. I then collected your payment as it were."

Upon hearing the day Big Paulie got shot brought up, the Chief opened his hooded eyes wide, and if there is such a thing as the corners of a man's mouth tightening to show anger, then both ends of the Chief's mouth probably squeaked inside because there was no more skin left to roll in. The Chief obviously was thinking that as long as he had to kill a priest he might as well kill him spectacularly. The young gangster next to the Chief, Tough Tony, couldn't contain himself. "Where is Frankie Five Hundred now?" Tough Tony moved his chair away from Great Big.

"I'm trying to listen to this man talk," the Chief said. The other gangsters sat motionless.

Cosgrove dwelled on the fringes of the subject, on time and place, attempting to allow his confession to develop candidness as he went along. He thought that perhaps by bringing out this particular case, that of Frankie Five Hundred, and tying it to others, such as the shooting of Big Paulie, which he already had just introduced, he could spark some fear into the souls of these people, although this was not his primary interest, cheap, grubby homicides in a nation stained with deeper sin.

Cosgrove said that Frankie Five Hundred had been gone for a long time now. Many hours.

The Chief shrugged. "That means that my friend Frankie should be walking through this door at any moment," the Chief said.

The young hoodlum at the table was anxiety ridden and the Chief once more warned him to behave.

Cosgrove plucked a shrimp from the Chief's plate and started to eat, but he felt compelled to stop and say to the Chief that, as far as he, Cosgrove, could time it, the gangster Mr. Frankie Five Hundred had disappeared from the basement of the church sometime the day before.

"Yesterday," the Chief said.

Cosgrove nodded.

"Who was watching him?" the Chief said.

Cosgrove pointed at Great Big.

"The cannibal," the young hoodlum said, pushing away from the table.

The Chief put food in his mouth and chewed slowly. He swallowed and pointed to the platter of seafood. "Tell him to eat something," the Chief said to Cosgrove.

Cosgrove spoke to Great Big in Yoruba. Great Big shook his head. Cosgrove looked at the Chief uncertainly.

The Chief's voice dropped to a whisper. "I asked the man to have something to eat with me."

Cosgrove went back to Great Big, whose answer was curt.

"What did he say?" the Chief said.

"He said he wasn't hungry," Cosgrove said.

The Chief thought this over. The young hoodlum standing at the table gasped. Then the Chief said, in a voice rising to a wail, "The cannibal ate Frankie Five Hundred!"

Terrified by Great Big, the thugs slid away in terror, except for the Chief and his chief enforcer, Jerry the Jew, who was called that because he was Jewish. The Chief grabbed Cosgrove from one side and Jerry the Jew got him from the other and they both pushed very hard against Cosgrove, causing Cosgrove to pop out from between them.

Cosgrove ran for the door. Great Big bent over and sank his teeth into Jerry the Jew's shoulder, much as a horse bites a groom, and Jerry the Jew let out a horrible scream, as if a shoulder bone had been shattered. Great Big opened his mouth wide and wanted to bite the Chief's head off and now even the Chief gave way. He fell backward to prevent his whole head from going inside Great Big's mouth.

Great Big followed Cosgrove outside, and they returned to the church by a route so circuitous that it took two hours. They took up existence in the church basement, protected from everything but the dim emptiness. Once Cosgrove peered out an upstairs window in the rectory and saw a car parked up the street, at the top of the gully. Standing by the car were three mean and lean young guys dressed to kill. Scouts. The Chief was only a phone call away.

Two days later, only a lonely picket was out there, sitting in the car. Cosgrove dispatched Great Big out the back door. Great Big moved through the weeds to the car, whose driver, Tough Tony Messina, was slouched in the front seat listening to a Frank Sinatra tape. Tough Tony had one hand on the wheel and the other was being used for finger snapping to Sinatra's singing. Great Big stood up at his full height next to the car. Immediately, Tough Tony turned gray. His fingers were stilled. Tough Tony jabbed a shiny shoe at the gas pedal. The car stalled. Great Big put his face against the window. Tough Tony slapped both hands on his chest and tried to breathe. Great Big pulled his hand back, apparently to smash the window. Tough Tony's tongue popped out of his head and his eyes rolled. Hearing Cosgrove leave the rectory on the run, Great Big turned from the car. Cosgrove ran with his left arm pumping and his right hand spread over the jacket so he could at all times feel the envelope with the five hundred in it.

———————

Heading to the bus, Cosgrove and Great Big found Seneca and Baby Rock walking down the street, holding hands. "I took Baby Rock to my aunt's house so he could get all cleaned up good for his new job," Seneca said.

"How do you like the job?" Cosgrove asked Baby Rock.

Seneca said, "Baby Rock be likin' the job." Baby Rock nodded. "Baby Rock say they have ribs there." Baby Rock nodded. "Chinee ribs." Baby Rock laughed. Seneca pouted. "Now what he be needin' is a roof. Disco Girl win the roof and they won't give it to her. Baby Rock won that roof, too."

"How is that?"

"He tell you. Tell him, Baby Rock."

"My sister be puttin' my name on the application as a dependent. If she won the roof, I won, too."

"So if you be married, you get the roof," Seneca said.

Suddenly, Cosgrove felt a burst of brilliance, and he grabbed Seneca and Baby Rock by the arms and rushed them aboard the bus. When they got off in downtown Brooklyn, he went up to a patrol car and received directions to Borough Hall and Cosgrove and Great Big walked the two kids up the steps of the old building and to the county clerk's office. There was no line.

"It's a shame to see them doing it so young," the clerk said. "But they got you helping them, Father, I guess it's great." The clerk had Baby Rock and Seneca fill out forms and Cosgrove sign as the guardian and there were no records requested, for in Brooklyn the Roman collar is stronger than cables holding a bridge.

Outside, Cosgrove checked the clock in the Borough Hall tower, for Baby Rock had to be at work by 10:30. He had an hour. "Hurry now. You're a workingman," Cosgrove said. It was a little before ten when Cosgrove, Baby Rock, and Seneca arrived at the East New York Income Maintenance Center and Cosgrove banged hard on the special supervisor's door and Harold Feinberg opened it.

"You cheap cur! You robbed Disco Girl of her house."

"She was not legally married." Feinberg exulted. "That is the rule."

"Well, if you check her entry, Baby Rock is on it. And Baby Rock is now going to be legally married in front of your eyes."

He thrust the marriage license into Feinberg's hands. "This must be a fake," Feinberg yelped. Cosgrove smirked. "Be off with you." He snatched the license back and called out to Elise Mabrey and some of the other women and they gathered around and Cosgrove, reading from the license, said, "You are to witness the wedding of Ms. Seneca Jackson and Mr. Basil ('Baby Rock') O'Dwyer."

Seneca shook her head. "Baby Rock and me have to be engaged first."

"What does that mean?"

"Baby Rock, you be wantin' to get married?" Baby Rock nodded. Seneca stood up straight. "We be engaged. Now we be married."

Cosgrove hurled his voice out as if presiding in a great cathedral. "Seneca, do you take Baby Rock for your lawful wedded husband, to love, honor, and cherish, forsaking all others, in sickness and in health, till death do you part?"

"I be," Seneca said in a small voice.

Elise Mabrey and the other women cried.

"And do you, Baby Rock . . ."

It was over quickly and Cosgrove had the women sign as witnesses and he pushed Baby Rock and Seneca on their way. Holding hands, they ran to Baby Rock's job in the Chinese restaurant.

"Now Baby Rock gets the house," Cosgrove said to Feinberg.

"Oh, we'll see." Feinberg chuckled. "The license is probably invalid because of the girl's age."

"God has joined them," Cosgrove said.

"Perhaps," Feinberg said airily. "But I will check you out to the ends of the earth and I am certain I can find a way to block you and your charges from getting what you want. Who are you people to try to slip around my ruling?" he said.

This depressed Cosgrove, for he felt that Feinberg probably would be able to obstruct as he pleased. Well, you tried, he thought glumly, now best be on your way.

———

Getting off a subway at Jackson Heights, where they would catch the bus for the airport, Cosgrove and Great Big were in a dim hallway between staircases and here was a door with a sign that said, BAR. Of course Cosgrove would not go into such a place, for he had to get to Ohio, but upon thinking he decided that there were many planes to Ohio, and into the bar he went, patting the envelope in his inside jacket pocket, the five hundred in twenties nestled there safely, God bless this Frankie Five Hundred's soul, and I will deal with that later and at length in the sanctity of the seminary in Ohio, he told himself.

He and Great Big first walked into an empty lounge room and took a staircase up to a large dim bar that was empty in the midmorning. A gaunt, bald man was dusting bottles. His eyes fell on Great Big and widened, but the shine of fear went away as he saw Cosgrove's collar and heard his voice.

Cheerfully, the barman served rye and soda water in little glasses and Cosgrove flipped one down, ordered another, and drank it as quickly and almost as enthusiastically as Great Big. They had a couple more and Cosgrove, looking out on the gray cold morning, was satisfied that they had all day for planes and certainly could use some warmth and pleasurable drink, so he settled at the bar with Great Big and gave a long, thoughtful sigh.

The benighted adventure now was over. He at first told himself that it certainly had been a horrible experience, but on another drink he scolded himself for this attitude. He and Great Big were alive, and this is the only reward a human being truly should expect, that of being allowed to breathe in the morning. That simple act of breathing of course is proof that man comes from God, and, Cosgrove reminded himself, one must never forget it. The most learned people have never been able to understand what causes a baby to take its first breath. Oh no, nobody understands that without professing a belief in God. The second thing is, how can humans, all other senses stilled, sound asleep, know enough to breathe?

Furthermore, Cosgrove scolded himself, he should be ecstatic that events had allowed him to come to America, for certainly he had discovered things about America. The poor were everywhere and would be with us forever, was that not in the oldest of stories, in the very tale of the Agony? Of course he had made a promise to Disco Girl to assist her in finding someplace to live, but this was unimportant when matched against his duty to go to Ohio and prepare a most forceful presentation of his case to the Pope's speech-writers.

Think of the opportunity that God has handed you, Cosgrove told himself, to influence all of Catholic thought everywhere. Good boy yourself, Cosgrove! He had another rye, bought cigarettes, touched the thrilling twenties in his jacket pocket, brought another of them out and into play on the wet bar, and considered over new rye whether he had discovered in his subconscious one way to address the complexities of the true religion and its relation to modern science.

He thought that the church could not block the proper advancement of science, but at the same time, if the only way to get the male sperm was to have the man masturbate, then there was no way for scientific advancements to be countenanced in the facts of sin. Somewhere, however, there was a way around this that was acceptable theologically and scientifically. He, Cosgrove, exposed to America the most, merely had to come up with the correct answer and he would be a most powerful figure in the Vatican. Good boy yourself, Cosgrove, have another and think on!

For a moment, Cosgrove saw Disco Girl in his mind. You really should have gone to see her, he told himself. Sadly, he thought of Disco Girl in the G Building lobby. By now, he had completely forgiven her for trying to push his poor

face into that black bush of hers. Oh, he understood that
the black bush could destroy the world, but that was in
a general sense; the individual must always be forgiven.
At the G Building, Disco Girl couldn't even get the doctor
to look at her. Cosgrove remembered the doctor's just wav-
ing a hand, his eyes not even bothering with Disco Girl's
naked body, and saying in such a bored voice, "Please
get dressed."

Here in the bar, Cosgrove had another drink and stared
out at the old El whose pillars were streaked with rust. The
street under the El was lined with small shops, the side-
walks crowded with blacks and Hispanics. Cosgrove de-
cided that this would be the last drink and they would leave
for Ohio. As he threw his head back to down that last good
drink, he saw outside the saloon window a young woman,
cheerful, her face smooth and round, carrying a baby in a
faded snowsuit into the subway. He noticed that the woman
was holding a little boy by the hand. Cosgrove saw that the
mother was wearing green fabric summer shoes on the cold
wet pavement and the little boy's sneakers did not appear
new. He closed his eyes against this sight and swallowed his
drink quickly, for he and Great Big had to get the plane to
Ohio, where they would have both comfort and an impor-
tant duty.

———————

At 2:00 P.M., Cosgrove and Great Big were crowded into the
rear of the van in front of the Flatbush Arms Hotel with
Disco Girl sitting in front of them. She had a baby in the
crook of each arm and Great Big had the third baby, the
Oriental, a blanket over all but her slant eyes, in his lap.
The driver, a bald black man, wore a blue rain jacket with

some sort of gold lettering on the back proclaiming WELFARE WORKER. In the front seat sat a white woman with short dark hair and glasses and protruding teeth. She introduced herself as Arlene Schneider, and the moment the van moved she turned around and lectured Disco Girl. "Now, you know, this is your last chance. If you do not take the apartment we show you today, you must go all the way down to the bottom of the ladder. You must go back and live in a shelter and work your way up to a hotel. This lottery is totally new to us. We must see if it works. But you are a player. So today is so awfully important for you. It is three-and-two day on the batter."

"Why are there only three chances?" Cosgrove said.

"Because the rules are patterned after baseball. Three strikes and you are out."

A woman with Arlene introduced herself as Ms. Saturday. When she was asked her first name she said, "Just Mizzz." A light-skinned black with light red hair, she held a new black briefcase on her lap. "I am from the Bureau of Child Welfare," she said. "I must see that the apartment they furnish this young woman and her children is up to livable standards for the children. If not, she cannot have the children in the apartment. If she takes an improper apartment, then we take the children away from her on the spot. I merely call the precinct to have this done."

"What happens," Cosgrove asked, "if she does not take the apartment today, which is her third strike, as it were?"

The two women shrugged.

"I be out," Disco Girl said. "I be back to tryin' commotions at the G Building."

The van rocked over streets of deserted old apartment

houses whose vacant doorways fronted broken streets. They reached a street that was a block from the ocean in Coney Island, a street that was the difference between Heaven and Hell, a street of frame houses that had been burned and an apartment house with a narrow, dark entrance that was stuffed with children.

"Crack-a-Jack?" one of the kids said.

At the end of the dark hallway, Arlene and Ms. Saturday banged on a door and a dog snarled and tried to scratch his way through the door. The superintendent, a Puerto Rican in a straw hat, opened the door slightly, slipped out so the dog, whose yellow teeth showed in the opening, couldn't rush out to bite the visitors. He led them up three flights to a landing on which one apartment, doorless, was charred from a fire. Inside, men stood in the half light and smoked glass crack pipes. A young woman in a housedress and old sweater was knocking at the door of a second apartment and when it opened two men in undershirts looked out. She handed them money, and they gave her two plastic crack vials.

The superintendent opened the third apartment and showed Disco Girl in. The ceilings were rust-stained from water dripping through and the floors sagged noticeably underfoot. Garbage was piled in corners, old garbage, soda bottles, and potato chip bags, and in the kitchen new plaster chips showed that rats had been eating a large hole around the pipes.

"I could fix it up," Disco Girl said sorrowfully.

Cosgrove looked for a bathroom. "It's right out in the hall," the superintendent said. "It's all right. You only got two apartments using it up here. Know how many hours a day a bathroom goes empty? Bathroom is empty twenty-three hours a day. Maybe even high-class buildings should have two, three families using the same bathroom."

Ms. Saturday, standing in the doorway, said, "Who is in the other apartment?"

"I don't know. I just rent. You want to know who they are, you go ask them."

"I have seen enough," Ms. Saturday said. "I'm sorry," she said to Disco Girl, "but if you move in here, you must surrender your children to my agency."

"And if you don't take this apartment, you must go back to a shelter and start all over again," said Arlene Schneider, her teeth seeming to protrude more, as she was speaking with pursed lips.

Disco Girl looked at Cosgrove and her face further saddened when she saw that he had no solution. "I don't know why I told myself you be helpin' me," she said. "I know more than you do."

On sad legs, she walked out of the apartment and went out to the van, where Great Big was throwing the babies up in the air like Indian clubs, and although they were too young to understand fully what was going on, they gurgled in delight.

Cosgrove was mortified because he had no helpful thought for Disco Girl. But then, he had nothing particularly helpful for the Pope, either. Howard Beach, a little perhaps, but somehow one major new thought must flare inside his brain and be introduced in a magnificent display of Catholic articulateness, subject, verb, object, one sentence connected to the other to form a flow, yet always simple; one does not require a complex sentence to introduce a complex thought. Think on, Cosgrove! He winced. He couldn't even assist this poor wretch, Disco Girl. He huddled in the van and tried to think.

Arlene Schneider told the driver, "Let us off here," as she ripped a blank off a pad and handed it to him. "Here is the address for their shelter for the night." She and Ms. Saturday walked off.

In the van, Cosgrove's head drooped and he fell asleep. Nausea awoke him; the van was rocking to a stop in traffic that was thicker than grass. By now it was dusk and past. The driver gave it one more stop and start, shook his head, and turned onto a street where the potholes caused the van to bounce so high that Cosgrove was certain he would throw up. He also realized that he had a fierce need to urinate. The driver said that they were assigned to an armory all the way over in a high-class part of Manhattan because the shelters in Brooklyn and lower Manhattan were chock-full. "Take us about twenty minutes," the driver said.

Cosgrove sat in pain and the van bounced up to East Sixty-fifth Street, turned, and rocked to another halt. Ahead, the wide avenue was motionless with traffic that had the cross streets blocked. On the side street in front of the van, limousines were triple-parked in front of a place that was obviously a restaurant, but one that was so important it had no neon sign. His personal plumbing causing agony, Cosgrove yanked the van door open and ran for the double-glass, lace-curtained restaurant doors. Entering the place at this moment were the two oldest blond women he perhaps had ever seen, diamonds swinging from their earlobes. Behind them came two elegantly dressed ancient men, shuffling. Cosgrove rushed in ahead of the two old women and immediately inside a maître d' looked up in horror at Cosgrove, who had the smell of welfare life all over him. This prompted the maître d' to try to place his body in front of Cosgrove, who made a proper selection of directions. He headed for a spot at the far end of the bar, which was so crowded with old people — ancient people to be factual — awaiting tables that Cosgrove caused the maître d' to be stacked up against the old people, a pickoff.

At the end of his short dash, Cosgrove found he had been correct, and he flew into a splendid men's room. Emerging, he had to pass the bar, where an old barman in white linen and matching hair placed drinks in wrinkled hands that shook.

"Barman, I've an idea," Cosgrove said. "Serve your drinks in the heaviest glasses available. It will help these poor old souls to hold them without so much spillage. Look about you."

The old people gasped and inspected their clothes and in doing so they of course put their glasses on the bar and Cosgrove snatched a martini and threw that down with a gulp, saw a large white wine, which took a couple of slugs, and by the time the maître d' rushed up, Cosgrove had somebody's big vodka and soda and he was down to the lime when Puerto Rican janitors enthusiastically carried Cosgrove to the door, which the maître d' held open.

The maître d' knew immediately that he had made a mistake, but such was the glee of the Puerto Ricans that it was too late to stop them from heaving Cosgrove high into the air, where he flew directly into two old women, huddled in their fur coats and nearly being blown over by the wind on the street. One woman, having no balance at all, fell with her ankle under her, and it cracked like a stick. The other woman was so concerned about choking on her false teeth that she clapped both hands to her mouth and cared nothing about balance and of course tumbled to the ground with limbs clearly injured but her hands still at her mouth to prevent choking on false teeth.

Since Cosgrove was pitched so high into the air, one of his shoes just happened to graze the hand of an approaching old man, who hollered in pain, for the shoe chipped a wrist bone.

A heavy woman alighting from a car with a pad and pen in her hand screamed out, "You have just visibly damaged New York nightlife."

The van was just pulling out of the street and going to what was obviously a public building of some sort, the armory, of course, on the far side of the wide avenue. Cosgrove thought the grass plots in the center of the avenue looked familiar. With that first truly great rush of whiskey warmth, he walked straight out into the wide street, headlights playing on him as the cars either stopped or whisked around him. How jolly, he thought, and he caught up with the van at the entrance to the armory, which was under a long canopy.

More old women in furs and men in scarves and white hair, if indeed they had any left, walked up the steps under the canopy. As Disco Girl, Great Big, and the babies got out of the van, another large black man in a welfare worker jacket and two soldiers closed in on them and had them wait against the wall until the rich were off the stairs under the canopy. Then the soldiers led the welfare van riders into the building, with its gold lights on old wood and pictures of great past generals. Immediately inside two young women were seated at a desk with a discreet sign on it saying, WEST-MINSTER KENNEL CLUB COMMITTEE.

Clearly, from a distance of many yards behind them,

which is the closest Cosgrove and the others were allowed to come, the old women thought it was delightful to be in such a masculine place as the armory and the old men looked at the pictures of the past generals knowledgeably. They strolled along a polished wood hallway toward the elevator.

One of the women admired the dress of another, and the one in the dress said, "When I got this in Bloomingdale's, I found it so disgusting. When you used to buy something for a thousand dollars and more, at least they put you off in a corner where you had some privacy and people didn't have to notice. When I picked this out the other day, I was standing with everyone else, a cattle run, and I found it all so distasteful. They had shopgirls paying four hundred dollars for a blouse right next to me. I couldn't decide whether they were trying to bring me down to the shopgirls' level or bring the shopgirls up to mine. At any rate, I think that store has lost its standards."

When they were gone, the soldiers and the man in the welfare worker jacket rushed Cosgrove and the five with him through huge double doors and into the gloomy drill shed of the armory, where, far down the end, behind a green canvas partition, they saw hundreds of cots covered with paper sheets and people sitting stooped over on the edges of the beds. There was a low murmur from the few who spoke to each other. Cosgrove seized the first cot in his way and flopped on it in fatigue from his day and in befuddlement from the whiskey. Disco Girl and Great Big, their arms full of babies, put two of them on one cot and Disco Girl jammed pacifiers in their mouths. The third, Latasha Yee, the Oriental, was snuggled in her arms. Disco Girl wearily stretched out on the cot. Great Big took the one next to her;

his head and most of his back were on the bed, and the rest of him hung over the end. In the rafters of the huge drill shed, they heard the sound of birds chirping vespers.

Now James Woods, wearing a security guard uniform, walked past, and upon seeing Cosgrove he issued greetings. "Are you our guard?" Cosgrove asked sleepily. "No, this is my home," Woods said. "I got no home so they give me a day job guarding the rent-check computer. Make me jealous, I guess. This is my place to stay at night. 'Thanks a lot,' I told them. Do you know what they told me? 'Take it or sleep under the trees.'"

Woods went to find a cot. Cosgrove reached out and took the little Spanish baby's hand and the child gripped firmly and Cosgrove, smiling, fell asleep in the huge drill shed. The birds chirped their evensong.

The first sound in the pale light of early morning was "Shit in my eyes!"

James Woods's head came up and his hand began to wipe the bird dung from his face. This of course woke Cosgrove and he stared straight up to where pigeons flew through the air and their droppings came down through the morning light and hit the people sleeping on the cots under plastic blankets. Cosgrove suddenly was splattered just under the nose, and he froze when he thought that some went into his mouth, which he felt was a ridiculous thing to contemplate until he saw all over the drill shed people spitting bird dung onto the wood floor. Hundreds of pigeons cooed as they strutted about the rafters, then took off into the early morning air and dropped dung on the sleeping people.

"My babies covered with shit," Disco Girl hollered.

Disco Girl's three babies' eyelids, covered with white bird dung, looked like white eye patches. Everywhere in the room the arising people were covered with about an hour's worth of bird dung. At this point, with few people even complaining, the green canvas was pulled back and two soldiers and a man in a welfare jacket shouted, "All out!" Covered with bird dung, the couple of hundred people began to rise from their paper sheets. In the doorway stood a couple of black maintenance men holding brooms and a group of people in business suits, men and women dressed alike, and Cosgrove didn't notice that Bushwick and Sarah were in the group.

Cosgrove got up on a cot and began to scream. "I have discovered this country! Look up! Look up! And see these birds. Through all the ages they have been a symbol of beauty and peace. The doves released into the sky by His Holiness as a symbol of peace for the world. Dove in the sky. A sparrow on the bare branches of a tree, telling you that life is here even if leaves are not. Thrushes deep in the thicket calling out to the passerby. How settling! How calming! Birds at dusk, flying in magnificent formations through the sky.

"In Africa, when there was a thirst and hunger, always, one saw the hope of birds in the sky. Only at the most bitter end, when we could neither breathe nor see, did the ugly vultures appear. And of course they had an appropriate presence because at the end the natural order must prevail and someone must be devoured by someone else. But now look what you have been able to do in America. You have the bird stand for something lousy. If it was a vulture, I could understand. But you have taken the pigeon, the lovely plump pigeon, who dares to tiptoe up to man, who often even trusts the hand of man, you have taken this bird that walks amongst our feet, and think of that, isn't that a marvelous bird, he trusts us enough to walk with us. How marvelous. And we have made him the metaphor for America. A metaphor. Who here knows what a metaphor is?"

The people stood in silence by their cots with paper sheets.

"What sort of schools did you attend that they did not even teach you what a metaphor is? A metaphor is transferring a situation to something different, but yet with enough connections to the problem, by its presence in speech or on paper, to illuminate further the situation. Now I shall give you the metaphor for the times in which you live. The American metaphor. Oh yes, that is one thing we Irish are capable of doing. We do not tarry or dally with matters of the surface. We much prefer, in our less disciplined but far more talented way, to go to the core immediately. And, therefore, look about you and see the American metaphor, and you must excuse my language but I have seen it all now. Look about you and excuse my language, but here is the metaphor for America: 'Birds shitting on the people!'"

In the doorway, one of the group in business suits, Special Supervisor Harold Feinberg, sneered. "Now you see what we get here."

"Isn't he a priest?" Sarah asked innocently.

"Oh, he just is dressed that way. Catholics act much more responsibly. That is how you can tell the man is no priest. You never would see a Catholic priest making such a statement in a setting such as this. Oh no, this man is a fraud. Don't listen to a word he says."

"I don't think he's a fraud," Bushwick said.

"I think it's the first time the man has been lucid since he arrived here," Sarah said.

"No, he is a welfare thief. So is that big goon with him."
Feinberg pointed at Great Big. "I am the only person in the
city stopping these two and some woman and a couple of
kids they are using from falsely getting a house from this
city." He looked up at the clock. "See what they are doing.
I have to call the commissioner at breakfast."

Bushwick and Sarah picked their way through cots and
found Cosgrove wiping bird dung from himself and Disco
Girl wiping Latasha Yee's eyes with one hand and running
the other through her hair in hopes the bird dung would go
away. Cosgrove looked at Bushwick and Sarah in their busi-
ness clothes and said, "The weapons of surrender."

"Brooklyn!" A van driver in a welfare worker zipper
jacket was in the entranceway to the drill shed. Another
worker came out and called, "Bronx." There was general
movement. Sarah took Disco Girl's black baby, Bushwick
held her Spanish product, and Disco Girl carried her
Chinese, and together they walked out to the Brooklyn van.
James Woods walked with them, wiping bird dung off the
shoulders of his security guard uniform. They packed into
the van, which first went all the way crosstown to Eighth
Avenue, where the van negotiated through thick traffic and
came to a halt. "There they go, in the instruments of sur-
render," Cosgrove said tartly.

Bushwick turned around. He pointed at Cosgrove. "Do
you want to fight?"

"Of course. That is my life. I fight for Christ," Cosgrove
said.

"Then why don't you just follow us and see what hap-
pens. I have something you can do that would help every-
body in the city if you got away with it."

Bushwick told the van driver to wait for Cosgrove. He

and Sarah, acting as if they didn't know Cosgrove was be-
hind them, walked into a building. Cosgrove walked with
Woods. Inside the building, everybody showed a pass to the
guard at the desk and the guard studied each pass intently
and Cosgrove, by now so used to sneaking on subways,
slipped past the guard without causing the air to move and
waited for Woods, Sarah, and Bushwick at the elevator,
which they rode to the ninth floor, where, as another guard
carefully inspected Woods's pass, Cosgrove flopped on his
hands and knees and gave it the full turnstile crawl, straight-
ened up, and waited.

Bushwick sauntered by and said, out of the side of his
mouth, "You go inside and just look for the two drums for
the rent. The drum and the backup drum. They'll be
marked. They got them in racks. You take them out of here
and you'll have some big shots walking around thinking of
suicide."

"We can't promote death," Cosgrove said.

"What do you think we do all day?" Bushwick said. "We
just try to keep it quiet."

Cosgrove wandered into the room with the white cabinets
and blue tops of the computer mainframes. Sitting in a cor-
ner office, Bushwick listened to a lecture by the head of the
computer room. He glanced over his shoulder and saw Cos-
grove strolling about. Right over Cosgrove's head was the
big sign, NO BULKY COATS ALLOWED. And here was Cosgrove
in a floppy black raincoat — a filthy raincoat, too — and he
had a cigarette jammed in the corner of his mouth and a wild
look on his face as he paced about the room. Bushwick nod-
ded solemnly to Cosgrove.

The director of the systems room and the assistant direc-
tor were explaining that all the tapes were kept on drums

and that, for each category, there were a tape and a backup tape kept in canisters on the racks. And Cosgrove paced the room and his eyes scoured the cream-colored canisters, each with its tape markings down the spine, and he saw one tape that said, "Two-Party Rent Checks" and he had it under his raincoat with one move and he froze as he saw a tall black in a striped Brooks Brothers shirt and dungaree pants and wearing low blue Nikes striding toward him so quickly that he was certain that he could not get away. "Excuse me," the tall black said. He reached past Cosgrove and slapped into the rack a canister whose tape marking said, "Two-Party Rent Checks BACKUP." Cosgrove ditched this under his raincoat as well and strode out.

In the circular lobby, James Woods was leaning on a counter and talking to a young woman, who indicated that Cosgrove had to show a pass to be allowed to go through the exit turnstile, and Cosgrove said to Woods, "See what I've learned in this country?" He ran up to the turnstile, slapped his right hand on it while hugging the bulging left side of his coat, and with one amazing pirouetting spinning leap he was over the turnstile. He faced the woman and bowed. "And that was taught to me on the number two train." The woman behind the counter broke into a giggle and Woods thought it was amusing and Cosgrove whisked out through double-glass doors to the elevator.

———————

"You be livin' here?" Disco Girl said, walking about what seemed to her to be the vastness of the empty rectory. One of her babies, the black one, was crawling on the floor and the other two were asleep on the only bed left in the place.

"Soon everybody will be living someplace," Cosgrove said. He sat on the floor, back against the wall, knees up, and wrote the second ransom note of his life, this one with deep anger rather than the trepidation of seeking ransom for Frankie Five Hundred. Or, to be precise, the late Frankie Five Hundred.

His note said,

I not only have your computer tapes but I fully understand their significance. I am not diabolical. I am merely attempting to prevent you from being consigned to the fires of Hell. No longer can I stand by and see people living as they do in this city. Therefore, you should immediately write down a plan to put all these poor people in a house and find them a job and submit the plan to me. By no later than midnight of Saturday. Have someone post your answer on the telephone pole in front of 365 Pine Street and depart immediately. If you remain in the area, it will be a sign of bad will and as you stand there the tapes will be destroyed. Do as you are told and catastrophe will be avoided.

Cosgrove ducked out and took the note to the East New York Income Maintenance Center and stuffed it into the in-house mail slot under the information windows, wheeled, and left. Nobody on the long lines noticed him. At 4:00 P.M., the atmosphere in the income maintenance center became one of the deepest and most silent apprehension and there was neither sound nor commotion as the great computer shootback from welfare center to welfare headquarters was supposed to begin. The lights blinked and the whirring tapes stopped dead in the main center and suddenly all two floors stopped and on computer terminals in maintenance centers all over the city, including here in the East New York center, there appeared on the screen, flashing urgently, the message "Please Log Off Immediately." The largest single industry in the greatest city on earth was at a standstill.

It was at that point, late of a Friday, and with only forty-eight hours to go to save his system, that Harold Feinberg, in talking with Bushwick Taylor, heard enough to promise Bushwick Taylor the job of special chief assistant. Bushwick, who wanted to get married soon, found the offer irresistible.

Cosgrove returned to the church basement on Friday evening to find Great Big and Disco Girl looking at each other lasciviously. Cosgrove found he didn't care anymore. Late that night there came sounds from the rectory above. People had broken in. In the basement, Cosgrove placed a finger to his lips. He and Great Big sat in silence for many hours. During the silence, Great Big's stomach recalled Africa. It was sometime after this, when there was complete silence in the place, that Cosgrove, from pure nervous exhaustion, fell asleep. And upstairs there was a loud sound in the church, as if someone had tripped over one of the broken kneelers that jutted out into the aisle.

In the basement Cosgrove awoke with a start and said to Great Big, "What's that?"

Great Big, awake and hungry, said grumpily that he would look. As Cosgrove figured that he, too, would have to climb stairs, he counseled waiting for another sound. Exhaustion overtook him and he fell off. Upstairs there was another sound, as if someone in anger had just kicked something. Great Big went upstairs, where Harold Feinberg was tiptoeing through the church in the darkness.

Imagine that fool Bushwick telling me not to come alone, Feinberg thought. If I had brought somebody with me, they would have two of us on television instead of just me. He had such dreams of gloriously carrying the tapes into a full New Opportunity meeting that he had no fear of the large cross in front of the church, even though, in growing up on Manhattan's West Side, he had been assured, in attempting to walk by a red-haired Irish kid at Blessed Sacrament School, that Jews were Christ killers. As he stepped from the deep shadows of a pillar, Harold Feinberg found himself being struck by pale moonlight, which came through a broken, uncovered stained glass window. The pale moonlight was hesitant at first, but a cloud drifted away and the pale moonlight developed far more intensity and revealed, for all to see, Harold Feinberg, holder of a master's degree in social work from Hunter College and of ambition unknown to reasonable man.

In the morning, Cosgrove's eyes watered as he swallowed. Red cabbage or horseradish or something like that.

Late that afternoon, Disco Girl, good and cold, pulled the large old metal handle of the furnace door, which creaked open. She wondered if there was anything to burn. Disco Girl stuck her head inside.

She let out a squeal that went up through the steam pipes. She ran over to Great Big and shook him. He refused to awaken. "I don't make a baby with no one like you," Disco Girl yelled at Great Big.

She scooped up her three babies and ran out of the church. Hearing her, Cosgrove jumped up and rushed after her. Disco Girl, arms full of babies, was down in the gully and up on the other side by the time Cosgrove was in motion.

"You don't understand," he yelled to Disco Girl.

"You crazy," she called.

Cosgrove knew that if she made it to the corner, she could summon others, and there was no way to prevent such an occurrence, for she had too much of a lead on him and those legs of hers were simply gliding along.

"You don't understand that you are the ones who are being eaten alive. The other people are the cannibals!"

"Nobody be eatin' my whole leg!"

"Of course they do. You just don't notice it because they do it to you and your babies a little each day."

Cosgrove thought this was good and profound. Disco Girl thought it was good and crazy. She disappeared around the corner. It took thirty seconds before Cosgrove saw the patrol car tear around the corner and stop dead when the two patrolmen spotted him trudging alone in the cold rain toward the church. The cops in the car appeared to be using the radio. Sure were. Soon the city was in East New York.

———

"Does he have them in there?" Pocantico Hills's personal envoy, an in-law dispatched from Westchester, said, pointing to the huge furnace. Cosgrove was crouched in front of it like a hockey goalie. His arms were folded across his middle, covering the two canisters of computer tapes.

"I don't know," Octavia Ripley Havermeyer said. "What does he have behind those arms?"

"That's just it," the head of the emergency service squad said grimly. "If these tapes are that important and he has them on him and we shoot him, we shoot the tapes, too. Can't do that, can we?"

"My Lord, no," Mrs. Havermeyer said.

"If you could find some way to shoot him without hitting

the tapes. I wish we had the Pinkertons here. They did it well for the family at Ludlow."

"I wish the mayor was here," the inspector in charge of the emergency service team said.

"Mayor?" Pocantico Hills said. "Why in the world would you need him? Politicians have nothing to do with this city. I can tell you that."

"But in case something goes wrong, if he's here he got to take the blame in the report instead of us."

"We don't know who the mayor is," Pocantico Hills said, in thought. His eyebrows raised. "But if you want a civil servant, we'll just have Jimmy Carter fly up here from Washington. It won't take long. We can wait."

"Excuse me," Octavia said.

"Oh, of course! Look what happens to me in tension. I completely forgot that we let Jimmy Carter go. Who did we replace him with? Oh, no wonder I didn't recall. Much too old to get downstairs on fast notice, much less all the way up here. No, let's just do this as is."

Cosgrove's little body twitched. The cops, unsure as to whether Cosgrove was an evil spirit or insane man, jumped back. They had spent an entire day outside the church, hoping the thing would all go away, and now, on a Sunday afternoon, they had finally stormed the place. The outside help they felt could be useful was gathered on the wood staircase leading from the church to the basement: Bushwick and Sarah, Disco Girl, Baby Rock and Seneca, and a dark, obviously Italian priest who was introduced as the Papal delegate. They faced Cosgrove, who crouched in front of the furnace. Behind him were cement steps going up to the back yard of the church. On these steps, head down to avoid hitting the ceiling, was a glowering Great Big.

"You didn't burn them?" Pocantico Hills called over the heads of the crouching, nervous police to Cosgrove, who was frozen in front of the furnace.

Cosgrove nodded.

Pocantico Hills vaulted the crouching police and rushed forward, trying to push Cosgrove aside. When Cosgrove didn't move quickly enough, Octavia Ripley Havermeyer simply reached around him and pulled open the furnace.

"What are these supposed to be?" she asked in frustration.

"Bones," a cop said, gagging.

As Octavia had a perfectly warm heart, the chill that ran through it caused her to feel sick. Octavia was beside herself with fear and of course could not look. She could not believe that she had allowed herself to be present at such ugliness. She stepped away from the furnace.

"Most cities are built on bones," said Pocantico Hills. "But never mind that. Where are the rent tapes?"

Cosgrove jumped up the cement steps, pulled one tape drum from under his coat, and shoved it into Great Big's mouth like a wafer. The first crunch stopped everybody. The tape drum clearly was damaged beyond repair. Great Big dropped it to the floor. Cosgrove held the other drum up and Great Big opened his mouth as wide as a whale's; one chew and the whole system, employing so many, producing so much, was gone.

"What do you want?" Pocantico Hills said.

"We won the roof!" Baby Rock yelled.

Disco Girl clapped. "We won the roof and you didn't give it to us!"

Cosgrove jabbed a finger at Pocantico Hills. "Disco Girl

won the lottery for a house and this man Feinberg wouldn't give it to her because she is not legally married."

"I don't understand this at all," Pocantico Hills said.

Octavia Ripley Havermeyer suddenly found herself, once again in command of a situation. "I won't waste any time reciting the facts. I shall tell you what I think. One, the regulation requires marriage. It is a pro-family rule, the house lottery."

"Disco Girl is not married, but Baby Rock's name is on the winning ticket," Cosgrove said. "And he is legally married to Seneca. I married them myself. This man Feinberg simply decided not to award the house."

On the steps, Baby Rock held up a marriage license. "It be like a big driver's license."

"Then it only requires Mr. Feinberg to sign off on the lottery result." Octavia called to another one of David Rockefeller's lackeys. "Could somebody find where Mr. Feinberg is now?"

"He be right behind you."

Octavia glanced into the furnace, closed her eyes for just this little moment, and said, "Very well. I shall sign off for him. Does that satisfy everybody? You get your house."

"That should do it," Cosgrove said.

Sarah Carter hung over the wood banister and screeched, "Don't be a fool, Cosgrove. One on one they fix anything. They refuse to fix the whole. Try for the whole."

"Maybe I won't be just settlin' for an apartment," Disco Girl said.

"She's right. Hold out. We can win," Sarah said.

"Oh sure. Man against tank," Bushwick said.

"Tell him to bite down hard on the tape and destroy the system," Sarah said.

"You can't do that or all the people will have no place to live," Bushwick said.

Sarah pointed in anger at Bushwick. "Don't listen to him," Sarah said.

Pocantico Hills waved and the Vatican delegate came down off the wood stairs and stood alongside him. "I know there has been a misunderstanding and it would have been so much easier for all of us if I had contacted you properly. But all this can be rectified. For now we truly do need your report."

"Yes," Cosgrove said, "but my report is not what it originally would have been. I have learned from the birds, just as certainly as if Saint Francis of Assisi had sent them to teach me. I know now that the problem in this country is the Poor, wh —"

"The Poor! They are our only property! You cannot do away with the Poor. Why, we would have no church. We need the Poor. On behalf of His Holiness, I command you to return their belongings to these people and to give me your report immediately. I will stand here and both collect the tapes and hear your report."

Cosgrove, standing there, holding this one thought of his own, perhaps the first idea of his life that was not tied solely to a rule of his religion, considered all this for a moment. He weighed a new belief against a command from his institution. Cosgrove's chin rose, his eyes blazed at the group about him, and he chanted, "In vitro fertilization! Surrogate mothers! Either they have too much sex in this country or they go the other way and they want babies without sex.

That is the ultimate confusion in this country. And I have the answer."

"What is it?"

"Ripped condoms! Sperm and egg can be mixed in a dish like an omelette and put straight back into the womb and be blessed by God, providing that the man has not masturbated. What he must do then is to wear a condom. Oh, I am sorry to use the word but I must, for he can only wear a ripped condom. If he uses an unripped condom, that is birth control and that is most sinful of all, next to abortion and masturbation. With my ripped condom, he can have heavenly union with his lawfully married wife and immediately afterwards rush that remainder of his sperm in the pocket of the condom if there are any to the doctor's office. Think of it. This overcomes all objections. He is not using a contraceptive if it is broken. He is not masturbating. He is mated in deepest love with his wife and because of a physical defect the sperm cannot reach the egg and fertilize it unless there is help from modern science. So I have done it. I have made the connection. I have the answer to at least one part of America's great and only problem."

"Marvelous," the Papal delegate said.

"You are truly a demented man," Sarah Carter yelled.

Pocantico Hills said to Cosgrove, "You are a genius."

"Am I? How jolly."

"Now let me have the tape."

"Of course," Cosgrove said, reaching inside his coat.

"And tell the cannibal to behave," the police commissioner said. "We are going to put leg irons on his wrists."

"On Great Big?"

"Oh yes," Pocantico Hills said. "Look what this big fellow of yours has done. We must commit him immediately so the tale never gets out."

Cosgrove and Great Big were up the cement steps and into the yard in back of the church, on the edge of the high weeds. Great Big went ahead too far and Cosgrove was running furiously, so he could shove the second drum, the backup drum, into Great Big's mouth and let him eat it like a wafer. At which point an oversized police emergency service truck, lit like a jukebox, tried to run down Great Big, who plunged into the bullrushes.

All the police and agents from everywhere now chased Cosgrove, who held the backup tape drum under his arm. He cut to the left. Men in suits, probably federal agents, closed in. He headed to the right. Uniformed police went for him. One obviously had athletic training, football probably, for he did not move as Cosgrove ran at him and suddenly tried to veer off, to fake the man out of the way. The uniformed cop stood with his feet rooted, arms out. He would not be faked and this gave Cosgrove no more running room. Cosgrove put the drum in the crook of his wrist like a discus, and he whirled. Whirling, whirling, whirling, gathering speed and strength from the speed flowing into his arm, and as hands tore at Cosgrove, he bellowed and, rocking his body as Jim Sheridan of Mayo did in the All-Ireland Games at Croke Park in Dublin, Cosgrove threw the drum into the air like a discus, and soar it did and spin it did, wonderfully high and moving with such speed that in midair the cover came off and the computer tape went into the air like a ribbon, miles of tape billowing in the air, snaking through the sky and landing in the bullrushes, draping the high weeds like decorations on an endless Christmas tree. There was a shriek. Those hands not pummeling Cosgrove on the ground were sent into the weeds to gather carefully, so carefully, the tape. The head of the computer room was there to rewind it with his personal hands. Nobody did anything else. Great Big was forgotten as they tended to Cosgrove and the tape.

"What do we do with this man?" one of the commissioners said, looking at Cosgrove.

"Punish him."

"How?"

"Send him home."

"Ireland," Cosgrove said numbly.

~~~~~~

At Kennedy Airport, three federal immigration agents put him in his seat on the plane at 8:00 P.M., and only when the plane whined off into the night and flew through the dark sky to Shannon in the West of Ireland, in the rain, did the immigration agents leave.

Great Big would be impossible to find, the police felt, because he could simply run into any black neighborhood and be another basketball star, of which they all look alike whether in a park or in the professional leagues. Still, Great Big remains on the most-wanted list because, in the history of New York City, he was the first and only cannibal who was black.